Issues in Design and Technology Teaching

Design and technology encompasses such a wide range of skills and specialisms that it can be difficult for students on initial teacher training courses to cover all aspects of the subject in real depth. The challenge for those training to teach the subject is to develop expertise in at least two of the diverse specialist areas, as well as in the core principles of design and technology. This can mean that there is little opportunity to engage with underlying, but important, theoretical issues.

Issues in Design and Technology Teaching identifies and examines important concerns in this subject, seeking to challenge preconceptions and stimulate debate about this relative newcomer to the National Curriculum. Key areas addressed are:

- **Issues of definition**: getting to the roots of the concepts of designing and 'design and technology' and their educational value
- **Issues in the classroom**: issues involved in planning and assessment and the role and implementation of new technologies
- **Issues in the school context**: gender as a concern in design and technology, with an examination of boys' performance in this area
- **Issues beyond the school**: ethics, values and attitudes in design and technology, and a discussion of professional development and industrial partnerships.

Issues in Design and Technology Teaching provides support for trainee teachers and newly qualified teachers in primary and secondary schools, helping them to reach informed judgements about the subject they are teaching.

Su Sayers, Jim Morley and Bob Barnes and are all tutors in Design and Technology at the Manchester Metropolitan University.

Issues in Subject Teaching series

Series edited by Susan Capel, Jon Davison,
James Arthur and John Moss

Other titles in the series:

Issues in Design and Technology Teaching

Edited by Su Sayers, Jim Morley and Bob Barnes

London and New York

First published 2002
by RoutledgeFalmer
11 New Fetter Lane, London EC4P 4EE

Simultaneously published in the USA and Canada
by RoutledgeFalmer
29 West 35th Street, New York, NY 10001

RoutledgeFalmer is an imprint of the Taylor & Francis Group

© 2002 Selection and editorial matter, Su Sayers, Jim Morley and Bob
Barnes; individual chapters, the contributors

Typeset in Goudy by
Prepress Projects Ltd, Perth, Scotland
Printed and bound in Great Britain by
Biddles Ltd, Guildford and King's Lynn

British Library Cataloguing in Publication Data
A catalogue record for this book is available from the British Library

Library of Congress Cataloging in Publication Data
  Issues in design and technology teaching / edited by Bob Barnes, Jim
Morley and Su Sayers
    p.cm. – (Issues in subject teaching series)
    Includes bibliographical references and index.
    1. Design, Industrial – Study and teaching (Elementary) 2. Design,
Industrial – Study and teaching (Secondary) 3. Technology – Study and
teaching (Elementary) 4. Technology – Study and teaching (Secondary)
I. Barnes, Bob (Robert) II. Morley, Jim (James William) III. Sayers, Su,
1945– IV. Issues in subject teaching.

  TS171.4 .I87 2002
  745.2'071–dc21   2001048814

ISBN 0–415–21685–0 (hbk) /seb
ISBN 0–415–21686–9 (pbk)

Contents

Illustrations

Figures

Tables

Contributors

Steve Bartlett was a sociology teacher and head of department in a large comprehensive school before becoming an area coordinator for the Technical Vocational Educational Initiative in the late 1980s. He has since worked as a senior lecturer in education at the University of Wolverhampton and is currently reader in education at Chester College of Higher Education.

Diana Burton was a social studies teacher and head of year in a large comprehensive school until the late 1980s. She has since worked in teacher education at Manchester Metropolitan University and is currently head of education programmes within the University's Institute of Education.

Melanie Fasciato is a senior lecturer at the Manchester Metropolitan University. She has taught in primary, middle and secondary schools and published textbooks and other materials for teachers and pupils at Key Stages 2, 3 and 4. She has made contributions to a variety of websites. She has been involved with the Assessment and Qualification Alliance (AQA) in a number of roles for several years.

Tony Hodgson was a teacher in schools for many years, before becoming a lecturer in higher education. His work has always been concerned with electronics and information and communications technology (ICT) in design and technology, with a particular focus on its implementation in schools-based technology. He is a consultant to many BAE SYSTEMS' educational intitiatives and manager of their International Teacher Training Centre at Loughborough University. Recent development work has included the design of on-line teaching and learning materials for computer-aided design and manufacture (CAD/CAM) systems.

Nicholas Houghton has extensive, international art and design education experience as a teacher, administrator and researcher. He has worked in the following sectors: secondary, further, higher, adult and teacher education. As well as writing about craft, he is interested in the history of ideas and its relationship to art and design education.

Steve Keirl has taught primary and secondary design and technology in England and Australia, lectured at the Universities of Tasmania and South Australia (where he coordinates design and technology teacher education courses). He has also published and has given keynote addresses at state, national and international design and technology conferences. Steve's research interests include the philosophy of design and technology education and the understandings of technological literacy for democratic life.

Mike Martin is currently lecturing in technology education at the University of Central England. He has taught in the UK and abroad and maintains a keen interest in sustainability issues in design and technology. Whilst working as an education officer for Intermediate Technology, Mike published educational materials encouraging teachers to look at design and technology in different cultures.

Rachel Mason is Professor and Head of the Centre for International Art Education and Research at the University of Surrey, Roehampton, in London and has taught art education in England, Australia and the US. She is a former president of the National Society for Education in Art and Design and a vice-president of INSEA (International Society for Education through Art). She is well known for research and publications on multicultural and international art education and recently edited the book *Beyond Multicultural Art Education: International Perspectives* with Doug Boughton.

Jim Morley is currently a principal lecturer in design and technology in the Institute of Education at the Manchester Metropolitan University. Formerly a teacher of three dimensional design in a progressive Leicestershire school, he inherited leadership of what was arguably the first compulsory design course for pupils of secondary-school age during the late 1970s. After a period of reseach leading to a higher degree, Jim moved into higher education, retaining contact with the work of schools as an A level external examiner.

Su Sayers currently teaches design and technology to primary and secondary specialists at the Manchester Metropolitan University Institute of Education. Following her MPhil, she worked both as a freelance textile designer and as a researcher, later becoming subject co-ordinator for home economics at Middlesex University. She has been a Chief Examiner for A level and an examiner for GCSE textiles. Other experience includes participation in an artists' group delivering community/educational art and craft projects.

Sue Shore is an experienced design and technology teacher and was Head of Design and Technology at Landau Forte College from 1998 to 1999. She has spent time teaching in New Zealand and is currently a design technology teacher and acting head of department at a girls' college there.

David Spendlove is a senior lecturer in design and technology education at Liverpool John Moores University, having previously been a senior teacher and head of department. He is a teacher fellow for the GTEP (Gatsby Technical Education Project) and has an MA from Loughborough University. He is a member of the Design and Technology Association editorial board and has published work on a range of subjects including CAD/CAM, concept modelling, gender issues and raising attainment.

Kay Stables is currently Pro-Warden with responsibility for students at Goldsmiths College, University of London. She is Reader in design and technology education and a former head of the Design Department. Recently she has conducted an evaluation of the Design Museum's 'Mystery Box' Outreach Programme and an evaluation of Middlesbrough Education Action Zone's Enriching Literacy through Design and Technology Project. She is currently undertaking a pilot research project for Design and Technology Association into the impact of Pro/DESKTOP™ Software in schools (with Richard Kimbell and Tony Lawler). She is currently engaged in further evaluations for the Design Museum and is directing a research project exploring assessment approaches for the Royal Society of Arts Opening Minds Project.

Torben Steeg is a lecturer in education at the University of Manchester where he runs the Post-graduate Certificate of Education (PGCE) design and technology course and supports all PGCE students in meeting the Teacher Training Agency's National Curriculum for information and communications technology (ICT). He has research interests in design and technology, ICT, science, mathematics and the interactions between them and, within design and technology, in systems thinking, control technologies and the uses of ICT to support learning. His publications include a wide range of curriculum materials, research papers, articles and training materials developed to support courses for serving teachers. He is a member of the editorial board for Electronics Education and of DATA's Initial Teacher Education Advisory Group.

Introduction to the Series

This book, *Issues in Design and Technology Teaching*, is one of a series of books entitled *Issues in Subject Teaching*. The series has been designed to engage with a wide range of issues related to subject teaching. Types of issues vary among subjects, but may include, for example: issues that impact on Initial Teacher Education in the subject; issues addressed in the classroom through the teaching of the subject; issues to do with the content of the subject and its definition; issues to do with subject pedagogy; issues to do with the relationship between the subject and broader educational aims and objectives in society, and the philosophy and sociology of education; and issues to do with the development of the subject and its future in the twenty-first century.

Each book consequently presents key debates that subject teachers will need to understand, reflect on and engage in as part of their professional development. Chapters have been designed to highlight major questions, to consider the evidence from research and practice and to arrive at possible answers. Some subject books or chapters offer at least one solution or a view of the ways forward, whereas others provide alternative views and leave readers to identify their own solution or view of the ways forward. The editors expect readers of the series to want to pursue the issues raised, and so chapters include suggestions for further reading, and questions for further debate. The chapters and questions could be used as stimuli for debate in subject seminars or department meetings, or as topics for assignments or classroom research. The books are targeted at all those with a professional interest in the subject, and in particular: student teachers learning to teach the subject in the primary or secondary school; newly qualified teachers; teachers with a subject coordination or leadership role, and those preparing for such responsibility; mentors, tutors, trainers and advisers of the groups mentioned above.

Each book in the series has a cross-phase dimension. This is because the editors believe it is important for teachers in the primary and secondary phases to look at subject teaching holistically, particularly in order to provide for continuity and progression, but also to increase their understanding of how children learn. The balance of chapters that have a cross-phase relevance, chapters that focus on issues which are of particular concern to primary teachers and chapters that focus on issues which secondary teachers are more likely to need to address, varies according to the issues relevant to different subjects. However, no matter where the emphasis is, authors have drawn out the relevance of their topic to the whole of each book's intended audience.

Because of the range of the series, in terms of both the issues covered and its cross-phase concern, each book is an edited collection. Editors have commissioned new writing from experts on particular issues who, collectively, will represent many different perspectives on subject teaching. Readers should not expect a book in this series to cover a full range of issues relevant to the subject, or to offer a completely unified view of subject teaching, or that every issue will be dealt with discretely, or that all aspects of an issue will be covered. Part of what each book in this series offers to readers is the opportunity to explore the inter-relationships between positions in debates and, indeed, among the debates themselves, by identifying the overlapping concerns and competing arguments that are woven through the text.

The editors are aware that many initiatives in subject teaching currently originate from the centre, and that teachers have decreasing control of subject content, pedagogy and assessment strategies. The editors strongly believe that for teaching to remain properly a vocation and a profession, teachers must be invited to be part of a creative and critical dialogue about subject teaching, and encouraged to reflect, criticise, problem-solve and innovate. This series is intended to provide teachers with a stimulus for democratic involvement in the development of subject teaching.

Susan Capel
Jon Davison
James Arthur and
John Moss
December 2001

Part 1

Issues of definition

1 The challenge for design and technology education

Jim Morley

Introduction

The challenges of teaching and learning within design and technology may arguably be regarded as unique within the school curriculum. The educational process deals with an activity that, by the nature of design problems, may be ill-defined at the outset and may lead to a range of varied, and perhaps equally justifiable, 'finished' outcomes. In this sense, the challenge for the pupil implies a problem or situation to be addressed, which requires recognition, rationalisation and negotiation of important factors to achieve a resolution. For the teacher, this implies an openness to situations that engage learners in the processes of designing. As Kimbell *et al.* (1996) have shown, the degree of openness, or otherwise, of learning situations remains one of the most difficult curriculum management challenges for design and technology teachers, and it involves risks for teachers and learners alike.

This chapter seeks to identify the requirements for 'challenge' and 'risk' in the context of the emergence of a rationale for designing as an indispensable component of design and technology education. It is argued that this has become the central feature of a new 'practical scholarship' (a term which I shall use to imply thought in action), changing our aspirations for a practical education to meet the needs of every child living in a modern industrial society.[1]

Why has the nature of practical education changed?

For a comprehensive review of the importance of making, and its changing place in the curriculum, the reader should consult Chapter 4 in this book. The issue in this chapter is the emergence of designing as a component of practical education and the rationale for its inclusion in the curriculum for all pupils of compulsory school age. This is particularly important in understanding the purposes of design and technology education for every child, regardless of vocational or career aspirations, and provides the key to understanding the unique challenge that design and technology requires us to address.

Models of practical education in the elementary schools early last century were based upon society's aspirations for a skilled workforce. These were, for girls: to take up menial, poorly paid employment or become wives and mothers; and for boys: to respond to a perceived collapse in the competitiveness of British industry (Penfold 1988). Practical activities were therefore largely pre-vocational in nature. To some extent developments following the 1944 Education Act, including the establishment of a tripartite system of secondary, technical and grammar schools, could have consolidated the pre-vocational nature of practical work in schools, but technical schools were not set up in sufficient numbers nationally to have a major influence on practical education. Instead, a more common bipartite system of secondary modern and grammar schools became the norm, with practical activities, and particularly those seen to be 'technical' in nature, most often confined to secondary modern schools and thereby to pupils of lower ability.

To a large extent pre-vocational intentions were continued by these schools, with woodwork, metalwork and technical drawing for boys, and needlework and home economics for girls. There were, however, an increasing number of teachers who questioned the previously held assumptions 'that the acquisition of manual skills', which were seen to be 'of little direct relevance to the society in which [pupils] were maturing, had to precede educationally more fulfilling goals' (Penfold 1987: 34).

The developing argument was accelerated throughout the 1960s and early 1970s by futuristic writers such as Alvin Toffler. In his book *Future Shock*, Toffler advocated education for change, a dynamic approach to education, based on a process that would enable pupils to cope with change confidently, rather than the teaching of specific knowledge and skills, which would soon be obsolete in a rapidly developing, industrial society (Toffler 1971). Although the debate here was not confined to establishing a rationale for the place of practical education in schools, some teachers of practical subjects welcomed his arguments. They recognised the need for a wider role for their subjects, and one which would place them closer to the educational debate about the relevance of what they were doing. Toffler clearly fuelled the debate about the concept of 'transferable skills', the role and status of knowledge, and the notion of educational approaches having to be 'process' rather than 'content' led if they were to be a viable preparation for life in a rapidly changing society – in short, approaches to education which would not become obsolete with changes in scientific and technological knowledge. The challenge to teachers and educationalists was quite different to that presented by a pre-vocational model of education. It was a significant change from the security of identified bodies of knowledge and skills that were thought to be directly useful to pupils moving, most likely (by virtue of the stratified education system of which they were part) into specific technical occupations.

The excitement about the possibilities of an education system designed to cope with the changes of the late twentieth century was consolidated in the 1970s by a group of senior figures from industry, education and the arts, who advocated 'education for capability'. So sure were they that the traditional approaches to education were in need of fundamental overhaul that leading figures, such as Patrick Nuttgens (an architect), Sir Alex Smith (Director of Manchester Polytechnic) and Andrew Fairburn (Director of Education for Leicestershire), placed prominent advertisements in the national press. These declared their commitment to an education system that should be essentially creative and foster 'capability'.

What should practical education in the early twenty-first century be like?

Developments in the curriculum

The following section is intended to alert the reader to some of the landmarks that occurred during a key time in the development of the new subject of design and technology.

During the 1960s and 1970s, few teachers looking for a new and more meaningful role within the school curriculum, beyond pre-vocational approaches to education, would have directly identified with the 'education for capability' movement. Teachers often advocated an educational justification for their subjects, which was based on the wider values of making and associated with the pride and confidence that come of doing something well.[2] Cynics might say this challenged teachers' views of their recognised domains of knowledge and expertise least. Others responded differently to what was more generally and increasingly recognised as the challenge to education posed by a modern industrialised society.

A significant landmark in acknowledging the importance of the cognitive processes of 'thought and exploration' in a new model of practical scholarship was reached with the publication of the Crowther Report (1959). As Penfold reported, in a journal article entitled 'From handicraft to craft design and technology':

> Crowther argued pervasively for an 'alternative road' approach to education to enable the country to benefit from the capabilities of all its young people. The report advocated the rehabilitation of the word 'practical' in educational circles even though it was aware of its ambiguity: 'practical' carrying pejorative overtones, frequently being construed as the opposite of 'academic'.
>
> (Penfold 1987: 35)

The report strongly refuted such a view and identified the tradition to which the pupil of practical subjects should aspire as '... the modern one of the mechanical man whose fingers are the questioning instruments of thought and exploration' (Ministry of Education, cited in Penfold 1987: 35).

Project Technology

In 1967, the Schools Council declared that the objective of its Project Technology pilot study was '... to help all children to get to grips with technology as a major influence in their lives, and as a result, to help more of them to lead effective and satisfying lives' (Schools Council, cited in Penfold 1987: 37).

As well as producing useful teaching materials, the teams' activities extended to research programmes that included enquiry into the educational value of technological project work and the development of creativity – activities which, though dependent on practical work, looked beyond the acquisition of knowledge and practical skills. Project Technology was notable for keeping the teaching of technology at the forefront of debate about the role of practical education, despite the resistance with which it was met by many 'handicraft' teachers of the time. It was seen by its supporters as a way of dealing with technological issues and problems which could be realised in school workshops.[3] In terms of curriculum development, it contributed much to the perception of the relevance of practical activities in schools, and was certainly part of a practical tradition that advocated 'project-led' approaches to tasks, rather than project work solely as a means of reinforcing scientific principles (an approach to the teaching of technology which was popular with some science teachers). These initiatives passed to the National Centre for Schools Technology at Trent Polytechnic, and they were influential in the teaching of technology through a 'systems approach' which, though acknowledging the importance of 'content', used it as a part of a process of education that helped pupils to deal with real problems.

The Keele Project

Despite the success of Project Technology in addressing the new challenges of practical education, what has now become universally known as the Keele Project caught the imagination of many more 'craft' teachers. The pilot study, 'Education through the Use of Materials', suggested approaches to craft work that combined the teaching of skills with the stimulation of pupils' own creative ideas (Schools Council 1969). It examined a number of contexts in which this might happen, including 'recreation' and 'design for living'. These were to offer wider relevance to the study of a variety of practical subjects and pupils' future roles in society.

Perhaps the Keele Project was more attuned to the backgrounds and aspirations of the majority of handicraft teachers of the time and, though clearly advocating a 'problem-solving' approach to practical education (a term that was to dominate debate and teaching in initial and in-service teacher education for many years), it was clearly located reassuringly, as declared by the title of the pilot study, in 'Education through the Use of Materials'. In the summary of the pilot study, entitled 'Ways Forward', the report states:

> … teachers have realised more clearly that craft skills, although important, are only a contributory factor in pupils' intellectual and personal development. This development is increasingly seen to be of an individual nature, involving goals with labels such as inventiveness, creativity, and initiative – qualities that are seen as essential for a full occupational, domestic, or leisure role in an advanced industrial society. It is an emphasis on thinking and expression in which knowledge and skill are supportive.
>
> (Schools Council 1969: 33)

Clearly, there is more than an indication here that certain skills were regarded as transferable. Without developing the rationale that would support such a statement, the report nevertheless highlights one of the fundamental challenges to the teacher, and one to which this chapter will return later: 'For the teacher the difficulty lies in striking a balance between teaching necessary skills and leaving time for the critically important creative use of skill.' (ibid.).

Developments in design education

The Keele Project was undoubtedly influenced in part by developments in design education. Protagonists of this movement included teachers of art, who did not have the same regard for knowledge and skill that was commonly the source of security for many traditional teachers of handicrafts or technical studies. Some of these teachers were looking for a wider justification for their subject within the context of an industrial society and spurned the notion of art education as an exclusive and talent-centred activity.[4]

Peter Green, who was something of a guru at the time, through his books for teachers and in a paper presented to a conference of the National Association of Design Education, summarised the importance of education in design as follows:

> Design Education is not about instilling good taste or buying wisely or making nicer and better things. Design Education is about the impact of Technology and the man-made environment on our lives – and our response. Increasingly we live in a designed, packaged and planned world. The evidence of crucial man-made decisions surround us and determine the nature of our lives. Design Education is about the response to this problem.
>
> (Green 1985: 57)

In highlighting that we have become 'passive consumers' of other people's decisions and increasingly likely to be confronted with more choices made on our behalf, Green advocated the importance of young people experiencing the processes of 'how decisions are arrived at' and 'how we can evaluate and measure their appropriateness':

> This, in formal terms, is what Design Literacy is about. One activity giving such experience is Problem Solving... but we are looking for any activity that allows us to test/exercise our decision making and practical skills – and which gives us the chance to test our decisions.
>
> (Green 1985: 59)

Though there is not a cognitive rationale for the transference of process skills acquired through practical activities, the argument and belief inherent in the statements of design educationalists is persuasive. Green goes on to explore David Pye's notion of 'the workmanship of risk' and 'the workmanship of certainty' (Pye 1968: 4–8) as a model for 'the creative and imaginative skills of hypothesis':

In the workmanship of Certainty you can't exercise your guess. In the workmanship of Risk rough work is the basis for perfect work (as the sketch is to the picture). In the workmanship of Certainty there is no rough work, no seeing if my idea works.

(Green 1985: 59)

In an article written in 1967 examining the Design Education Movement, Kate and Ken Baynes stated:

… Only with the dissatisfaction of a younger generation of teachers, who have felt the inadequacy of the traditional teaching methods, has craft begun to grope its way along the tricky path from cosy certainty of learning known hand techniques towards a broader consideration of the construction and function of objects in an industrial society.

(Baynes, cited in Penfold 1987: 39)

Two crucial issues are restated in this reference: the concern for an appropriate education in the context of an industrial society, and the need to progress from 'the workmanship of certainty' and all the associations this has with pre-vocational models of practical education.

Between 1973 and 1976, the Department of Education and Science funded an inquiry at the Royal College of Art, led by Professor Bruce Archer and his team, into 'Design in General Education'. By May 1975, one of its stated propositions was as follows:

There exists an area of human experience, knowledge and action, centred on man's desire and ability to mould his physical environment to meet his material and spiritual needs, which is as important to his well-being as such well-recognised areas of learning as literacy and numeracy. We call this area of experience, knowledge and action, 'design'.

(Archer 1975: 1)

While seeking to define a third main area of the curriculum: 'wroughting' alongside reading and reckoning, and 'designacy' alongside numeracy and literacy, the inquiry did not seek to locate the activities of 'design' in any one existing curriculum area.[5] It suggested instead that many subjects may deal with the issues inherent in 'design', particularly the practical subjects, one of which it described as 'craft'. 'Design activity' was one of two important precepts on which curriculum activities were built, the other being 'design awareness'.

In a critique of the Royal College's inquiry, Anita Cross from the Open University stated that: 'If Design then, is to be considered as basic to general education, it must be amenable to the usual meanings of basic or general education, i.e. an education which is, in principle, non-technical and non-vocational.' Cross asserted that design would only achieve parity with other disciplines by:

… providing instruction in concepts and methods of enquiry appropriate to life-long learning, and attempting to foster an understanding and appreciation of the contributions that design activities and specialisms make to the individual's life and the lives of others.

(Cross, cited in Penfold 1987: 42)

Here, two particularly important principles emerge. The first is that the position of design can only be justified in general education if it is of wider relevance than pre-vocational experiences; and the second is that one of the central values of a design education for all is the acquisition of skills which are of 'lifelong' relevance to individuals. The clear implication here is that the processes of enquiry conducted in schools should be transferable to other situations throughout life. That it is 'design activity' that will engage pupils in a manner that will achieve this is central to these discussions, as it is to those who believe that 'design awareness' in a modern industrial society is also a significant part of the rationale for design education.

The fact that these issues were maintained as important precepts underpinning the eventual introduction of design and technology in the National Curriculum in 1990 is not only due to the apparent educational relevance of these arguments, but also the result of high-profile support for design education from organisations such as the Design Council (*Design Education at Secondary Level, 1980),* and the prime minister of the day, Margaret Thatcher, who declared herself a 'design addict' during a BBC television programme in 1985. In Mrs Thatcher's case, the need to address the country's balance of payments problems through the regeneration of British industry was widely regarded as an important factor in this support. The influence of this kind of thinking and of the TVEI (Technical Vocational Educational Initiative), which was introduced in 1985 to address the long and uncomfortable relationship between the needs of industry and education, could have taken 'practical scholarship' back to a pre-vocational model of practical training. This did not happen; instead, the increasingly high-profile consideration of design and technology and its place in general education persisted into the National Curriculum we have today.

In defining the nature of design and technological activity in schools, the interim report of the National Curriculum Working Group, set up to determine the nature of the subject, made the following statement:

We address now what is at the heart of design and technology, namely the special characteristics which are the ultimate warrant for its inclusion as a foundation subject in the National Curriculum. What is it that pupils learn from design and technological activities which can be learnt in no other way? In its most general form, the answer to this question is in terms of capability to operate in the made world. The goal is increased 'competence in the indeterminate zones of practice'. Distinctions are sometimes drawn between:

| 'knowing that' | and | 'knowing how' |
| 'propositional knowledge' | and | 'action knowledge' |

'homo sapiens' (man the   and   'homo faber' (man the maker)
understander)

Whilst it would be misleading to imply that the components in these polarities are mutually independent, it is the second in each pair which is indicative of what is distinctive about an education in design and technology.

(Department of Education and Science (DES) 1988: 3)

In *Design and Technology for Ages 5 to 16*, which documented the proposals resulting from a period of consultation following the interim report, the following statement is made:

The inclusion of design and technology as a foundation subject in the National Curriculum is a recognition that the capability to investigate, design, make and appraise is as important as the acquisition of knowledge.

(DES 1989: 1)

The importance of these statements in indicating what it is that underpins the curriculum in design and technology cannot be overstated: developing the capability to operate in the made world, understanding the importance of knowledge in action, of investigation and appraisal and, not least, the idea that confidence and capability in the process skills associated with designing will provide useful and transferable skills for future life.

Conclusion

This is not a review of all the influences that have historically led to the introduction of design and technology to the National Curriculum. For that the reader should use the references at the end of this chapter to initiate a wider enquiry. The intention here has been to alert the reader to some of the 'landmarks' which may impart a better understanding of the challenge for a new practical scholarship in schools and the context of its role in a rapidly changing, industrial society. It is clear that the needs have been perceived as less pre-vocational and more generally 'educational' in nature; less of a preparation for the minority to undertake very specific practical activities, and more of a preparation for the majority for the common challenges that will confront them in dealing with modern life. This implies less dealing with the 'cosy certainty' of very specific bodies of knowledge and practical skills where outcomes are predictable ('the workmanship of certainty'), and more of the appropriate use of knowledge and skills in relation to problems that pupils are striving to resolve ('the workmanship of risk').

The challenges are clear, but how will they be managed? In essence, when we have a curriculum that, for whatever reason, is skills- or content-led, the educational process may be predictable. Where there is any intention to expose pupils to the generic processes of research, hypothesis, decision making and appraisal, we necessarily have degrees of uncertainty and risk. The nature of that uncertainty and the approaches to managing the challenges of 'risk' are discussed in Chapter 2.

Questions to consider

1   To what extent is any model of practical education dependent on the selective or non-selective education systems of which it is part? (Studies of comparative systems of education in the Netherlands and Germany appear to reveal quite different priorities.)
2   As we have seen, art teachers had a significant role in the development of the Design Education Movement. Consider the relationship between design and technology and art and design in the National Curriculum. How similar are the objectives of each?
3   It is arguable that models of pre-vocational education in this country, which were designed to address the often uncomfortable relationship between the needs of industry and the wider needs of society (such as the TVEI), have not fulfilled their full potential. Do you consider this is so?
4   To what extent can a model of design and technology for all contribute to the needs of industry?

Notes

1   Further discussion of ideas about the rationale for design and technology is to be found in Layton, D. (1993) *Technology's Challenge to Science Education: Cathedral, Quarry or Company Store?* Buckingham: Open University Press.
2   Students of Loughborough and Shoreditch Training Colleges, two of the main training institutions for teachers of 'Handicraft', were encouraged to aspire to the highest standards of skill and finish, in keeping with 'Arts and Crafts' values and the Edward Barnsley tradition.
3   Over 500 schools participated in the Schools Council's 'Project Technology' initiative under the overall control of project leader Geoffrey Harrison, based at Loughborough College.
4   One of these was Peter Green. Formerly a teacher, Green's influence increased as a teacher trainer at Hornsey College of Art in the early 1970s. Later, in 1985, as Dean of the Faculty of Art and Design at Middlesex Polytechnic, he delivered a paper to a conference of the National Association of Design Education, entitled 'Design education – a historical perspective'.
5   For further discussion of this idea, see Archer, B. (1979) 'The three R's', *Design Studies*, 1 (1): 17–20.

References

Archer, L.B. (1975) 'A closer look at the relationship between the broad concept of design in general education and its component parts', Paper 5, presented at the Design in General Education Summer School, July 1975, Royal College of Art, London.

Department of Education and Science and the Welsh Office (1988) *National Curriculum Design and Technology – Interim Report*, London: DES.

Department of Education and Science and the Welsh Office (1989) *Proposals of the Secretary of State for Education and Science and the Secretary of State for Wales. Design and Technology for Ages 5 to 16*, London: HMSO.

Green, P. (1985) 'Design education – a historical perspective', paper presented at the National Association of Design Education Conference, Haywards Heath Sixth Form College, London, pp. 53–61.

Kimbell, R., Stables, K. and Green, R. (1996) *Understanding Practice in Design and Technology*, Buckingham: Open University Press.

Penfold, J. (1988) *Craft, Design & Technology: Past, Present and Future*, Stoke on Trent: Trentham.

Penfold, J. (1987) 'From handicraft to craft design and technology', *Studies in Design Education Craft and Technology*, **20** (1): 34–48.

Pye, D. (1968) *The Nature and Art of Workmanship*, Cambridge: Cambridge University Press.

Toffler, A. (1971) *Future Shock*. London: Pan Books.

Further reading

Eggleston, J. (1976) *Developments in Design Education*, London: Open Books.

Eggleston, J. (1997) *Teaching Design and Technology*, Buckingham: Open University Press.

Green, P. (1974) *Design Education, Problem solving and Visual Experience*, London: Batsford.

Schools Council (1969) *Working Paper 26, Education through the use of Materials: the Possible Roles of School Workshops in the Education of Secondary-school Pupils*, London: Evans and Methuen Educational.

2 How can we meet the challenges posed by a new model of practical scholarship?

Jim Morley

Introduction

The contention of the previous chapter is that the challenges now facing us in design and technology are present because our aspirations for practical scholarship in schools have led us to a new relevance in relation to the society in which we now live. Those aspirations manifest themselves through the processes of 'designing', with knowledge and making skills the important means to an end (knowledge and thought in action), not ends in themselves. What the processes of designing bring to practical scholarship are degrees of uncertainty which are a prerequisite for 'the creative imaginative skills of hypothesis' (Green 1985: 59).

Do we understand the processes of designing?

For most teachers of 'craft' or technical subjects in the 1970s, 'problem solving' would have been their first experience of a 'process-led' approach to practical work. Though introduced by design educationalists, such as Peter Green, author of *Design Education, Problem Solving and Visual Experience* (Green 1974), the term ('problem solving') permeated other interest groups in practical education and was certainly popularised through the widely accepted Keele Project (Schools Council 1969). While generally recognised today as only part of what we mean when we talk about the processes of designing, the ways in which it was interpreted and enacted in schools have parallels with the more comprehensive processes associated with designing. It is perhaps natural that the majority of teachers, used to the 'cosy certainty' of technical procedures leading to predictable outcomes, sought to systematise ways of approaching problems to make 'tangible' inherently abstract processes for the benefit of both themselves and their pupils. As far as many of those who had previously celebrated 'problem solving' as an exciting and relevant approach to practical scholarship were concerned, it had by the 1980s become a tired and lifeless concept in the minds of many. Even Peter Green who had clearly been an early advocate, declared in 1985: ' "Problem Solving" is a bit of jargon. It is just a natural non-selfconscious, everyday activity.' (Green 1985: 59).

Green appears to make this statement as if needing to exorcise that which initially had been a useful concept but had subsequently become a misused and inflexible process. What at first was regarded in the singular as 'the design process' suffered similarly, though, in fairness, this was at the hands of not just teachers, but also those design theorists who were looking for ways of identifying and describing what was happening when people design. The notion in educational circles that it was design process skills that were the transferable element of a new practical scholarship, and thereby the source of the rationale for relevance in our changing society, may also have contributed to the development of a 'process model' that could be applied to many situations, often inflexibly.

Two immediate challenges, therefore, face the current teacher of design and technology. The first is to understand the processes of designing so that they may be articulated through teaching; the second is to understand that which is transferable to other situations and contributes to 'lifelong learning', a widely held precept to the relevance of practical scholarship for all.

'Design process' or 'designing': singular or plural?

By the time the interim report of the National Curriculum Working Group had been published in 1988, important work on the nature of design and technological activity had been started by the Assessment and Performance Unit (APU), by way of developing a framework for its assessment. This work had a formative influence on the working group's perception of designing. Referring to what was often called 'the design process', the report states:

> ... we avoid the use of this term in its singular form in our report. Different kinds of designers – graphic, product, system, environmental – do not all go about their work in identical ways and what they do cannot be captured in algorithmic form. In this connection we regard as salutary the warnings in the APU report, *Design and Technological Activity: A Framework for Assessment* (HMSO, 1987), against any linear, rule-bound view of what the activity of designing entails.
>
> (DES 1988: 11)

Earlier than this, Professor Bruce Archer of the Royal College of Art warned:

> Design is not a linear activity which begins with problem definition, continues with ideas generation, follows with ideas evaluation and terminates with solution description. Human beings don't think like that.
>
> (Archer 1974: 3)

Later, in his book *How Designers Think,* Bryan Lawson, an architect and psychologist, mischievously published his map of the 'walking process' with, as he put it, 'apologies to design methodologists who like maps' (Lawson 1980). The implication here is that 'designing' is a natural, largely subconscious process.

It is, however, hard to blame teachers, whose role it is to improve pupils' designing skills, for trying to explain, classify or 'map' this unseen process which they were being encouraged to see as central to the new relevance of their subject area. In some ways the maps were useful in highlighting constituent parts of a process which pupils should be aware of. For example, one could reasonably say that 'evaluation' is an important component of designing, which will always be present, but it is less reasonable to suggest it occurs only after a solution has been made, as some linear design maps suggested (Figure 2.1; Kimbell *et al.* 1991: 18). Some who appreciated the subtlety of what was increasingly recognised as an interactive process strove for ever more revealing diagrams. These inevitably became increasingly confused (Figure 2.2).

In acknowledging the potential guidance these models of designing provided for the kinds of activity that should be present in design and technology, the APU cautioned:

> … they have equally been dangerous in prescribing 'stages' of the process that need to be 'done' by pupils. Used unsympathetically, the approach can reveal a greater concern for 'doing' all the stages of the process than for combining a growing range of capabilities in a way which reflects individual creativity and confident and effective working methods.
>
> (ibid.: 19)

It is easy to appreciate, therefore, how the wish to make an abstract process explicit can lead to an unnatural perception of order and stages in the process. The tendency may, in part, evolve out of a wish to make more certain the 'workmanship of risk' (Pye 1968: 4–8), to bring order and guidance to processes where, in the context of design problems, it does not exist. The APU clearly illustrates the outcome of over-slavish adherence to linear models of designing, fearing that 'stages' in the process may no longer be seen as 'active capabilities', but instead '… the process of design and technology becomes a series of products, (The Brief, The Specification, The Investigation, etc., etc.)' (Kimbell *et al.* 1991: 19)

Readers who have observed work produced for public examinations will appreciate how efficiently packaged each of these stages may appear and how isolated each can become from the next:

1   research that has no bearing on the development of ideas;
2   solutions selected from a number of alternatives for which there is no apparent justification in design development;
3   evaluations written without reference to original intentions.

Figure 2.1 A simple linear model. Reproduced from Kimbell *et al.* (1991: 18) with permission from HMSO.

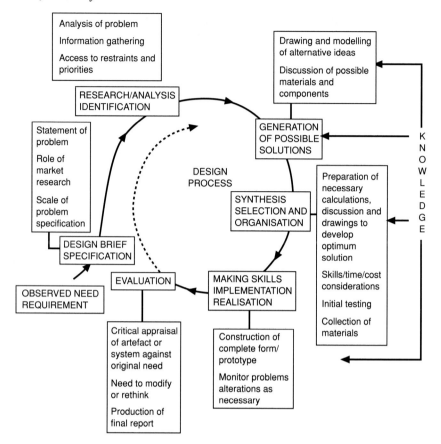

Figure 2.2   Interactive design process model. MEG 1986, CDT Design and Communication
GCSE Syllabus. Reproduced with permission from OCR.

The challenge here is clear: we must take extreme care not to fragment the
processes inherent in designing through unsympathetic 'formatting' and packaging.
In short, the risks must be maintained to ensure the integrity of the activity,
otherwise its educational relevance is compromised.

Can design and technology claim to foster 'transferable skills'?

Are we justified in our assumptions that the processes of design and technology
contribute to transferable 'life skills' and thereby to the rationale for the place of
design and technology in the compulsory school curriculum? The historical
references used in Chapter 1 point to a growing sense of belief that justification
for the inclusion of practical subjects for all pupils resides in a transference of
process skills inherent in the activities of designing. There is a sense that if pupils

are involved in research, pursuit of the solution of problems, testing, and evaluation in contexts related to their study of design and technology, then these skills will usefully translate into other post-school contexts, regardless of pupils' vocational aspirations. In examining the motives underlying design and technology, the APU acknowledge the 'instrumental' and 'educational' arguments for its inclusion in the curriculum. Some see it as a means of helping pupils into industrially related employment and thereby increasing the nation's productivity (a not too dissimilar rationale proposed for practical activities in the elementary schools of the early 1900s). Others argue that its purpose is to enhance the education of all pupils as autonomous, capable individuals (a view shared by design educationalists of the 1960s and 1970s). It would, of course, be nonsense to suggest that these motives are mutually exclusive, but the APU report conceded that:

> Increasingly the debate is being resolved in favour of a broad educational interpretation of design and technology… and in the schools context we must see the outcome of the activity not as three dimensional artefacts but as enriched and rounded young people.
>
> (Kimbell *et al.* 1991: 18)

The educational value of those activities, inherent in design and technology, to a curriculum that should meet the requirements of the twenty-first century were described in the original proposals for the National Curriculum as follows:

> It must stimulate originality, encourage enterprise and emphasise quality. It also needs to help pupils to develop a flexible approach to the problems and opportunities they will face in a rapidly changing society.
>
> (DES 1989: 1)

Clearly, there is a significant consensus about that which design and technology may contribute to pupils' later lives, but is this acceptance merely an 'act of faith'? Some educationalists now question the notion of the transferability of skills and aptitudes learnt in one context being readily applicable to another. In an examination of this issue, Hennessy and McCormick are highly critical of:

> … the expectation upon pupils to assimilate an all-purpose 'design process'…

> … the research on expert problem-solving and situated cognition points to the conclusion that the idea of a general problem-solving capability that can be used in a variety of contexts and subject areas again has little empirical justification.
>
> (Hennessy and McCormick, cited in Banks 1994: 98)

In essence, the theories emerging from studies of 'situated cognition' indicate that procedures adopted to solve particular problems may have a unique relationship to the subject matter or context in which that problem exists. In short, the procedures we adopt to solve one set of problems may not readily transfer to different contexts. It is easy to see how the emergence of such theories can be used to challenge some of the assumptions for the relevance of design and technology in the National Curriculum. In the interim report of the Design and Technology Working Group there does, however, appear to be some understanding of the subtlety of this issue:

> From what we know of the transfer of learning, the likelihood of transfer of a pupil's capability to undertake successfully a design and technology task is increased by a carefully graduated application of procedures and ways of operating in one context to another different, but not too dissimilar one.
>
> (DES 1988: 8)

What the research appears to do is to further undermine any notion that there is one effective design process, and it should provide further evidence, if any were needed, that rigid adherence to sequential procedures rarely helps pupils to solve specific problems or transfers to others later in life. This does not invalidate a commitment to the notion of transferable skills. What Hennessy and McCormick emphasise is the need for pupils to realise that there are multiple ways to solve any problem. They acknowledge:

> … situation specific learning by itself can be very limiting, precluding transfer when familiar aspects of a task are changed. Decontextualised knowledge is potentially a powerful aid which helps us master complex situations and results in far greater flexibility.
>
> (Hennessy and McCormick, cited in Banks 1994: 102)

There is some evidence, they suggest, that the extension of the theories associated with situated learning to different contexts and settings may encourage pupils to perceive a variety of different problem-solving strategies and increasingly be prepared to try them. This must be accompanied by teachers making explicit to their pupils cognitive strategies that may be appropriate to solving particular problems and, most importantly, 'metacognitive' strategies, that is, 'thinking about their thinking', which will strengthen their 'decontextualised knowledge'. Hennessy and McCormick point out that most of the research, though promising, has been carried out in languages and mathematics education; there is clearly a need to undertake similar studies in design and technology. The notion of decontextualised knowledge clearly keeps transferable cognitive skills on the agenda, though we should not be complacent about our claims. Teaching strategies which make these skills accessible are underdeveloped and overdue.

We are not looking for a single multipurpose process but, increasingly, a self-conscious recognition by pupils of many possibilities. Encouraging pupils to ask themselves questions about what they are doing, and why, may improve their ability to approach new problems in new contexts with confidence. In this respect, the following extract from the 1989 National Curriculum proposals might be considered prophetic:

> Another feature of progression is the ability to reflect upon practice and from this make explicit the concepts, procedures and strategies involved so that these can be carried over and applied consciously to new design and technological situations.
>
> (DES 1989: 9)

Hennessy and McCormick emphasise that a preponderance of activities that require pupils to work holistically may not provide opportunities to focus on the sub-processes of designing, such as research or generating ideas. Activities that focus on these issues may contribute to a growing understanding by pupils of approaches that may be useful and therefore relevant in different situations.

Some of the devices are already in place, because suggested strategies for the delivery of the National Curriculum (for instance, focused practical tasks (FTPs)) are an acknowledgement that it may be desirable to focus on a particular activity in which learning is enhanced by its removal from the overwhelming complexities of considering many aspects of designing in a holistic project. FPTs are most often used to enable pupils to acquire specific context-related knowledge or practical skills but are generally underused for making explicit the more abstract processes of designing. There is still a considerable challenge for teachers to develop appropriate pupil activities to address this. Pupil self-assessment may also focus attention on objectives for a learning challenge, encouraging greater transparency of the processes involved.

Process or content: 'risk' or 'certainty'?

The evolution of a model of design and technology in general education in which the capability sought is more than the acquisition of specific knowledge and practical skills presents particularly rigorous challenges to the teacher. Where the purposes of practical education have been instrumental and pre-vocational in nature, prescribed knowledge and skills have contributed a sense of security and certainty to what is to be taught. Where the purposes of practical education are predominantly 'general', as is the case with design and technology, there is less certainty about the knowledge and practical content of what is to be taught. This is particularly the case if we believe that it is the processes engaged in when designing that are a substantial source of the relevance of design and technology for all. For how can we know what knowledge and skills will be relevant to a process which is design, and therefore context-led? There has been considerable debate about this issue for many years and, despite changes to the way that knowledge and content have been specified in the National Curriculum 'orders', the subject has taken something of a 'middle road' approach to the issue. In referring to the knowledge component of design and technology, the interim report stated:

One position, strongly advocated by some experienced professional designers, is that the body of knowledge in support of design is unbounded; designers have the right and duty to draw upon knowledge from whatever sources seem likely to assist them in the quest for a solution.

(DES 1988: 10)

In contrast, the working group noted the 'prevailing orthodoxy' in secondary school teaching of subjects related to design and technology, and found 'relatively narrow veins' of knowledge. While the members of the group felt that they could not justify the latter and had considerable sympathy with the former (recognising, significantly, that some primary school practice may approximate it), they also recognised the daunting challenge of the complete openness of the situation. They proposed an 'intermediate position', in which knowledge would be prescribed in sufficient detail to give support and guidance to teachers, but which would be less restrictive than in the past. This was clearly important for those teachers coming from backgrounds in home economics, handicraft and project technology, where the need to teach particular knowledge and skills was perceived as an essential foundation to allowing pupils to engage in practical activity. In contrast, a minority of teachers, sympathetic to the central importance of 'designing' to practical scholarship, were more comfortable with an 'as and when required' approach to the teaching of knowledge and practical skills, and, since the early 1970s, many had been writing their own 'Mode 3' design-led syllabuses. These often did not specify particular knowledge and practical skills as part of course content. In essence, however, the scale of uncertainty and therefore challenge, posed to most teachers by a completely design-led approach to the relevance of content, had been contained by the National Curriculum Working Group's view of this issue.

In any design-related activity, however, there must be risk. There must be sufficient openness to encourage pupils to gain experience of the 'creative imaginative skills of hypothesis'; 'this is my guess – let's see if it works'. Indeed, if we believe in the 'workmanship of risk', we must accept uncertainty, trial and error (Green 1985: 59):

When we modify our prototype, it is, quite flatly because we guessed wrong. It is eminently true of design that if you are not prepared to make mistakes, you will never make anything at all. 'Research' is very often a euphemism for trying the wrong ways first, as we all must do.

(Pye 1983: 27)

The challenge to teachers is very clear: how can the risks inherent in work, which must embody degrees of uncertainty, be offset against the need for pupils to achieve success in their learning? The pressure to achieve good examination results, in the context of published schools' league tables, threatens to compromise what needs to be achieved in design and technology education:

In the current political climate, there is caution about how much freedom should be given to schools, teachers and learners to be creative. There are concerns that:

- it might not show immediate gains in knowledge, skill and understanding;
- valuable time might be wasted;
- creative success is difficult to measure and not subject to universal agreement.

(Davies 1999: 101)

It is understandable that teachers and learners should be cautious in such a climate. Anxieties for both, even where the aims and objectives of the design and technology curriculum are clear, can lead to an overvaluing of the end product as a tangible outcome rather than as an achievement of 'process objectives'; of destination rather than journey; and of 'doing all the stages' rather than striving for increased understanding of how they might interact meaningfully. In short, it can lead to striving for 'the workmanship of certainty'. Even without these pressures, the challenges are not insignificant, and teachers' understanding and attitudes to them are crucial in achieving the aims and objectives of design and technology. Many teachers of design and technology come from technical backgrounds (this is still true today of many mature entrants to teacher education), so it is unsurprising that they are concerned about how knowledge and making skills are delivered. It is naturally assumed that understanding of content and improvement in practical skills is achieved by undertaking tasks that progress from simple to complex. In general, this approach has been less well articulated in the case of process skills associated with designing. Classroom activities, particularly at Key Stage 3, have sometimes been dominated by the need to improve knowledge and practical skills, with concessions to the processes of designing being made only by offering limited choices in the nature of the outcome. In the worst cases these choices have manifest themselves in superficial preferences: the colour of a lid or the number of bends in a wire figure. These amount to solution restrictions and not exciting possibilities that will challenge pupils. This is evidence once again of 'safe work', of tightly constrained tasks offering security (ibid.: 104).

Total openness, however, representing the highest level of challenge for teachers and pupils, is clearly 'high risk' with all the attendant anxiety stemming from risk of failure. Roberts and Norman point out:

Design and Technology teachers might like their students to be engaged in open-ended problem-solving (i.e. ill-defined or wicked problems), but that alone would hardly be a realistic curriculum (the ability to address, effectively, such classes of problems, might however be a legitimate performance objective).

(Roberts and Norman 1999: 126)

How to achieve this objective must be given all the attendant care and concern for the escalation of experience that knowledge and practical skills appear to receive unquestioningly. Clearly the scenario outlined below is unacceptable and, in a perverse way shows how, 'When design gets too easy it becomes difficult' (Pye 1983: 35):

> I once watched a class of infants brought up on free activity methods, attempting to make paper hats for a Christmas party... One child finally evolved a very inadequate copy of a crown he had previously seen. The rest merely copied him. The argument is that the child should be free to choose what sort of hat he wanted, and that in finding out for himself how to achieve this end, valuable educational experience would be gained.
>
> (Bantock, cited in Kimbell 1982: 13).

Kimbell used this illustration to argue that the apparent openness and freedom in this situation (in which one might have reasonably expected pupils to exercise their creativity and decision-making skills), is so overwhelming that there is no freedom at all. The first child to bring form to any idea on the basis of previous experience is rapidly copied. If a comparable activity were run today it would clearly not foster the desired capability. Indeed, in its way, it is as ill suited to achieving this capability as an exercise that requires all pupils to make identical outcomes. Clues as to how this might have been made into an acceptable challenge are partly inherent in the quotation. Pupils could have been furnished with experience of other hats and head-gear, of carnivals and festivals, thereby providing some support for what party hats might be like. They could have also been furnished with experience of a range of materials, which, by the nature of their qualities, might have stimulated ideas. In both instances this provision would help define the parameters of the activity so that the teacher could plan resources and demonstrations ensuring pupils would have a source of experience from which they could draw their ideas and exercise their decision-making skills. Altogether a much more manageable challenge with less risk of pupil failure; appropriate definition and provision by the teacher of the context in which decision making will be encouraged and, crucially, 'support and guidance' rather than 'solution restrictions' are more likely to lead to a favourable outcome (Kimbell 1982). This is indicative of the central importance of teachers' attitudes to this issue.

Further guidance as to how pupils might experience increasingly challenging situations may be found in the way in which the National Curriculum in design and technology defines the achievement of capability:

> Pupils should be taught to develop their design and technology capability through combining their designing and making skills with knowledge and understanding to make products.
>
> (Department for Education 1995: 2)

This might be represented diagrammatically (see Figure 2.3) and, if we apply the same rationale to learning how to cycle (cycling capability), we might rationalise the learning process according to Figure 2.4.

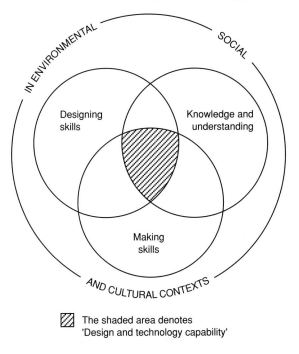

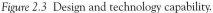 The shaded area denotes
'Design and technology capability'

Figure 2.3 Design and technology capability.

In recognising capability, Farrell and Patterson use a similar analogy:

> ... progression in capability cannot be represented in simple incremental steps. Like riding a bicycle you learn by concentrating on different aspects – pedalling or steering. Then quite suddenly you get the hang of it. You practice some more, in different circumstances or with different equipment, and gradually become more capable. Increasingly you can handle more variables and different challenges with broader and deeper understanding.
>
> (Farrell and Patterson 1993: 7)

Critically, the same authors remind us that: 'Capability is more than a collection of separate abilities' (ibid.: 3).

If capability is represented by the shaded portion of each diagram in Figures 2.3 and 2.4, the necessity of abilities being exercised together and with coherence in appropriate contexts is obvious. It is, however, possible to learn to cycle by focusing on 'pedalling and steering' as a stage to achieving full capability. (I am sure many of us have experience of willing parents holding the saddle, thereby temporarily removing the complexities of 'balance'.) As previously argued, it is entirely appropriate that the teaching of design and technology can assume a particular focus. This is helpful in defining stages in teaching where we feel increasingly able to trust students to undertake different levels of open-ended activity. As a way of managing risks for teachers and learners alike, we should be careful, however, not

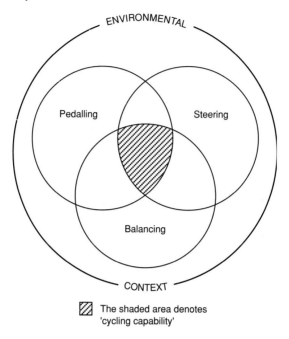

Figure 2.4   Cycling capability.

to neglect those aspects that can less easily be seen, for example 'balance' (in cycling) and designing skills (in design and technology education).

Conclusion

The source of an appropriate model of design and technology for all in general education must lie with the potential to foster skills that are transferable to new situations and thereby relevant to us all in the society in which we live. This must imply that specific bodies of knowledge and skills are not fundamentally taught as ends in themselves but contribute to the means by which pupils may engage in creative decision making and whereby outcomes to projects are made in order to make visible and test that decision making.

We have seen that there is considerable commitment to the view that the capabilities that this educational process has the potential to foster are transferable to new situations if our teaching aspires to encouraging pupils to be increasingly 'self-conscious' about how they are approaching the challenges inherent in their projects. As the processes engaged in when 'designing' are at the heart of fulfilling our aspirations for design and technology education for all, we must ensure that the challenges this necessarily implies are sufficiently open to allow pupils to exercise their decision-making skills. In managing those challenges, however, teachers must ensure the risks are not overwhelming.

As we have seen, pressures to succeed, and to be seen publicly to do so, threaten to drive teachers to models of practical education where success may be more certain and challenges have predictable and, arguably, more easily measured outcomes. Such a model of practical education cannot, in this authors view, be sufficient to sustain a rationale for design and technology education for all.

Questions to consider

1   Is the structure, content and assessment of GCSE examinations sympathetic to the maintenance of appropriate pupil challenges in design and technology education?
2   In practice, how can focused practical tasks be structured to develop the skills of designing?
3   How can the role of pupil self-assessment contribute to developing pupils' 'metacognitive' awareness (that is, pupils' 'thinking about their thinking')?
4   It is evident that 'mapping' the processes of designing can contribute to both understanding of the process and over-restrictive practice; can this apparent conflict be rationalised? (Consider the APU model of 'the interaction of mind and hand'; Kimbell *et al.* 1991: 20.)

References

Archer, L.B. (1974) 'Design in general education', Paper 4, presented at the Design in General Education Summer School, July 1974, Royal College of Art, London.

Banks, F. (1994) *Teaching Technology*, Buckingham: Open University Press.

Davies, T. (1999) 'Taking risks as a feature of creativity in the teaching and learning of design and technology,' *Journal of Design and Technology Education*, 4 (2): 101–8.

Department of Education and Science and the Welsh Office (1988) *National Curriculum Design and Technology – Interim Report*, London: DES.

Department of Education and Science and the Welsh Office (1989) *Proposals of the Secretary of State for Education and Science and the Secretary of State for Wales. Design and Technology for Ages 5 to 16*, London: HMSO.

Department for Education (1995) *Design and Technology in the National Curriculum*, London: HMSO.

Farrell, A. and Patterson, J. (1993) *Assessment in Design and Technology*, London: Hodder and Stoughton.

Green, P. (1974) *Design Education, Problem Solving and Visual Experience*, London: Batsford.

Green, P. (1985) 'Design education – a historical perspective', paper presented at the National Association of Design Education Conference, Haywards Heath Sixth Form College, London, pp. 53–61.

Kimbell, R. (1982) *Design Education. The Foundation Years*, London: Routledge and Kegan Paul.

Kimbell, R., Stables, K., Wheeler, T., Wosniak, A. and Kelly, V. (1991) *The Assessment of Performance in Design and Technology; The Final Report of the Design and Technology APU Project*, London: Evaluation and Monitoring Unit, Schools Examination and Assessment Council (SEAC).

Lawson, B. (1980) *How Designers Think*, London: Architectural Press.

Pye, D. (1968) *The Nature and Art of Workmanship*, Cambridge: Cambridge University Press.

Pye, D. (1983) *The Nature & Aesthetics of Design*, London: Herbert Press.

Roberts, P. and Norman, E. (1999) 'Models of design and technology and their significance for research and curriculum development', *Journal of Design and Technology Education*, **4** (2): 124–31.

Schools Council (1969) *Working Paper 26: Education through the use of materials: the possible roles of school workshops in the education of secondary-school pupils*, London: Evans and Methuen Educational.

3 Designing – what does it mean at Key Stages 2 and 3?

Melanie Fasciato

Introduction

The subject of design and technology concerns our relationship with the made world and our attempts to shape it to fulfil our needs and desires. To invent and improve is a basic human instinct. Technology is inextricably linked with design because, without appropriate technology, we would not be able to make the things we want and need. Although the term 'design' is used in other contexts, for example 'art and design', it is the use of the term 'design' in association with 'technology' that will form the focus of this chapter. As a school subject, design and technology is defined more by process than by content. It is the process of designing, supported by the implementation of appropriate technology to produce high-quality products, which forms the basis of National Curriculum design and technology:

> Pupils should be taught to develop their design and technology capability through combining their design and making skills with knowledge and understanding in order to design and make products.
>
> (Department for Education (DFE) 1995)

Designing is a complex process which needs to be understood by teachers if they are to enable their pupils to get the most from the subject. The importance of teachers' subject knowledge and understanding and its association with pupil achievement is emphasised by the Office for Standards in Education (Ofsted) in its inspection findings review:

> … teachers' subject knowledge was very strongly associated with high standards of pupils' achievement. Where teachers had good subject knowledge, they were more confident in planning and implementing learning tasks, more skilled in asking relevant questions and providing explanations and in using the National Curriculum programmes of study…
>
> (Ofsted 1995)

This chapter will deal with a number of fundamental questions:

- What is designing?
- What is designing in the National Curriculum?
- What is the 'design process'?
- What are the problems associated with using the 'design process' in schools?
- How do psychologists explain the process of designing?
- When are children ready to produce design drawings?
- What other design tools should children use?

What is designing?

This is perhaps the first question that needs to be asked when considering designing as an activity for pupils. We know that designing exists as an adult occupation; it is not an activity which has been invented for pupils to carry out in school, such as, for example, tossing coins to provide data for probability statistics. Individuals have always needed to make decisions about how to tackle problems that threatened survival and how to create ways of enhancing the quality of life. As the division of labour became more distinct, so the social structure of Western society became more complex, and certain design activities were given separate identities by associating them with particular professions. Many of these design professions now have high status, and designers are often viewed as being gifted and creative.

Research into design is recognised as an academic discipline, and many definitions of design have been produced, for example Archer (1965), 'a goal directed problem solving activity'; Jones (1970), 'to initiate change in manmade things'; and Matchett (1968), 'the optimum solution to the sum of the true needs of a particular set of circumstances'. Papanek (1992) states that 'all men are designers' and that, 'design is basic to all human activity'. Papanek's definition of design is a useful one to consider: 'Design is the conscious and intuitive effort to impose meaningful order'.

These definitions have some things in common: they all suggest that designing is not limited to those individuals who are involved with it at a professional level; indeed, they show clearly how we all design as part of everyday life. Design activities range from cooking a meal to composing a symphony, from designing to satisfy our own needs and desires to designing for a commercial market. Do the design skills that we teach our pupils enable them to impose meaningful order through conscious and intuitive effort, in line with Papanek's definition?

Are the design skills which professional designers carry out when designing clothes, chairs, houses and ships mirrored in the activities that we expect pupils to carry out in school? Perhaps, more importantly, as we have a statutory obligation to teach them, are they mirrored in the requirements of the National Curriculum?

What is designing in the National Curriculum?

The section of the National Curriculum document for design and technology, headed 'Developing, planning and communicating ideas', starts, as do each of the sub-sections, with the words, 'pupils should be taught to...'. Looking at the designing skills within in the National Curriculum programme of study, it is apparent that the emphasis is upon pupils making a conscious effort rather than using their intuition. The level and complexity of cognitive skills required by the designing activities vary, depending on the programme of study for the pupil's Key Stage and the attainment target level towards which the pupil is working. There is a prevalent misconception that designing is simply about drawing ideas on paper. A glance at the programme of study and the attainment target shows that it is not. We need to be mindful of the range of activities that are listed in the National Curriculum. A pupil will have to provide evidence of having met the following requirements in order to achieve a Level 3:

- generate ideas;
- recognise that their designs have to meet a range of needs;
- make realistic plans for achieving their aims;
- clarify ideas *when asked*;
- use words, labelled sketches and models to communicate the details of their designs;
- think ahead about the order of their work;
- choose appropriate tools, equipment, materials, components and techniques;
- identify where evaluation of the design and make process has led to improvements;
- identify where evaluation of their product has led to improvements.

[Paraphrased from the National Curriculum (DfEE 1999)]

This 'list' appears to suggest that there are certain elements that are common to all design tasks. Is designing *really* designing without having covered each of these elements? Should these elements be read as a linear process, one element leading to another? Is there a design process?

What is the 'design process'?

Both professional designers and teachers refer to 'the design process'. Perhaps it is this 'process' that will provide the answer. Teachers are encouraged to accept that there is a generalised procedure that pupils of all ages can use in order to come up with solutions to all design problems in a wide variety of materials, ranging from electronics to food. Since the 1960s, there has been a growing interest in analysing design methodology, or the process of design, and attempts have been made to equate design methodology with science methodology (for example the 1966 Birmingham Conference on 'The Design Method'). Design methodology appears to have much in common with scientific methodology, for example conjecture and testing. Layton (1993) explored aspects of the relationship between science and technology and design and technology in schools and considered the similarities and differences in the process models. Barlex (1991) compared the nature of modelling in science and design and technology at Key Stage 3. He concluded that it is an activity central to both disciplines and that both gave insight into pupils' thinking.

However, we need to remember that there is one major difference between design and science, namely, 'science is analytic; design is constructive' (Gregory 1966); in other words, science is concerned with 'how things are and design with how they ought to be' (Simon 1969). Design is used to tackle 'unstructured problems' (Frederikson 1984). These are problems that are complex combinations of factors that require individual solutions and the use of compromise. Their solution relies on a variety of information sources, both internal and external. They require intuition and affective response, the application of objective analysis and high-level cognitive skills. These elements may be combined to provide a means by which a design problem may be solved, but there are difficulties in establishing how these elements can be made into an understandable framework, or generalised procedure, which can be used by pupils as an aid to designing.

Frederikson (1984) suggests that a generalised procedure for problem solving can be created, but Cohen (1983) argues that the range of possible problems is so vast that there is little likelihood of their sharing sufficient ground for this to be possible. In the report of the Schools Council Design and Craft Education Project (Schools Council 1974) it was claimed that, through observation of designing and problem-solving activity in a number of different disciplines, a common pattern of activities could be determined:

> At the heart of the Project's work has been the development of problem solving approaches suitable for use in secondary schools... Students are encouraged to identify design problems, investigate them, produce and realise solutions, and finally evaluate end products.
>
> (ibid.: 1)

This is echoed in the definition given by the Design Council (1976) in its publication relating to the education of engineering designers. Yeomans, in his presidential address to the National Society for Education in Art and Design (NSEAD) annual conference in 1984, emphasised the similarities in the process as it applies to the craftsperson and the engineer. Yet too simplistic a definition should not be sought. If there were a common problem-solving process which was applicable to every unstructured problem, then all those who are involved in creative output would be capable of designing anything – and there have been few with the talents of Leonardo da Vinci.

Lawson (1980) argues that the activity of designing involves a multitude of elements, spontaneous as well as systematic. He cites a range of different designers (fashion, town planning, architecture, industrial, graphic and interior), and states that all of these design fields are related to the creation of an object, place or system which has a practical purpose and contributes to the visual environment, and they therefore belong in the same spectrum of activity. The elements of the design process are combined in different proportions, depending on the kind of design being undertaken, but there is such a thing as design methodology and each individual needs to develop his or her own process. It should be 'learnt rather than taught... for it is we, not others, who must design with it' (ibid.: 3). Lawson made a comparative study of the approaches employed by architecture and science students in tackling the same task. Science students began by trying to understand the problem, architecture students by looking at possible solutions that would lead them to an understanding of the problem. Darke (1978) also found this to be the approach most commonly used by architects.

Jones (1970) writes of a design method that consists of the design process and a design procedure. Design method is all the action taken while designing. The design process involves thinking skills and the design procedure concerns the communication of ideas, usually upon paper. He argues that the design method should be appropriate to the design problem that is being tackled, and, if necessary, a new design method should be invented. Whereas the thinking element, or process, should be as unconstrained as possible, the recording element, or procedure, should be rigorously undertaken. This definition takes into account the wide variety of possible design disciplines and problems, but there is an implicit recognition of the impossibility of defining the design process.

However, teachers are encouraged to accept that there is a generalised procedure that pupils can use to come up with solutions to all design problems, in a wide variety of materials ranging from electronics to food. Many different variations and adaptations of the design process model exist, some linear, others cyclic; some attempt to show the iterative nature of the process (Figures 3.1 to 3.3) but all have certain elements in common. Having identified a problem, the pupil establishes the needs to be met by the final solution, carries out research, generates ideas, details a specification, and plans and makes the final design, while evaluating at each stage. Pupils are usually asked to make explicit reference to each of these 'stages' in a design folder, transferring their own ideas and research on to paper in order to provide evidence that they have addressed each stage. But is this a realistic reflection of what actually happens when a pupil designs?

It cannot be denied that the design process has a beginning, because every 'project' undertaken in school starts at a specific point in the term. Teachers also impose a time limit, so the 'project' has an end. However, it is unravelling the 'muddle' in the middle that constitutes design which concerns us as teachers.

A study of Key Stage 3 children's problem-solving processes by McCormick *et al.* (1993) focused on the influence of the teacher in structuring the task and the effect of teacher intervention on children's problem-solving behaviour. They concluded that:

> … the design process is highly complex and not easily communicated. Children encounter different problems requiring different approaches, according to the kind of task and the stage reached in its solution… problem solving in [design and] technology may proceed in a very different way to that characterised by a holistic 'design and make' process.
>
> (ibid.)

However, great faith is placed in this systematic design process, and the GCSE examination boards use it as the basis of their assessment schemes. In many schools,

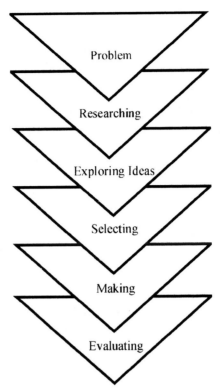

Figure 3.1 Design process model: sequential or linear design model.

this has led to a mechanistic view of a process that can be spontaneous and disorderly as well as systematic and methodical. Some designs are the result of 'happy accidents', whereby the designer has stumbled upon a solution when they least expected it, but unfortunately the design process adopted by many secondary schools does not allow for this. If a pupil cannot 'draw six, improve one and draw it up as a final design', they are unlikely to gain full marks from their design and technology teacher.

What are the problems associated with using the design process in schools?

In a study of the key factors that affect pupils' performance in Key Stage 4 project work, Atkinson (1993) concluded that some pupils are inherently creative and others are not. Within these two categories are two further divisions, those creative pupils who are able to design within the constraints of the GCSE examination design-process model, and those who are inhibited by it. Of those pupils who are not inherently creative, and this forms the vast majority of pupils, some are receptive to learning and using this design-process model, and others have conceptual difficulties with it and are demotivated. Obviously other, external, forces have a

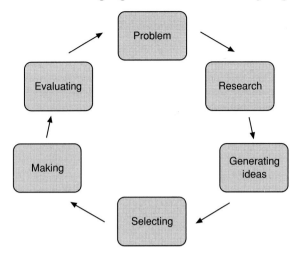

Figure 3.2 Design process model: cyclical design model.

bearing on achievement and motivation, for example, culture, context and parental and teacher expectations, but there are other factors associated with imposing a particular process model upon unwilling and ill-prepared pupils which are also important. These factors are: 'pupils' acquired modelling skills, conceptual skills regarding the process, inherent creative skills, the need for evidence for assessment causing the use of inappropriate forms of modelling by the pupils and cognition of the real process of designing' (Atkinson 1993).

Although there are elements that are common to most design activity, for example drawing up a specification and modelling, there is a major problem in trying to formalise the design process, as there are endless combinations of design contexts, design problems and designers. Each combination will generate a slightly, or radically, different design process, which in turn will result in a unique solution. The nature of the design process varies, depending on what is to be designed and who is doing the designing.

Welch and Sook Lim (1998) investigated the design strategies adopted by Year 7 students in Canada. They looked at whether the type of problem presented to these 'novice designers' determined the design strategies that they adopted. In a comparison between the design strategies used by the students in two different studies, they found that there was no significant difference in the strategies adopted to tackle two different types of problem. There was, however a significant difference between the strategies that the students adopted and the theoretical design process models. They concluded that:

> … students did not use two dimensional modelling to explore and communicate a design proposal, nor did they generate multiple solutions. They moved immediately to three-dimensional modelling but often lacked the requisite skills to develop their ideas. While students used the design

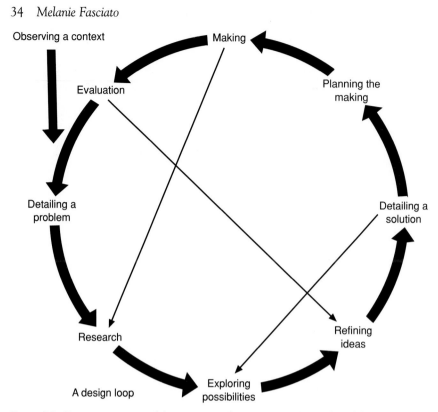

Figure 3.3 Design process model: interactive design process. Reproduced from Kimbell *et al.* (1987: 10) with permission from HMSO.

process skills identified in theoretical models their strategy was less linear and more iterative.

(ibid.)

In other words, whereas the students carried out some elements of the design process, they did not follow all of them, nor did they implement them in the order shown by many of the visual design process models.

Hopper and Downie (1998) studied the contrast between what teachers of design and technology in secondary schools believed to be the components of design and technology capability, how they taught these and the relationship between the teachers' professed educational objectives and the curriculum content and delivery models that they used. The authors are quite blunt about what they see as the failings of the design process that is used in schools:

By limiting the creative involvement of children to the employment of a linear and mechanistic 'design process' teachers run the risk of failing to fully exploit the potential of their subject to develop and nurture the skills, knowledge and personal qualities which they say are central to their subject.

(ibid.)

A solution to the problem of the imposition of *a design process* could be to allow a pupil to design and to chart the process as it occurs, with the teacher negotiating with the pupil. Pupils can thus design intuitively using the properties of a material, rather than having to choose a material that is appropriate for an already completed design, which did not necessarily take the properties of the material into account. Teachers need to question their reluctance to allow pupils to make the first thing that they decide upon. It is arguable that, rather than insisting that several alternatives are drawn on paper, which rarely reflects the process that the pupil actually used, the first idea should be drawn up in detail. The process can then be charted as changes are made as a result of evaluation. This would give a truer indication of the process that the pupil has undertaken and provide a useful basis for both formative and summative assessment. This notion of a 'process diary' has been promoted by Rogers and Clare (1994), and personal experience of using this with degree-level students suggests that it works, for both the students and the assessors. This leads us on to ask, what actually happens in our heads when we design?

How do psychologists explain the process of designing?

Designing is the end result of a series of complex thought processes. These thought processes will be employed by everyone who designs, whether they are children or adults. The process of human thought has been the focus of study of many psychologists who have formulated their theories within a variety of frameworks.

The behaviourist theory of human intelligence is based on the formation of associations by response to a stimulus. This is known as the associationist model. Berlyne (1965) suggests that patterns of thought are the result of an individual choosing from a variety of responses associated with each stimulus that they are given. The strongest link is chosen in each case and these links are in turn strengthened or weakened by experience. This theory regards goal-directed thinking and problem solving as a type of repeated mental trial and error. Lawson (1990) suggests that this model is applicable to imaginative thought or day dreaming, in which thoughts are allowed to wander, making associations where they will. Brainstorming is an example of this and can be a very fruitful method of designing.

Gestalt psychology has a long-established tradition of the study of problem solving, which is continued today in the popular works of Edward de Bono. The basis for Gestalt theories of thinking lies in the exploration of processes and the organisation of data, as distinct from the mechanistic behaviourist theory, which is based on building associations. Wertheimer (1959) considered that problem solving consists of first understanding the structural relationships of a situation and then reorganising them by using a number of different techniques, such as redescribing the problem and using analogies, until a solution is achieved. This forms the basis of a number of design techniques which are frequently used both professionally and in schools (see Shepard and Fasciato (1992) and de Bono (1988)). De Groot (1965) stressed the need to acquire the ability to recognise relationships and patterns and to take context into account in problem solving. In a study of chess players he showed how reading situations and recognising the patterns of games was used by experienced players as opposed to the reasoning skills employed by the less experienced players in their game. This has parallels with the problem solving associated with designing. Experience and familiarity are important factors in influencing the way in which a design problem is approached and the creativity of the solution. However, with experience often comes the ability to foresee problems and this can hamper creativity instead of aiding it. We take the 'soft option' because we choose to avoid taking risks and the possibility of making errors.

Gestalt psychologists are also interested in the representation of the external world in human thought, which links to the notion of designing. Bartlett (1932; 1958) conducted a series of experiments to show how having a schema, or internalised mental image, allowed the organisation of past experiences that could then be used to structure and interpret future experiences. He asked subjects to remember drawings and then to reproduce them after a number of different time lapses. Where the drawings were more meaningful to the subjects, their reproductions were more successful. It is in drawing upon internalised images of the external world that much design thinking is achieved. Where experience of the material world is meaningful and past knowledge can be used, reinterpretation of past experiences and their incorporation into new schema can take place: this is designing. Harrison (1992) produced research evidence to support this in his study of children designing model houses and using these to learn how to draw plans and elevations.

When the child is placed in the position of designer, Bruner (1961) states that it should be treated as a design professional and have information available to him or her. This should include existing products and a range of materials, as well as the opportunity to extend his or her own experience. This is supported by Laxton (1969), who, while discussing design education in schools, denies that children can be creative if they do not have experience to draw upon. The decision-making process is supported by four sources of information according to Markus (1969). He lists these as the designer's own experience, the experience of others, existing research and new research. It is the combination of these four that influences designers' thinking.

This is where contextual or critical studies of design play an important role. Since the revision of the National Curriculum, design and technology has included 'disassembly activities' in which children may analyse products of a similar type to that which they will be required to design, prior to designing their own product. This can take several forms including the investigation of existing products to help determine design criteria, the examination of historical objects followed by speculation about their use and modern equivalents, and the evaluation or testing of products prior to redesigning or improving them. The 'experience of others and existing research' are combined in this investigation of products.

When are children ready to produce design drawings?

As with all issues in developmental and educational psychology, opinions vary. The psychologist who pioneered work on the growth of understanding and the development of intelligence in children, Jean Piaget, identifies four stages of mental growth. The first two years of life are the sensory–motor phase, when the child is preoccupied with learning about the physical world and gaining motor control. Between the ages of two and seven, the child can reason intuitively, using imaginative play to build a mental model of the world. Notions of space, time, movement, speed, number, measure, whole and part, class and sub-class, and serial order are not yet settled. Structural concepts are in a constant state of flux; 'conservation', to use Piaget's term, has not yet been reached. It is not until the concrete operational stage of development, between the ages of seven and twelve, that the child can begin to deal with abstract concepts, and therefore enters the stage where it is ready to begin drawing abstract ideas on paper. However, it is not until the child reaches the age of twelve to fifteen that he or she can begin to reason logically and systematically, and is able to fully engage in drawing designs of the sort that adults can produce. Differences in the time taken to arrive at each of these stages should be taken into account. At early Key Stage 2, before the stage of concrete operations, when the world finally starts to make sense through the formation of schemes of operational thought, it may seem unreasonable to ask children to draw their designs on a sheet of paper before listing the resources they are going to need to make them. For many children, drawing on paper can be difficult and demotivating, especially when graphic skills are not taught. We carefully nurture skills of letter and number formation, of reading and manipulation of number, but we tend to leave graphic skills to chance. In our increasingly visual world, there is a growing need for the curriculum to be based on literacy, numeracy and 'graphicacy', where 'graphicacy' could be defined as communication in which words or mathematical notation alone are insufficient.

In the wake of the Industrial Revolution, designs no longer evolved to keep in step with the requirements of the customer, with gradual changes being implemented that were simply slight variations of a traditional design. The increasing rapidity of change in technologies and scientific understanding was such that consumer markets required radically different concepts, not variations on a traditional theme. The designer no longer experimented with designs by implementing changes to objects that they had themselves produced, for example the watchmaker and the blacksmith. Design intentions had to be expressed in ways that the people who were going to make the product could understand; this led to the development of 'design by drawing' (Jones 1970). Baynes and Pugh (1981) explored the development of engineering drawing and how it made possible the development of the steam engine. This was because concrete imaging methods, such as sketching, 3-D modelling and engineering drawing, provided a tool with which designers could not only explore their own ideas (thinking on paper) but also with which they could communicate with others who were involved in the designing and making of an object. However, drawing as a form of communication needs to be taught.

Egan (1995), commenting on the drawing behaviour of Key Stage 1 pupils, noted their preoccupation with 'aspects of task management'. The children all drew with relative fluency, but kept up a commentary on what they were doing ('now I have to put feet…') and how they were doing it ('now I need some blue…'). She suggests that, until a child feels confident in the mastery of the 'management tasks' of drawing, he or she is unlikely to be able to concentrate on wider aspects of design thinking.

Samuel (1991) explored how to combine Key Stage 2 children's making skills with their ability to draw. He recognised that making skills were generally further advanced than designing skills and that children often designed products that were impossible to make. He strongly promoted the idea of introducing constraints on making and carefully structuring their learning of design skills. The constraints suggested included limitations on materials and size, and he advocated involving the children in discussions about why these limitations were necessary (for example, the size of battery to be housed in a model lighthouse). He also promoted the teaching of drawing techniques that enable children to show hidden parts. This could be done by asking children to draw familiar objects from the top and side (see Harrison 1992), before requiring them to produce design drawings with the same elevations.

There are many skills associated with designing and some of these are generic skills, which are transferable to other areas of the curriculum, for example researching, brainstorming and prioritising. It is of vital importance that these are recognised as being skills which should be 'taught not caught'. It has already been suggested that children need to be taught skills of graphicacy, but research shows that there are other aspects of designing which also need to be taught.

What other design tools should children use?

One of the most important aspects of designing is modelling ideas in order to explore possibilities before making a product. Harrison (1992) looked at how pupils model their ideas at both Key Stages 1 and 2. He defined modelling as: 'a simplified representation of something created for a specific purpose'. He also categorised the purposes to which modelling is put: helping with thinking, communicating form or detail, and evaluating a design or selected features of it. He argued that at both Key Stages 1 and 2 most making is in fact modelling. Indeed, many teachers of Key Stage 1 and 2 pupils refer to the products that children make as their 'models'. Harrison's research involved studying the relationship between 2-D (drawing on paper) and 3-D modelling and the need for teachers to recognise the complexity of transitions between them. He concluded that asking children to model in 2-D, something that they are going to make in 3-D, was not a helpful approach. He found that some Year 6 children believed that 'if they drew around a hat (producing an elliptical shape on a piece of card), this would somehow make a hat shape'. Their ability to sketch ideas in 2-D for a 3-D hat was unrelated to their ability to draw a net or pattern that would produce a 3-D hat.

In the same study, children were asked to make small-scale models of houses using boxes provided by the teacher. They then successfully drew plans of their houses, by looking down into the rooms, after they had made the houses. A third group were asked to design their ideal house. They started by first drawing plans of their own houses, with some problems posed by the stairs. They then had to discuss and draw in 2-D the layout of their ideal house and model this in a choice of media: Lego, Quadro or cardboard boxes. Lego was relatively easy to use as it was used 'ground up' and the original 2-D plans were used to show the lines of the walls. Quadro was more difficult to manipulate as it required pupils to have a 3-D 'vision' of what the rooms would look like. The cardboard boxes were constraining because they only came in certain sizes. This last group did not refer to their 2-D plans at all. He concluded that the function of modelling was different at different times and that an ideal sequence for this design problem would have been:

1   Use Lego to think out your design for your ideal house.
2   Use a more permanent medium to make a corresponding model that you can detail and keep.
3   Make 2-D plans and a sketch of what you have made.

It is interesting to compare these findings with what Piaget had to say about the stages at which children are ready to use abstract reasoning and when they can reason logically and systematically. Lego provides an adaptable and easily constructed modelling medium which does not require children to use abstract reasoning as did the Quadro, or to compromise, as the boxes forced them to do. The Lego also provided a model from which children could take measurements in order to construct their finished product in another medium without recourse to their original 2-D plans. Thus, they moved from 2-D to 3-D modelling before making the final product.

Liddament (1993) suggests that models may be used not only as 'information carriers;... clarifying and enlarging upon information', but can also be used to teach ideas, concepts and conceptual relationships that are important in design and technology education. Do the skills of researching existing products, finding out what the end user wants, modelling in 2-D and 3-D, and using models to provide information for making a product, bear any relationship to those skills which professional designers carry out in the course of their specialised designing?

Conclusion

Design and technology is one of the National Curriculum subjects that requires children to develop and implement design skills. Design is made up of a very wide range of activities that encompass speaking, listening, reading, writing, drawing, mathematics, researching, planning and making 3-D models, as well as a myriad of other skills. It is a complex process that cannot be easily defined or conveniently squashed into a framework which, when imposed on children's design activities, ensures success every time. It can be both intuitive and conscious, yet we require the design activities of our children to be almost exclusively conscious because of the strictures imposed by 'the design process', which has been adopted by the design and technology establishment. In reality, children design using a range of different variations of the process, rarely incorporating all of the 'required' elements. In order to provide proof of having completed 'the process', design work is often faked or carried out retrospectively in a mechanistic way.

Children can design, but they need to be taught design skills. Additionally, the skills they use in design situations need to be negotiated with and nurtured by the teacher. Children need to have developed the necessary cognitive skills before they can be required to develop design skills. When children have reached the right stage of development, then these skills can be taught through design activities that feed into and enhance children's experience of design and technology. Design education is not simply about pupils coming up with ideas for things to make, it is as much to do with teaching them to handle change.

Design activity is basic to all human activity, every sentient person designs, but rarely would they recognise the 'design process' as being central to their own design activity. Design is the product of a series of complex thought processes that have been explained and described by psychologists in a number of ways. Experience and familiarity play an important part in designing, as well as the development and enlargement of schemas.

Design skills can be taught and developed, but designing is dependent upon context and individual preference.

Questions to consider

1   What do you think are the design skills that we should teach our pupils 'to enable them to impose meaningful order through conscious and intuitive effort' (Papanek 1992)?
2   The National Curriculum consisted of separate programmes of study for designing and for making until the 1999 revision. What do you think are the advantages and disadvantages of having a single programme of study that encompasses the two?
3   Harrison (1992) wrote that making is modelling at Key Stages 1 and 2. What do you think he meant and do you agree? When does modelling become making?

References

Archer, L.B. (1965) *Systematic Method for Designers*, London: Council for Industrial Design.
Atkinson, E.S. (1993) 'Identification of some causes of de-motivation amongst Key Stage 4 pupils in studying technology with special reference to design and technology', in Smith, J.S. (ed.), *IDATER 93: International Conference on Design and Technology Educational Research and Curriculum Development*, Loughborough University of Technology, Loughborough.

Barlex, D. (1991) 'A comparison between the nature of modelling in science and design and technology', in Smith, J.S. (ed.), *IDATER 91: International Conference on Design and Technology Educational Research and Curriculum Development*, Loughborough University of Technology, Loughborough.

Bartlett, F.C. (1932) *Remembering*, Cambridge: Cambridge University Press.

Bartlett, F.C. (1958) *Thinking*, London: George Allen & Unwin.

Baynes, K. and Pugh, F. (1981) *The Art of the Engineer*, Cardiff: The Engineering Council.

Berlyne, D.E. (1965) *Structure and Direction in Thinking*, New York: John Wiley.

Bruner, J. (1961) *The Process of Education*, Oxford: Oxford University Press.

Cohen, G. (1983) *The Psychology of Cognition*, London: Academic Press.

Darke, J. (1978) 'The primary generator and the design process', in Rogers, W.E. and Ittleson, W.H. (eds), *New Directions in Environmental Design Research*, Proceedings of EDRA (Environmental Design Research Association) 9, Washington, DC.

de Bono, E. (1988) *Practical Thinking*, London: Penguin.

De Groot, A.D. (1965) *Thought and Choice in Chess*, The Hague: Mouton.

Egan, B. (1995) 'How do children perceive the act of drawing? Some initial observations of children in an infant school', in Smith, J.S. (ed.), *IDATER 95: International Conference on Design and Technology Educational Research and Curriculum Development*, Loughborough University of Technology, Loughborough.

Frederikson, N. (1984) 'Implications of cognitive theory for instruction in problem solving', *Review of Educational Research*, **54** (3): 363–407.

Gregory, S.A. (1966) *The Design Method*, London: Butterworths.

Harrison, M. (1992) 'Modelling in Key Stages 1 & 2', in Smith, J.S. (ed.), *IDATER 92: International Conference on Design and Technology Educational Research and Curriculum Development*, Loughborough University of Technology, Loughborough.

Hopper, M. and Downie, M. (1998) 'Developing design and technology capability – rhetoric or reality?', in Smith, J.S. (ed.), *IDATER 98: International Conference on Design and Technology Educational Research and Curriculum Development*, Loughborough University of Technology, Loughborough.

Jones, J.C. (1970) *Design Methods: Seeds of Human Futures*, New York: John Wiley.

Lawson, B. (1980) *How Designers Think*, London: Architectural Press.

Layton, D. (1993) *Technology's Challenge to Science Education*, Buckingham: Open University Press.

Liddament, T. (1993) 'Using models in design and technology education – some conceptual and pedagogic issues', in Smith, J.S. (ed.), *IDATER 93: International Conference on Design and Technology Educational Research and Curriculum Development*, Loughborough University of Technology, Loughborough.

McCormick, R., Hennessy, S. and Murphy, P. (1993) 'A pilot study of children's problem solving processes', in Smith, J. S. (ed.) *IDATER 93: International Conference on Design and Technology Educational Research and Curriculum Development*, Loughborough University of Technology, Loughborough.

Matchett, E. (1968) 'Control of thought in creative work', *Chartered Mechanical Engineer*, **14** (4).

Papanek, V. (1992) *Design for the Real World*, London: Thames and Hudson.

Rogers, M. and Clare, D. (1994) 'The process diary: developing capability within National Curriculum design and technology – some initial findings', in Smith, J. S. (ed.) *IDATER 94: International Conference on Design and Technology Educational Research and Curriculum Development*, Loughborough University of Technology, Loughborough.

Samuel, G. (1991) 'They can never make what they draw', in Smith, J.S. (ed.), *IDATER 91: International Conference on Design and Technology Educational Research and Curriculum Development*, Loughborough University of Technology, Loughborough.

Shepard, T. and Fasciato, M. (1992) *Design and Technology Matters*, Cheltenham: Stanley Thornes.

Simon, H.A. (1969) *The Sciences of the Artificial*, Cambridge, MA: MIT Press.

Welch, M. and Sook Lim, H. (1998) 'The effect of problem type on the strategies used by novice designers', in Smith, J.S. and Norman, E.W.L. (eds) *IDATER 98: International Conference on Design and Technology Educational Research and Curriculum Development*, Loughborough University of Technology, Loughborough.

Wertheimer, M. (1959) *Productive Thinking*, New York: Harper & Row.

Yeomans, M. (1984) 'Art and Design: Interdependent or Interrelated?', Presidential address to the National Society for Education in Art and Design (NSEAD) Annual Conference, Bath, UK.

Reports and official publications

DfEE and QCA (1999) *The National Curriculum*, London: HMSO.

Department for Education (1995) *Design and Technology in the National Curriculum*, London: HMSO.

Design Council (1976) *Engineering Design Education*, London: Design Council.

Ofsted (1995) *Design and Technology: A Review of Inspection Findings*, London: HMSO.

Schools Council (1974) *Design and Craft Education Project*, London: Arnold.

4 The educational value of making

Rachel Mason and Nicolas Houghton

Introduction

Within the National Curriculum for both design and technology and art, 'making' is identified as an important element of the attainment targets. This chapter explores the place of 'making' in the school curriculum, and draws on research into craft education in secondary schools[1] carried out by the authors for the Crafts Council between 1994 and 1998.

Two things are important to state at the start. First, we come to the topic from an art background but understand design and technology and art as closely linked. Common attributes, according to Allison (1982), are:

- their shared concern with technical processes involving skills in the use or manipulation of materials;
- interactive relationships between the materials, purposes and processes employed in realising designs;
- the fact that these designs reflect the culture and period in which they are considered and produced.

While we accept that art is concerned more with the visual than the functional aspect of making, these issues are of equal importance and interest to design and technology teachers.

Second, we know the term 'craft' has negative connotations for some design and technology teachers. The Crafts Council defined craft education and/or making as 'active involvement in designing and making one-off individual artifacts that necessitates development of pupils' imaginative skills, visual sensitivity and a working knowledge of tools and materials'. We found this definition too narrow and sought one that is more inclusive of practice in design and technology.

One of the main questions we had to address in writing this chapter was: *is* making the same thing as craft? In our research, presented in a later section of this chapter, we found that pupils and teachers used the two terms interchangeably, as did the Crafts Council. The problem with the word 'making' for us is that, although it describes certain practical activities that take place in design and technology and art, it omits reference to the quality of pupils' achievement or effort. We found that craft education has been widely used historically to define making in the school curriculum. Although it has been interpreted in many ways (for example, as 'practical knowledge', 'technology', the 'design-and-make process' or 'intelligent making'), essential to them all is the notion of craft as a form of skilled knowledge that is acquired through engaging purposefully with materials and processes at first hand over time. The definition we finally arrived at, therefore, was that craft is skilled knowledge expressed through making and doing.

The way making is now being viewed and taught in schools has come about for different reasons. To help us determine why teachers and pupils responded to our questions the way they did, and the implications of this for the future, we reviewed the history of craft education. This is presented in the first section of this chapter below. Through this research into historical justifications for craft education in schools, we found that craft knowledge has traditionally been undervalued because it differs from numerate and literate forms of knowledge and is tacit. However, the research and arguments in the literature convinced us that this knowledge is essential for realising and understanding the sorts of designs, materials and processes that are central to design and technology and art. There are significant general educational benefits also to be gained from competence in skilled knowledge that deserve to be better known, and the arguments that people today use to justify the place of making in the curriculum are summarised in the final section of this chapter.

The origins of craft education

Formal craft education in Europe originated in the apprentice system, which came into being in the Middle Ages. It was regulated by guilds that represented the various trades (for example, tailoring, carpentry, masonry and leather work). Under this system, which was predominantly male, masters trained apprentices in a specific craft discipline over a number of years. Once they had achieved a high level of skill, apprentices submitted an example of craft work to be examined by another master. If successful, they became masters themselves.

Craft was also engaged in by women in the privacy of the home. In this context too it was learned through observation and practice but was seldom done for money. Contemporary educational theorists, such as Howard Gardner (1990), argue that apprenticeship, which employs intuition, touch and sight and relies on demonstration, observation and constant practice, remains the most effective way of learning craft knowledge.

Painting and sculpture were originally understood as craft.[2] During the fifteenth and sixteenth centuries, however, they gradually became known as 'art'. The social status of artists as opposed to craftspersons increased and a separation took place, in which art came to be viewed as much more important in society. Whereas people valued art as something produced by talented individuals who used their intellect and imagination (Greenhalgh 1997), they viewed craft as something more mechanical and as a form of labour, catering for their functional needs.[3]

The Industrial Revolution had a decisive impact on the useful crafts. Factory methods of production meant that traditional hand crafts survived only where there was a limited demand for specific products, such as, for example, local or luxury items (stone carving, bell making and carpentry), or where it was not sufficiently profitable to invest in the technology needed for mass production. However, industry also depended on skilled craft workers who were paid more than unskilled workers. Industry also adopted the apprentice system to train skilled workers.

One influential view of the Industrial Revolution is that mass production lowered standards of taste and making. The Arts and Crafts Movement, which flourished at the end of the nineteenth century, condemned production by machinery as a social evil and argued against a distinction between art and craft. William Morris, its unofficial leader, was uncompromising about this. He believed that all artists should see their true function as craftsmen, creating 'artistic' objects of daily use with their hands, rather than remaining aloof from society in a rarefied world of pure painting and sculpture. For Morris, civilisation could not exist without artistic objects, and these could not be made by machine.

The Arts and Crafts Movement influenced people's views of craft throughout the twentieth century. Ironically, it also influenced the establishment of design as a discipline and as a profession that serves the needs of industry. It is the importance that this movement attached to the quality of everyday objects that has attracted attention, whereas its opposition to industrial production has tended to be disregarded.

According to Macdonald (1970: 291), the roots of the term design lie in the Latin verb *designato*, meaning arrangement of order. In the Middle Ages, design usually signified the marking out or first stage of an artefact; however, during the fifteenth and sixteenth centuries it came to mean the inventive process for every type of artwork – hence the 'arts of design'. Whereas in the eighteenth century it tended to be associated with a 'lower art' of ornament, in the nineteenth century it resurfaced as the 'art' that is applied to functional objects, in order to make them more appealing, or beautiful.

The way in which craft education has developed in compulsory schooling reflects these early origins. There are useful and artistic strands in the school curriculum that overlap but are treated very differently. The useful strand has always been afforded lower status and remains gendered, in spite of the Sex Discrimination Act of 1975. For better or worse, each strand has been, and continues to be, influenced by the anti-industrial ethos of the Arts and Crafts Movement. Increasingly, during the twentieth century, they have both been influenced by new conceptions of 'design' and 'technology' that consider hands-on manipulation of materials to be less important.

Craft education in compulsory schooling

Girls' domestic crafts

A useful strand of craft education was introduced into compulsory schooling in 1870 in the form of needlework. At that time needlework was considered as fundamental for the education of girls as reading, writing and arithmetic for boys.

According to Attar (1990), it was intended to prepare working-class female pupils for menial, poorly paid employment, or to be mothers and wives. Between 1890 and 1910, however, the ideas of the Arts and Crafts Movement inspired some teachers to include 'decorative needlework' (techniques of embroidery) in schooling and involve the girls in developing original designs. The content of 'plain needlework' was typically very basic, centring on learning how to sew seams, hems or knit socks (Sutton 1967). In some schools, girls were taught other aspects of housewifery, such as laundry, cleaning, bed making, nursing the sick and home hygiene and cooking. It was believed that, by stressing the science of home management, the health and well-being of the population could be improved. Therefore, from 1900 these were gradually combined into a new subject, called domestic economy or domestic science (Yoxall 1965; Rutland 1997).

During the 1950s and 1960s a dominant view of a nuclear family living in an ideal nuclear home influenced policy and practice in this strand of craft education. The commonly held view that a function of schools was to train girls to become model housewives (Attar 1990) was reflected in a change of the subject's name during the 1950s from domestic science to home economics. However, there was little alteration to its emphasis on cooking and needlework. During the 1970s and 1980s, home economics continued to be taught mainly by and to females and for utilitarian reasons (Eggleston 1976; Attar 1990; Rutland 1997).

Industrial crafts and handicraft for boys

In the 1880s, a useful strand of craft education for boys entered the upper elementary curriculum in the form of industrial craft. It was viewed as a form of pre-vocational training, and the main reason it was introduced was public concern about a partial collapse of the apprentice system and an alleged loss of competitiveness of UK industry, which was attributed to a lack of suitably trained, skilled workers (Penfold 1988). 'Manual', 'technical' or 'industrial training', as it was variously called, was taught initially in separate school buildings. At this time, many pupils left school at the minimum age to enter trades and other manual callings. Craft education for boys became part of the grammar school syllabus after 1902, where it continued in an almost unbroken tradition right up to 1944. Taught in specialist workshops, the content consisted mainly of practical work in wood and sometimes metal.

According to Penfold (1988), Barnett (1986) and Taylor (1988), manual training in schools never achieved its vocational aim for three reasons. First, the school boards were unwilling to adequately fund it. Second, some teachers turned away from industrial craft because they were influenced by the Sloyd system of creative educational handiwork in Sweden[4] and the Arts and Crafts Movement. Third, it suffered from a problem of low status, because in the UK school system skilled knowledge has always been, and still is, considered inferior both to academic forms of knowledge and to creativity.

Nevertheless, as Eggleston (1976) has pointed out, craft teachers were adept at pursuing other aims. They consistently sought to develop technological understanding and aesthetic judgement (refinement of taste) in pupils through the use of materials. They also tried to develop a range of socially approved value orientations towards life. In particular, they promoted 'artisanal' values, such as respect for work and workmanship, the dignity of labour, honesty, integrity in the use of techniques and materials and avoidance of the easy answer. In addition, they were successful at opening up scholastic forms of knowledge to less academic pupils, through integrating them with practical knowledge.

The drift away from industrial training in this strand of craft education was reflected in a change of name to 'handicraft' early in the twentieth century (Blanchford 1961; Penfold 1988). Right up to the 1960s, the content of this strand consisted mainly of woodwork, with an emphasis on acquisition of basic technical skills (such as planing, sawing and chiselling). These were taught as a prelude to making simple artefacts for the home, such as book-ends, stools, pipe-racks, small tables and lamps. Metalwork was less common and focused on the skills of soldering, brazing, forging, instrument making, model engineering and hammered metalwork.

Although manual work was included in the examination system from 1917, it was scorned by universities and other potential employers. Consequently, entries remained bottom of the league table, along with home economics and needlework (Penfold 1988: 62). The 1944 Butler Act, which raised the school leaving age from fourteen to fifteen and restructured secondary education to a tripartite system of grammar, secondary and technical schools, could have given industrial crafts a new impetus. However, they continued to be afforded low priority by policy makers and handicraft was relegated to being a subject mainly for less academic pupils attending the lower status secondary schools. Moreover, the technical schools, which could have given industrial training a boost, were never funded in great numbers. To make matters worse, there was always a shortage of specialist teachers.

Handiwork for young children

Handiwork for young children had fundamentally different origins. In this case, the influence came from theories of child learning originating in continental Europe. The idea that the mind is trained by the hand and eye lay behind Froebel's 'occupations', practised by children under seven as early as 1854. Froebel believed that children learn best through sensory experience, symbolisation and play. The series of 'gifts' he created (innovative educational toys) were designed to show the qualities of forms and his related 'occupations' (structured games) were designed to help young children acquire concepts and skills (Sienkiewicz 1985). According to Sutton (1967), Froebel's concept of kindergarten education was not well understood and most infant teachers involved children in mechanical craft routines, such as paper-cutting, plaiting, cardboard modelling, stick laying, block-building, etc.

By 1905, hand–eye training, stressing accurate working habits and clear thinking, was advocated for older elementary children too. Hand–eye training was said to form 'habits of industrious, careful accurate work', was 'a valuable aid in the development of character', and it was believed that it 'awakens interest in the industrial side of national life' (Sutton 1967: 242). However, a different, more artistic, concept of handiwork, intended to develop aesthetic feeling for form, gradually developed. Handiwork (in lower elementary schools only) incorporated an increasingly wide range of materials and practical activities, including Plasticene modelling, paper-folding and -cutting, cardboard modelling, wire and string work and light woodwork. It was justified instrumentally on a great many counts: because, for example, it is 'natural' for children and assists their intellectual development; it illustrates number, geometry, history, and geography; it inculcates moral values attending to all useful work; and it also has the benefit of 'giving fun'.[5]

Aesthetic crafts

The influence of the Arts and Crafts Movement resulted in aesthetic crafts (such as leather work, book-binding, stencilling, basketry, pottery, enamelling and weaving) being introduced into elementary art around 1928. In 1926, the Hadow Report had made an impassioned plea for combining 'the various forms of practical instruction', arguing that 'the maximum educational benefits from practical work such as modelling, light woodwork, sewing and weaving occupations, are secured when they are combined with drawing and painting'. In suggesting they are closely connected, it recommended crafts in general, not only to teach vocational skills, but also to strengthen character and 'develop while at school tastes for occupations that they [children] can practise in their leisure time in later life' (Sutton 1967: 252–3). A strong case was made for offering girls a wider craft experience than needlework and it was argued that learning how to use tools is useful for both girls and boys so they can 'do small repairs in the home'.

In 1938, however, the Spens Report for Secondary Education formally separated 'aesthetic' from 'non-aesthetic' crafts, claiming that they could be taught either with an emphasis on the aesthetic aspect (as in weaving, carving, fabric printing and handwriting) or the constructional aspect, as in carpentry and woodcraft (Sutton 1967: 259). The report acknowledged another educational role of crafts, that of providing pupils with the sense of pride and satisfaction that comes from making something well.[6]

Aesthetic craft spread rapidly into secondary art lessons during the 1950s (Sutton 1967). Most often this took the form of studio pottery, but other crafts such as furniture making, hand-woven and embroidered textiles and jewellery were sometimes taught. At this time traditional handicrafts were experiencing a revival and the national system of drawing examinations was revised to include them (Carline 1968). Meanwhile, the subject was undergoing radical reforms, brought about by the discovery that children have their own mode of artistic expression, which is different from that of adults, coupled with the arrival of 'modern art'. The reforms were also backed by psychological theory which claimed that children have an innate need to communicate their emotions and thoughts. In response to these ideas, the expressive art movement proposed a freer approach to teaching art. This was intended to enable children to express their innate creative abilities through art and craft (MacDonald 1970; Thistlewood 1992).

The success of the expressive art movement owes much to Herbert Read. His influential book, *Education through Art* (1943), was widely interpreted as promoting art as the basis of education in general, on the grounds that it communicates with the realm of feeling and develops pupils' imagination and creativity. Because he understood talent as an innate ability within the child that a teacher encourages and releases, this aspect of art education was afforded precedence over teaching craft skills. By this time, the artistic and useful strands of craft education had moved poles apart. McCormick (1994) and Parker (1986) both allege that this dichotomy was class-based. Handicraft and domestic science were perceived to be pre-vocational education for the working classes, whereas art was perceived of as developing the talent and aesthetic sensibilities of the middle classes. Korsenik (1992) notes that in America art education has been justified as a vehicle for self-improvement, achieving a measure of refinement, and as morally and spiritually uplifting; and that it has always been free of any association with training and manual labour. This also appears to be the case in the UK.

A Ministry of Education pamphlet about metalwork, published in 1952, does not mention any vocational role for craft. Instead it argues that craft is important because it stimulates children's intellectual development, gives them confidence 'born of accomplishment', encourages discernment and promotes good taste. It claims that through creative experience in a variety of media, children can be led to appreciate and enjoy quality of craftsmanship and beauty. 'Discussing and planning, solving problems of construction, persevering in difficult operations, and realising that the finished work will be judged worthy of commendation or criticism' were recommended on the grounds that they are character forming. A similar justification for craft was proposed by Robertson in 1961, when she pointed out that completing an artefact from start to finish taught a sense of responsibility and perseverance and habits of sustained work.

Robertson (1952; 1961; 1989) grounds her comprehensive argument for craft as education of the senses and the refinement of touch in her observations of young children's intuitive response to the sensuous qualities of natural materials and immersion in playing with them. She proposes that the satisfaction of making is a legitimate educational goal in itself and that it is central to all children's general education, for a wide number of intrinsic and extrinsic reasons. These include instilling a deep, intuitive understanding of the properties and possibilities of natural materials; and teaching responsibility and intuitive thought and freedom through discipline. Robertson also repeats the traditionally held view of handicraft teachers that it helps pupils' academic work. However, it is important to note that she is adamant that craft education has nothing to do with development of the analytical skills that are central to learning in most other school subjects. Instead, she advocates teaching craft skills, 'because there is real satisfaction to be gained from making something well which will last and in which each part is skilfully fashioned' (Robertson 1952: 79).

Craft, design and technology

During the 1960s, 1970s and 1980s, the entire educational system underwent reform. This happened because society was experiencing fundamental changes in the technological and economic organisation of work, domestic life and leisure. The introduction of comprehensive schooling and raising of the school leaving age to sixteen, combined with the increasing realisation that, in future, most pupils would have several careers in a lifetime, signalled the need for new ways of dealing with less academic pupils. The traditional craft subjects (handicraft and domestic science) were neglected by policy makers, who considered the skills they transmitted had been rendered obsolete by scientific and technological advances and by the dramatic rise in consumption of mass-produced goods. In addition, their failure to stretch pupils' intellect and imagination was criticised at a time when schooling was moving away from emphasising memory, stored knowledge and passivity, towards adaptability, originality and participation. Conversely, however, the need to give pupils first-hand experience of the world through materials was also recognised as more important, given that second-hand experience was becoming available as never before through information technology and the mass media.

Throughout the 1960s, 1970s and 1980s a new way of thinking about practical knowledge in schools gradually emerged with the help of government funded research initiatives, such as the Technical Vocational Educational Initiative (TVEI).[7] It took the form of two separate reforming movements in the useful strand of craft education, centring on the twin concepts of technology and design. They were united in their desire to modernise the useful craft subjects through an emphasis on interactive process, not product. However, the design education lobby sought to transform that which already existed in schools, and the technology education lobby wanted to introduce something new. At first both reforms experienced considerable resistance from traditional handicraft and homecraft teachers. Nevertheless, by the 1980s, 'craft, design and technology' (CDT) was the accepted name for the single new subject that combined these strands (Down 1983; Penfold 1988).

According to Penfold, the design education movement emerged from dissatisfaction with traditional methods of professional training in art and reflected the general upsurge of interest in creativity at the time. Design education would give pupils the capacity to adapt, initiate, modify, solve practical problems and make design decisions creatively, in a variety of social contexts. It also embraced awareness of the need for aesthetic considerations to underpin the making of commercially successful, mass-produced systems and products. Work with materials that sought to promote investigative, creative, expressive and evaluative thinking on the part of children in response to identified human needs gradually became an important focal point of wood and metalwork. Although traditional craft skills pertaining to wood and metalwork, for example, continued to be taught, the process of practical problem solving was afforded greater educational importance than producing finished products (Down 1983). Craft teachers agreed to these changes because of their desire to raise the status of their subjects and give them academic respectability, but the concept of design never had more than lukewarm support from those wedded to making in the workshop. Despite the efforts at reform, most schools continued to refer to the subject as 'craft' during the 1970s, and it remained the province of low achievers.

Technology, understood as the results of human action and as bringing about change in, or exercising control over, the environment, originated in secondary schools as 'applied science'. It was officially introduced into the core curriculum in the form of mechanical engineering and electronics in 1985. In *The Curriculum 5–16* (DES 1988), the Department of Education and Science expressed the view that education through the use of materials was essential for all children because human beings are tool users and most students are destined for a life of productive action. It also argued that, because material culture depends on increasingly sophisticated technologies, it is necessary to initiate students into this culture during schooling. Within the CDT curriculum, the technology aspect emphasised learning about mechanisms, systems and components, rather than hands-on making of artefacts or products. It drew heavily on civil, electrical and mechanical engineering sources but ignored many other technologies, such as medicine and urban design. It embraced clothing in home economics as 'fibre science' and cooking as 'nutrition' and 'food technology'. Traditional craft teachers experienced difficulty delivering the new curriculum content, according to Penfold (1988), and were widely considered to be teaching low-status as opposed to high-status technology, which was taught in science.

CDT enthusiasts, therefore, held different views of how and why practical knowledge should be taught, although they all considered it had a central role in bringing about change and exercising control over the environment. For design education enthusiasts such as Baynes (1998), the primary purpose of CDT was to develop design awareness. It was about people shaping their environments though deductive reasoning and expressive work, and was not purely practical and utilitarian (Rutland 1997). The DES (1988) defined technology, on the other hand, as an area of experience, rather than a discrete subject. Likewise, the Engineering Council (1992) understood technology as a practical organisation of skills and knowledge, rather than a form of knowledge in its own right (although they accepted the need for a knowledge base in formal subjects such as science and mathematics). Technology for them centred on solving practical problems associated with specific skills disciplines (for example, mechanical engineering); and they criticised the way the essential elements of designing and making had become generalised problem solving in CDT without any specific knowledge base.

Technology was strongly promoted by the government in the 1980s for vocational purposes in successive attempts to establish closer links between industry and schools.[8] The TVEI, which was funded by the Department of Industry, the introduction of city technology colleges and the rapid expansion of engineering and industry training courses under City and Guilds, Business and Technical Education Council (BTEC) and General National Vocational Qualification (GNVQ) were all intended to make practical subjects more vocational. The additional equipment and materials provided for by funding under the TVEI made it possible for some schools to offer high-level alternative skills-based courses in vocationally orientated technological studies, ranging from computer studies and information technology, through to electronic music and photography. Traditional craft teachers were supportive up to a point. However, they argued that the skills-based knowledge these initiatives promoted was being erased by an ever-increasing emphasis on qualifications and examinations, which tested other forms of knowledge such as communication skills and conceptual and analytical thinking.

Art, craft and design

Parallel changes took place in art during the 1960s, 1970s and 1980s with the inclusion of design subjects such as 'graphics' and 'fashion and textiles'. There was a steady increase throughout this period in 'basic design' teaching, which reflected the values of a society of mass consumption. Design was sometimes associated with making children more discriminating consumers (Taylor 1992; Schofield 1995). Meanwhile, the concept of craft was increasingly linked to the production of high-quality goods for the wealthy. The arrival of an 'avant-garde' in the history of craft for the first time (Frayling 1990) also meant that it was equated with 'fine art' and originality was considered more important than craft skills. Although some professional 'craftspeople' embraced new technologies, craft education in art tended to resist this development.

Until very recently, and with the exception of consumer-orientated rationales, craft has tended to be justified in art on psychological and general education, not economic, grounds. Throughout the 1960s, 1970s and 1980s, it continued to be valued for expressive reasons, as a means of educating the whole person and as offering a different experience from other school subjects. In the tradition of the Arts and Crafts Movement, it was sometimes associated 'romantically' with transmission of heritage and nostalgia for the past. The perception of craft as providing solace in a rapidly changing society is nicely illustrated in a speech at a DES conference to art, CDT, design and home economics teachers in 1985, which praised the virtues of professional craftsmen (Jeffrey 1985: 73).

Craft, design and technology in primary schools

Design and technology was introduced into primary education during the 1980s, being variously called 'primary engineering', 'craft' and 'design and make'. Primary-age children had experienced using card, paper, clay, fabrics, everyday materials and construction kits in making activities for many decades, within the discovery approach to learning emanating from the philosophy of John Dewey. Design and technology, however, demanded a more active involvement of children in practical work. There was more emphasis on the design process (that is, on involvement in processes related to defining and meeting needs, generating ideas, designing and making plans and on implementing and evaluating them). At primary level, making in design and technology tended to focus on resistant materials, such as card, wood and construction kits rather than on non-resistant materials such as textiles, food or graphic media. Although Ritchie (1995) claims this movement suffered from being a watered-down version of secondary CDT and from confusion about the distinctive natures of science, design and technology, he points out that this was the first time the importance of the design process had been acknowledged at this educational level.

The National Curriculum and craft

How craft is thought of and taught in UK secondary schools now is fundamentally affected by the passing into law of the 1988 Education Reform Act. The National Curriculum (DES 1989) specified twelve required foundation subjects with attainment targets, which listed the skills, knowledge and understanding pupils must attain at completion of the four Key Stages. One of these twelve subjects was 'technology', the name of which was subsequently amended to 'design and technology', and another was 'art'. Design and technology was compulsory until pupils reached the end of Key Stage 4, usually at age sixteen, and art was compulsory until pupils reached the end of Key Stage 3, usually at age fourteen. Common explanations given for the introduction of the National Curriculum are:

- It was the political will of government to control the work of teachers.
- There was widespread concern that pupils' educational experience was too variable and uncertain (Eggleston 1996) to meet the needs of commerce and industry (Steers 1995).

One outcome of its introduction was anxiety that skills-based learning was being diminished (Mason and Iwano 1995).

Although technology was, in part, an amalgamation of home economics and CDT, it was presented as a brand new interdisciplinary subject for all children, linked to science, business studies, art and mathematics (Eggleston 1996). According to Kimbell (1985: ii), it was so innovative, teachers had to 'make it up as they went along'. In its original manifestation, it was divided into technology and information technology 'capability' – capability signifying a concern with practical action (Barlex 1998). The unique educational contribution proposed for the subject as a whole was learning the capacity to operate effectively and creatively in the made world through the design and make process. It was stressed that pupils were expected to apply both knowledge and skills to solve practical problems.

The technology orders specified four attainment targets – 'identifying needs and opportunities', 'generating a design', 'planning and making' and 'evaluating' – but made no reference to craft. According to Eggleston (1996), it was the problems teachers new to this kind of work were experiencing, coupled with inadequate resourcing, that caused Her Majesty's Inspectorate (HMI) to report that standards of practical work were falling. Criticism was also expressed that pupils were only experiencing low technology making and not doing work that led to completed artefacts. The vocational lobby argued they were not being equipped with the kinds of skills required by UK industry and that lessons ought to be less theoretical (Eggleston 1996). In 1992, new orders for design and technology were issued, with more emphasis on skilled making. This time there were two attainment targets only: 'designing' and 'making' (Eggleston 1996). Then, in 1995, the Dearing Committee's recommendations for further changes were accepted, which allowed for the possibility of craft to continue to be taught in this subject. According to Brecon (1998), the new order was broadly welcomed as a decent compromise, flexible enough to allow teachers with a traditional craft approach to follow their inclinations, alongside others with a twenty-first-century, 'high-tech' view of school technology.

In the case of art, the English National Curriculum orders had two attainment targets: 'making and investigating' and 'knowledge and understanding of art'. Although the term craft was originally excluded, the revised orders specified that art should be interpreted within the document to include 'art, craft and design'. Craft was not defined, however, although the orders stated it could include pottery, textiles and jewellery. Moreover, reference was made to 'artistic heritage and traditions', but not to 'craft heritage and traditions'; and to 'quality of expression' rather then 'craftsmanship'. According to Robinson (1995), the consequence of National Curriculum art has been more picture making, and Hughes (1995) claimed that craft continues to exist only if and when schools make a choice to employ trained craftspeople to teach it. The proposal in the original orders that art teachers could contribute to the aesthetic aspects of the technology curriculum did not come about and making has become ever more separated in the two subjects.

Pupils' and teachers' views of craft

This section of the chapter summarises our findings about teachers' and pupils' views of craft in secondary school from the national survey we carried out for the Crafts Council. When we used the term 'craft' in the first stage of this research, it elicited mixed responses from both design and technology and art teachers. Most art teachers considered it is impossible to distinguish craft from art. Design and technology teachers were evenly divided in their opinions about it. One half claimed the concept of craft is redundant in post-traditional society, whereas for the other half it represented a 'traditional' approach to teaching skilled knowledge, with which they firmly agreed. However, the majority of all design and technology and art teachers were adamant that making is a very important general educational tool. Three-quarters of them stated that it has intrinsic educational value, for which they gave three main reasons. First, it fulfils a basic human need for sensory experience. Second, it enables pupils to develop important forms of knowledge and skills which are unavailable to them in other school subjects. Third, it provides an intuitive approach to acquiring knowledge, through hands-on experience with materials. Many of them understood this to be a unique form of knowledge acquisition that is valuable in its own right. As one design and technology teacher explained:

> Making is different from other areas of the curriculum, the pupils behave in a different way because of the different relationship. You can address their

learning differently, particularly those who find written work very daunting. Turning the two-dimensional into the three-dimensional doesn't happen anywhere else and also, the application of a broad range of knowledge, through to the final effect of everything you know coming together to produce something which will last.

Teachers repeatedly mentioned four extrinsic or general educational reasons for teaching craft. First, it brings personal fulfilment. Second, it develops 'higher order thinking skills' including problem-solving, imagination and ideas, managing time, coordinating resources, etc. Third, it enables knowledge and understanding of all kinds to be demonstrated in tangible form; and fourth, it reinforces and contributes to knowledge and skills developed in other school subjects.

At the same time, they were very concerned that 'making' and 'craft' are low-status concepts in society. Typical comments were 'society doesn't value it' and 'the way education is going there is less emphasis on it'. As noted in the introduction, the concept of craft was understood to be very problematic by large numbers of design and technology teachers in particular, as the following comments show:

> There has been a de-craft or non-craft focus in schools for so long that really positive work needs to be done to improve its status in relation to art and that of skills.

> Before we can get anywhere, we need to raise the profile of the crafts.

The second part of the Crafts Council research investigated Key Stage 3 and 4 pupils' views of making and of craft, which are extremely positive. We established that design and technology and art are very popular with pupils in this age group and that they very much prefer making to any other aspect of learning in these subjects. Typical comments were:

> I like working with my hands, using my hands to actually construct something.

> You have something to show for your time. There is all that research and stuff and that takes time, but it's worthwhile. When I've made something, it feels really good. To other people it might not matter, but to me it does. I think people are missing out if they don't get a chance to do things like that.

> Designing and making, because I like drawing my design and when I make it its exciting.

Pupils of this age clearly gain enormous personal pleasure and satisfaction from hands-on experience of and engagement with materials and processes. When the research interpreted making more broadly to encompass the much wider range of craft activities actually practised in society in comparison with schools, it established that involvement by pupils in DIY, sewing, cooking and fixing bikes, clothes, furniture and electrical goods at home is commonplace. The finding that the majority of them participate in making activities outside school conflicts with a widely held view within education, therefore, that they are in decline:

> In our cellar there's a complete Victorian kitchen range which I have put back together again with my brother. We repaired all the panel doors and re-hung them, as well as dismantled and repaired a mangle.

The pupils in this research expressed interesting views about why making at home is preferable to making in school and how it should be taught. For example, they like making at home because it gives them greater ownership over projects, they can spend more time on them and there are no distractions from other pupils. They praised teachers who physically demonstrated practical processes and were critical of those who did not. They almost unanimously rejected evaluation as a component of the design and make process but were very keen to acquire practical knowledge and skills:

> I don't <u>have</u> to make it at home and I don't <u>have</u> to do what I'm told, what and where and how. I like it better at home because I can ask for help when I want and need it and not when the teacher thinks I've done something wrong.

Moreover, pupils are keenly aware that making skilfully is not a question of innate talent and ability. They find it demanding and challenging educationally. In this research they were able, during interviews, to articulate reasoned judgements about quality processes and outcomes and to explain their personal strengths and weaknesses:

> My clock [is the best thing I made]. It was very curvy and I carved it all out. There was a sun and it had flames around it and I had done it all on a coping saw – all on my own – and I filed it as well and the finishing paint was very... was all different colours, blotched together and I really liked the effect it had and enjoyed making it.

They also recognised that making in design and technology and art serves different educational purposes and had strong views about which subject they prefer, how it should be taught and what they do and do not like to make at school:

> Well we were told to make a money box and there was no research material there at all apart from shop catalogues which we were supposed to go though and find anything that we liked. I just couldn't. I refused to get into it because I just thought it [the project] was so badly thought out and I made a very naff money box.

Arguably, one of the most important findings to come out of the research, in view of the current tendency towards a broad approach to practical learning, was that pupils' motivation for making is positively affected by the level of skills they are able to acquire within a particular discipline base, and vice versa. The majority very much preferred working with the materials and processes in which they had developed the highest degree of technical competence and were dismissive of 'cardboard technology':

> It's easy if you know what you are doing, but it's difficult to learn to use new tools and things. But once you learn, it's easy.

Most significantly, perhaps, pupils were convinced that learning to make has a high educational value and will be useful to them in their future lives:

> You can't just have knowledge all the time. I mean making involves the future; it's a thing you have control of.

> Um, I think it will be [useful] yeah, because it might be the grades in the other subjects that get you a job but having good grades in practical subjects shows you are more independent, more practical.

> If you can't make anything, you won't be able to do nothing!

Contemporary rationales for making

The historical review, in the first section of this chapter, identified artistic and useful traditions of craft education dating back over 100 years in which making is central. Sometimes they have been viewed as discrete subjects and sometimes as having things in common. Whereas making entered schooling for vocational reasons, there are other reasons why it has been valued. A recurring problem is that making has been afforded a very low status. Attempts have often been made to improve this situation by emphasising its contribution to the development of cognitive abilities in pupils, such as creativity, practical problem solving and/or design thinking. For the same reason it has sometimes been subsumed within the more prestigious concepts of technology, art and design. However, in none of these is it viewed as essential. At the present time, the term craft is discredited as is shown by its absence from National Curriculum policy.

Our analysis of both past and present justifications for making as an aspect of both design and technology and art suggests it has been valued broadly for four main reasons. First, for vocational reasons: as something which contributes to the nation's economy, in the sense that it prepares students for the workforce. Second, for social and/or cultural reasons: as something that helps individual students to fit into and adapt to present-day society or contributes to its future development. Third, for child-centred and psychological reasons: as something which positively affects the development and well-being of individual pupils. And fourth, for knowledge-based reasons: as a unique form of knowledge which is important in its own right. To help us arrive at our own conclusions about its relevance at this particular time, we shall discuss each of these in turn.

Vocational rationales

Although making in the useful strand of craft education has consistently been promoted for pre-vocational reasons, we are sceptical about this. The vocational rationale has a poor record of success historically and schools do not have the necessary resources to respond to the rapid pace of industrial and technological change. On the other hand, we do not agree with the populist view that there will be no employment opportunities for pre-industrial forms of making (crafts) in the twenty-first century[9]. Society still needs skilled artisans in a variety of occupations such as catering, car mechanics and hairdressing. Whether schools are the right places to acquire this kind of knowledge is another matter.

When the concept of vocational training is extended to include the notion of 'transferable skills' it may have more mileage. Although we need to be cautious about this (Eisner 1999), research evidence may be emerging that learning to make in school contributes to employability in general. A study at Middlesex University (Cave *et al.* 1998), found that employees rated 'practical competence' much higher than cognitive abilities and personal qualities. Moreover, although the craft graduates studied by Cusworth and Press (1998) did not obtain employment immediately after completing their specialist training, it was subsequently found useful for a wide range of jobs.

The vocational argument for making is really an economic one. In this connection, Roberts and Baynes (1998) suggest that the emphasis on mass production that underpins present government policy for design and technology is misguided, because consumerism is more important to the nation's economy than production. They cite the dramatic rise of public concern for lifestyle and the expansion of DIY- and craft-based hobbies as evidence that, as an act of consumption, other forms of making contribute very significantly to the UK economy. If these developments were taken seriously by government, design and technology would cover a much broader range of making traditions than is currently the case.

Socio-cultural rationales

A dominant rationale for making in both strands of craft education during the first half of the twentieth century was that the discipline involved in fashioning well-crafted objects by hand inculcates positive citizenship attributes and values such as hard work, perseverance and attention to detail. (This is a rationale that Japanese technology and art teachers take very seriously to this day.) The second half of the twentieth century saw the development of more future-orientated rationales for the social benefits of making. This is particularly the case in the useful strand of craft education where terms like technology and the design and make process have been substituted for craft. In this way, making is understood to contribute to the development of useful mental capacities.

The design and technology teachers who participated in our research subscribed to both positions. Whereas some of them reiterated Robertson's (1952; 1961; 1989) view that making an artefact from start to finish teaches a sense of responsibility, perseverance and habits of sustained work, others valued its role in developing 'higher order thinking skills' such as problem solving, imagination and ideas. The view that making contributes to the development of problem-solving abilities that are useful practically, both in the workplace and in everyday life, is well supported in the literature (e.g. Sternberg and Caruso 1985; Schön 1991) and is something with which we concur. However, we consider the increasing tendency to promote skilled knowledge as an adjunct to other forms of knowledge to be misguided because it underplays its intrinsic educational benefits.

That making contributes to pupils' life enhancement and thus to society in general is something schools in Switzerland, Japan and Sweden take very seriously. In this connection, another recurring social justification, especially in the artistic strand of craft education, has been that it contributes to the refinement of aesthetic value or taste. (In design education, which is linked to consumerism, this rationale was also economic.) This view is no longer tenable. Whereas modernism once preached something called 'good taste' to which everyone was supposed to aspire, post modernism posits a variety of taste cultures all of which are meaningful to the people concerned. The concept of aesthetic value has continuing significance, however, because skilled knowledge always involves judgements of quality on the part of the maker about the manipulation of materials and processes and about fitness for purpose.

Perhaps because of our art background, we also consider knowledge of making in the past an important social and cultural aim for two reasons: first, because our understanding of present and past technologies is interconnected; and, second, because there are good grounds in the literature about craft for arguing that traditional forms of making can play a key role in bringing together communities of people of diverse backgrounds. The cultural and multicultural potential of making (understood as skilled knowledge or craft) is something education systems in other countries appear to recognise but is not usually taken very seriously in the UK.

Child-centred rationales

There is a long tradition of making in the artistic strand of craft education being valued and justified for psychological reasons. For example, reference is sometimes made to its role in the creative and aesthetic development of the individual child. However our historical research shows that psychological child-centred rationales are not just restricted to art. (Creativity is viewed as a positive attribute of design thinking in the useful strand too.) Moreover, the most common justification for making given to us by both design and technology and art teachers in our survey was a psychological one – that it brings personal fulfilment and develops a sense of pride. With reference to the pupils' views, we think it is important to point out that pride is a consequence of the acquisition and demonstration of 'skilled knowledge' not just making *per se*.

Another recurring rationale for making is that it helps children who are low academic achievers to succeed with scholastic forms of learning. Whereas this is typically framed as an equal opportunities issue, we believe it addresses more fundamental educational outcomes and aims. As many of the design and technology teachers who participated in our survey observed, the reason making reinforces and contributes to knowledge and skills in other school subjects is that it enables them to be demonstrated in tangible form. In other words, it offers all children an alternative mode of learning that elevates hand labour to a position of primary importance. Howard Gardner's (1990) theory of multiple intelligence, which challenges the standard hierarchy of mind over body and thought over physical labour, is informative in this regard.

According to Gardner, there are six distinct forms of knowledge (linguistic, logical/mathematical, musical, spatial, personal and bodily kinaesthetic), which are value-neutral in the sense that there is no biological basis for placing them in a hierarchy. (Each type of cognition arises in response to specific environmental conditions and serves different cultural needs.) Bodily kinaesthetic knowledge is intuitive, according to Gardner. It is acquired through sensory perceptions and motor actions and tapped chiefly through the stimulation of these capacities; and it is mastered by observation, direct involvement and informal coaching, analogous to the manner in which early or non-scholastic forms of learning are ordinarily acquired. (He notes that in their early years of life people acquire a considerable amount of knowledge simply by virtue of their interactions with physical objects and other persons.) Because so many cultural practices, ranging from catching a ball to driving a car and dancing, necessitate learning physical skills, it is a form of knowledge all individuals must attempt to master and integrate with the other knowledge forms over their lifetimes. Gardner believes craft education is particularly conducive to the development of bodily kinaesthetic knowledge because it is so intimately tied to labour (doing) and the physical handling of materials and it demands exceptional motor control.

Of particular importance for our findings about the low status of craft education is his observation that Western civilisation falsely privileges linguistic and mathematical intelligences (probably because they are most useful in business, war making and academic careerism). Whenever these two forms of intelligence are used to predict success and failure, he notes that bodily skills become relegated to the lowest levels of the hierarchy.

Knowledge-based rationales

Making has been justified in both strands of craft education as a unique form of knowledge which is pleasurable in itself and to which every child has a right. Like Gardner, Robertson (1952; 1961; 1989) is adamant that the skills and knowledge it develops through the senses differ fundamentally from the analytical skills and knowledge that characterise other school subjects. Its particular educational contribution, in her view, is the development of intuitive thought and an understanding of the properties and possibilities of materials through the refinement of touch. Anthropological theory strongly supports her claim that the satisfaction gained from making is a legitimate educational goal in its own right, although this is unlikely to be heeded by policy makers in the current socio-political climate.

For example, Dissanayake (1992) explains the pleasure children feel in 'making' as a consequence of a biological predisposition in humans to be makers of tools and to use them to contribute to the prosperity and well-being of society and to leave their mark on the world. Like many anthropologists, she is unwilling to distinguish craft from art[10] and explains the latter as a form of behaviour called 'making special' with roots in the tool-making and ceremonial practices of our ancestors. In this connection, she notes that every single study of pre-modern societies stresses the social as well as the economic function of made objects and artefacts and that they serve to embody the norms of social groups and to articulate their deepest social values. (For example, she views the care and control bestowed upon weapons and tools as a metaphor for the care and control the person wishes to execute in using it.)

Gell (1992) writes about productive and artistic technologies as components of a technical-cultural system or domain. The characteristics of all technologies, for Gell, are that they invoke knowledge and skill, involve work, are attended by uncertain outcomes and are dependent on poorly understood processes of nature (ibid.: 57). His case for art as a form of magical technology is too long to present in full in this chapter. In brief, however, he understands the power of artwork to move people as resting on the technical prowess (magic) which gives rise to them and which casts a spell over viewers so they see the real world in 'enchanted form'. For Gell, productive and artistic technologies both serve essential social functions in that the former provides the means for production of subsistence and goods and the latter is the means whereby we are persuaded of the necessity and desirability of the social order. Like Gardner, he is highly critical of the tendency in Western civilisation to play down the significance of the technical–cultural domain, given how utterly dependent we are on it in every department of life.

We sympathise with the view expressed by the DES (1988) in *The Curriculum 5–16* that education through and in the use of materials is essential for all children because the majority are destined for a life of productive action. Moreover, the claim that they should be exposed to the newer forms of making in society, on which material culture now depends, is persuasive. (Even though it is possible to counter this by arguing that, in an age of virtual reality, hands-on experience with materials and processes is important also because it helps children to deal with concrete reality.) But while we do not wish to deny pupils access to the newer technologies, we agree with traditional craft teachers that is it is rash to devalue 'craftspersonship' and the opportunity to capitalise on the educational advantages of physically making something. In other words, that the real and abstract design and make distinction is important.

So what is distinctive about craft education as opposed to technology and design? Press and Cusworth (1996) use craft, as opposed to design, where a person is engaged fairly directly in both making and an end product. Must the product be a physical one or can *it* be virtual? This is the million dollar question we find difficult to resolve.[11] Whilst we accept that the concept of craft is problematic at a time when making is experiencing a fundamental paradigm shift, it connotes something very important educationally – namely, the skilled knowledge that is derived from fashioning artefacts, artwork, systems and objects competently and well. Our research found that what pupils and teachers valued most about making was the concrete learning achievements and sense of control over the environment that is facilitated by skilled knowledge. Such educational benefits only accrue where aesthetic judgements (judgements of quality) about the manipulation of materials and processes are recognised as important in the design and make process and where making operates within a specific discipline base. These considerations are neglected in National Curriculum policy for both design and technology and art.

Conclusion

The question remains, does making have any distinctive educational virtue in the twenty-first century? Having investigated historical and contemporary justifications for craft education and shown that it is popular with pupils, we have arrived at the following arguments in its favour, if, and only when, it is understood as skilled knowledge or craft:

1   Making, in itself, is inherently pleasurable and is a critically important biological drive. The pleasure people feel at handling and 'crafting' physical materials is inextricably linked to the tool making and ceremonial functions of our ancestors and making plays an essential part in human evolutionary development. Initiating students into artistic and productive technologies is important educationally because they have been crucial to human survival and these needs have not gone away.

2   Practical knowledge (knowing how) is as integral to life experience as scholastic or academic forms of knowledge (knowing that). There is theory in the literature (for example, Sternberg and Caruso 1985; Schön 1991) to support the view that knowledge acquired tacitly through the hands-on experience of making is central to the acquisition of practical knowledge which is useful in human decision making, both at work and in everyday life. Making in schools builds confidence in this kind of knowledge.

3   Making is central to all pupils' learning, much of which takes place intuitively and is tapped through the stimulation of sensory perceptions and motor actions. Whereas schooling as a whole tends to concentrate on developing linguistic and mathematical intelligence, skilled making (craft) is uniquely conducive to the development of bodily kinaesthetic intelligence (Gardner 1990). This form of intelligence is wrongly viewed as inferior.

4   The relative balance needed between making and other forms of knowledge in the school curriculum is difficult to determine at a time when new

technologies are increasingly blurring these boundaries. However, we find the argument for students experiencing some form of skilled making through an apprenticeship mode of learning very persuasive. The danger is that in trying to intellectualise this kind of intelligence, we run the risk of destroying its essential character, which is that it is tacit and intuitive and acquired through hands-on experience.

Notes

1   The ideas presented in this chapter result from research into craft education in design and technology and art courses in secondary schools. This research, which had two parts, was sponsored by the Crafts Council and carried out by a team of four researchers at Roehampton Institute, London between 1994 and 1998. The first part took the form of a questionnaire survey of all secondary schools in England and Wales, and the second part involved interviews with 126 teachers and 239 pupils in selected schools. Records of observations of lessons, questionnaire analyses and other information about this project can be found in three research reports located in the Reference Library at the Crafts Council (Mason and Iwano 1995a; Mason and Bedford 1997; Mason and Houghton 1997) and at the University of Surrey Roehampton Learning Resources Centre. The Crafts Council published two executive summary reports (Mason and Iwano 1995b; Mason 1998).

2   Although we think there are good reasons for including painting and drawing in our definition of craft, the survey of craft education reported in this chapter was restricted to making in ceramics, textiles, metal and wood.

3   This separation of art and craft was reinforced by the foundation of the first formal academies in Europe for teaching the arts of design (drawing, painting, architecture and sculpture). These institutions combined skills training with the 'scientific' study of ancient history together with principles of symmetry, proportion, anatomy and perspective. Meanwhile, craft continued to be taught through the apprenticeship system as a trade.

4   According to Penfold (1988: 31), Sloyd translates into English as 'any form of skilled hand activity'. He points out that this system of educational handiwork, which originated at Naas near Gothenberg, emerged from a country that, at the time, was almost entirely unindustrialised.

5   Handiwork was taught by teachers who were largely unskilled in crafts and was limited by a lack of any specialist facilities.

6   Until 1946 it was unusual for craft to be taught as a subject within art in secondary schools. The art syllabus consisted mainly of drawing and painting and was justified as hand–eye training, to develop accuracy of observation, concentration of mind and disciplined effort. It was also recommended, particularly for girls, for the purposes of developing their appreciation of beauty and refinement of taste (McCormick 1994; Sutton 1967).

7   Penfold (1988) and Eggleston (1996) both make extended reference to these developments. In particular, they mention *The Design and Craft Education Project* and *Project Technology*, and the work of the Assessment Performance Unit (APU) and a related project, established by Richard Kimbell, at Goldsmiths College.

8   Vocational education enthusiasts, according to Sanderson (1993), argue that liberal education aims belong to a past social reality when the UK had easy mastery over the world economy, a class structure and deference was paid to the church. They have outlived their purpose in the present political, social and economic climate.

9   According to Hogbin (1992), there are four possibilities for craft in industry: industrial craft such as piece-work (which is rapidly disappearing because of robotics); prototype craft (e.g. one-off pieces for building the machines to make machines); design

production of craft or interpretation work for well-known concepts, such as a chair or cup, produced in limited numbers; artistic craft – exploratory work making one or a series of pieces.

10   According to Metcalf (1997), one reason art is different from craft is that the art world continues to promote the primacy of verbal and linguistic intelligence and disparage any other kind of intelligence or even accept there may be a blend. The craft world on the other hand accepts the meanings of felt experience and the body and remains loyal to tradition, medium process and skill.

11   For Press (1998), craft is a process to do with manipulating a medium, and what the medium is, is not really relevant any more. It is about mental processes involved in manipulating the medium and there is some connection between the person who is manipulating and the product. There will always be that connection with the product. The craft part is actually manipulating the medium to reach that point which is the end product for the person doing the manipulation.

References

Allison, B. (1982) 'Identifying the core in art and design', *Journal of Art and Design Education*, **1** (1): 59–66.

Ashwin, C. (1975) *Art Education Documents and Policies*, London: Society for Research into Higher Education.

Attar, D. (1990) *Wasting Girls' Time: the History and Politics of Home Economics*, London: Virago.

Barlex, D. (1998) Examining GCSE design and Ttechnology: Nuffield insights. *Journal of Design and Technology Education* **3**(3): 249–53.

Barnett, C. (1986) *The Audit of War: the Illusion and Reality of Britain as a Great Nation*, London: Macmillan.

Baynes, K. (1998) 'Education for living, social changes and crafts', unpublished conference paper, presented at Learning through Making and Making a Living, 25–26 November, British Library, London.

Blanchford, G. (1961) *A History of Handicraft Teaching*, London: Christophers.

Brecon, A. (1998) 'Reviewing design and technology for the year 2000', *Journal of Design and Technology Education*, **3** (2): 101–5.

Carline, R. (1968) *Draw they Must: a History of the Teaching and Examining of Art*, London: Edward Arnold.

Cave, J., Neale, J. and Tufnell, R. (1997) 'Learning through making: competencies and capabilities', unpublished research report, Middlesex University, Barnet, UK.

Crafts Council (1995) *Pupils as Makers: Aspects of Crafts in Secondary Schools*, London: Crafts Council.

Cusworth, A. and Press, M. (1996) 'Defining craft in the 1990s', unpublished research report, Art and Design Research Centre, Sheffield Hallam University, Sheffield.

DES (Department of Education and Science) (1988) *The Curriculum 5–16*, London: HMSO.

DES (Department of Education and Science)/Welsh Office (1989) *Proposals of the Secretary of State for Education and Science and the Secretary of State for Wales. Design and Technology for Ages 5 to 16*, London: HMSO.

DES (Department of Education and Science) (1992) *Design and Technology for Ages 5–16*, London: HMSO.

Dissanayake, E. (1992) 'The pleasure and meaning of making', *American Craft*, **55** (2): 40–5.

Dormer, P. (1997) (ed.) *The culture of craft*, Manchester: Manchester University Press.

Down, B. (1983) 'Problem-solving, CDT and child centerdness', *Studies in Design Education, Craft and Technology,* **6** (1): 38–43.

Eggleston, J. (1976) *Developments in Design Education,* London: Open Books Publishing.

Eggleston, J. (1996) *Understanding Design and Technology,* Buckingham: Open University Press.

Eisner, E. (1999) 'What do the arts teach?', *RSA Journal,* **2** (4): 42–51.

Frayling, C. (1990) 'The crafts in the 1990s', *Journal of Art and Design Education,* **9** (1): 91–100.

Gardner, H. (1990) *Art Education and Human Development,* Los Angeles: J. Paul Getty Trust.

Gell, A. (1992) 'The technology of enchantment and the enchantment of technology', in Coote, J. and Shelton, A. (eds), *Anthropology and Aesthetics,* Oxford: Clarendon Press, pp. 40–66.

Greenhalgh, P. (1997) 'The history of craft', in Dormer, P. (ed.), *The Culture of Craft,* Manchester: Manchester University Press, pp. 104–15.

Hogbin, S. (1992) 'Morals of the story', *Crafts,* Sept./Oct.: 6–19.

Hughes, A. (1995) 'Creating cross-curriculum connections', in Prentice, R. (ed.), *Teaching Art and Design,* London: Cassell.

Jeffrey, R. (1985) 'The crafts in schools', *Journal of Art and Design Education,* **4** (1): 73–81.

Kimbell, R. (1995) 'Uncertain crossings', *Times Educational Supplement,* 20 October, Technology Supplement, p. ii.

Korsenik, D. (1992) 'Structure and transformation in art education', in Thistlewood, D. (ed.), *History of Art and Design Education: Cole to Coldstream,* Harlow: Longman.

McCormick, R. (1994) 'The coming of technology in education in England and Wales', in Banks, F. (ed.), *Teaching Technology,* London: Routledge.

MacDonald, S. (1970) *History and Philosophy of Art Education,* London: University of London Press.

Mason, R. (1998) *Craft Education in Secondary Schools at Key Stages 3 and 4: Pupils as Makers,* London: Crafts Council.

Mason, R. and Bedford, D. (1997) *National Survey of Craft in Art and Design and Technology at Key Stages 3 and 4 in England and Wales. Part 2: Teachers' Views,* unpublished report, University of Surrey Roehampton Learning Resources Centre.

Mason, R. and Houghton, N. (1997) *National Survey of Craft in Secondary Schools. Pupils as Makers: Their Motivation for and Perceptions of Craft Education at Key Stages 3 & 4,* London: Roehampton Institute.

Mason, R. and Iwano, M. (1995a) *National Survey of Craft in Art and Design and Technology Curricula and Courses at Key Stages 3 and 4 in England and Wales,* unpublished report, University of Surrey Roehampton Learning Resources Centre.

Mason, R. and Iwano, M. (1995b) *Pupils as Makers: Aspects of Crafts in Secondary Schools in England and Wales,* London: Crafts Council.

Metcalf, B. (1987) 'Craft, art, culture and biology', in Dormer, P. (ed.), *The Culture of Craft,* Manchester: Manchester University Press, pp. 67–82.

Ministry of Education (1952) *Metalwork in Secondary Schools,* Pamphlet 22, London: HMSO

Parker, R. (1986) *The Subversive Stitch,* London: The Women's Press.

Penfold, J. (1988) *Craft Design and Technology: Past, Present and Future,* Stoke on Trent: Trentham Books.

Percy, C. and Triggs, T. (1990) 'The crafts and non-verbal learning', *Oral History,* **18** (2): 37–43.

Prentice, R. (ed.) *Teaching Art and Design: Addressing Ideas and Identifying Directions,* London: Cassell.

Press, M. and Cusworth, A. (1988) 'New lives in the making: the value of craft education in the information age', unpublished research report, Art and Design Research Centre, Sheffield Hallam University, Sheffield.

Press, M. and Cusworth, A. (1996) 'Defining craft in the 1990s', unpublished workshop manuscript, Art and Design Research Centre, Sheffield Hallam University.

Read, H. (1943) *Education through Art,* London: Faber and Faber.

Ritchie, R. (1995) *Primary Design and Technology: A Process for Learning,* London: David Fulton.

Roberts, P. (1998) 'From making things to making sense: the educative role of practical making activity', unpublished conference paper, presented at Learning through Making and Making a Living, 25–26 November, London: British Library.

Robertson. S.M. (1952) *Creative Crafts in Education,* London: Routledge and Kegan Paul.

Robertson, S.M. (1961) *Craft and Contemporary Culture,* London: Harrap.

Robertson, S.M. (1989) 'The refinement of touch', *Journal of Art and Design Education* **8** (3): 241–5.

Robinson, C. (1995) 'The National Curriculum for Art: translating it into practice', in Prentice, R. (ed.), *Teaching Art and Design: Addressing Ideas and Identifying Directions,* London: Cassell, pp. 124–33.

Rutland, M. (1993) 'An MA student's critical evaluation of design and technology', *Design and Technology Teaching,* **25** (2): 25–8.

Rutland, M. (1997) *Teaching Food Technology in Secondary Schools,* London: David Fulton Associates with Roehampton Institute.

Sanderson, M. (1993) 'Vocational and liberal education: a historian's view', *European Journal of Education,* **28** (2): 189–207.

Schofield, K. (1995) 'Objects of desire by design', in Prentice, R. (ed.), *Teaching Art and Design: Addressing Ideas and Identifying Directions,* London: Cassell.

Schön, D. (1983) *The Reflective Practitioner: How Professionals Think in Action,* New York: Basic Books.

Sienkeiwicz, C. (1985) 'The Froebelian kindergarten as an art academy', in Wilson, B. and Hoffa, H. (eds.), *The History of Art Education,* proceedings of Pennsylvania State Conference, Reston, VA: National Art Education Association, pp. 125–37.

Smithers, A. and Robinson, P. (1992) *Technology in the National Curriculum – Getting it Right,* London: Engineering Council.

Steers, J. (1995) 'The National Curriculum: reformation or preservation of the status quo?', *Journal of Art and Design Education,* **14** (2): 129–38.

Sternberg, R. and Caruso, D. (1985) 'Practical modes of knowing', in Eisner, E. (ed.), *Learning and Teaching: the Ways of Knowing,* Chicago: University of Chicago Press, pp. 133–58.

Sutton, G. (1967) *Artisan or Artist. A History of Teaching of Art and Crafts in English Schools,* Oxford: Pergamon Press.

Taylor, M. (1988) 'CDT: a perennial identity crisis', unpublished MA dissertation, University of London, Institute of Education, London.

Taylor, R. (1992) *The Visual Arts in Education: Completing the Circle,* London: Falmer Press.

Thistlewood, D. (1992) *Issues in Design Education,* Harlow: Longman.

Yoxall, A. (1965) *A History of the Teaching of Domestic Economy,* Bath: Cedric Chivers.

Part 2

Issues in the classroom

5 How should current technologies be implemented in the design and technology curriculum?

Tony Hodgson

Introduction

The issues raised in this chapter will focus, primarily, on those concerned with the teaching of technology in UK secondary schools. Many issues will also be of interest to those concerned with science and technology in primary schools and initial teacher training in higher education. Considering these issues will help to focus on the nature of technology education and how it may be implemented in schools, so it is useful to begin by considering the original remit for the working group which first fashioned the National Curriculum subject of technology.

> In approaching its task the working group is to view technology as that area of the curriculum in which pupils design and make useful objects or systems, thus developing their ability to solve practical problems. The working group should assume that pupils will draw on knowledge and skills from a range of subject areas, but always involving science and mathematics... They should also learn about the variety of modern materials and technologies in use in the industrial and commercial world.
>
> (DES 1988: 86)

It is interesting to reflect on the extent to which this original specification for technology in the National Curriculum has been met, and to consider the nature of technology as a curriculum subject and its relationship with a subject called design. There is no doubt that the subject we know as design and technology is an excellent vehicle for education, but it is equally clear that there are many different views about subject content, focus and pedagogy that should be included. What is it that pupils should know, understand and be able to do after studying design and technology?

Despite a number of attempts to identify this in National Curriculum documents, there is still a great deal of interpretation required by teachers and, consequently, a wider range of subject definitions than the National Curriculum aimed to encourage. My own view is that the original remit is a reasonable descriptor and that it suggests a particular focus and purpose for the subject that has rarely been met in practice. Design and technology education should be about developing technological awareness and capability; these should be developed in the context of applications which appear real to the learners so that they can readily identify with the relevant principles, concepts and issues. The educational tasks and activities undertaken by learners should reflect current technologies, underpinned by relevant fundamental principles. Designing and making things is an excellent way of exposing pupils to technology, allowing them to learn about and apply technology in real contexts, thus providing relevance and motivation.

This does not mean that activities need to emulate those of industrial, product or graphic designers, unless, of course, these lend themselves to the primary purpose of developing technological capability. That is, pupils should design and make things not for their own sake, or even to learn about designing and making, but to develop an awareness and capability in technology that is relevant to the general aims and aspirations of education and society. For this reason the particular technologies that are selected to be part of a curriculum should reflect current technology, but in a way that will focus the more general aims of a design and technology curriculum. A section in the new National Curriculum, headed 'The importance of design and technology', describes some aims for design and technology:

> Design and Technology prepares pupils to participate in tomorrow's rapidly changing technologies… Through design and technology, all pupils can become discriminating and informed users of products, and become innovators.
> (DfEE 1999: 15)

Should the technology we teach be an end in itself, or should it be the means by which we achieve the aims of our technology curriculum?

Rather than discuss the definition of technology or the range of technologies that a curriculum should contain, this chapter will consider issues concerned with two particular areas of technology – computer-aided design and manufacture (CAD/CAM) and electronic systems. Both will be related to design and technology education in schools by considering the extent to which it is possible or desirable to reflect current practice, which fundamental principles and concepts are involved and how teaching and learning might be developed. Having considered what technology may be relevant, the notion of using technology to teach technology is discussed in the context of computer-aided learning.

Computer-aided design and manufacture

Bearing in mind that designing and making activities are central to the teaching of technology, the use of computers to enhance these activities is likely to be a key area of technology to be included in the curriculum. This is particularly true because information technology (IT) is considered to be a key skill that may be taught through design and technology activities. The teaching of IT is important for its own sake, and an awareness of the potential of the technologies involved, together with experience of using these technologies, is an essential element of any curriculum. Teachers should also look to focus on specific areas of IT that will enhance the teaching and learning of their own subject area.

Design and technology lends itself to the development of IT capability through a very wide range of applications and hardware. Including CAD/CAM in course work is just one of these, but it illustrates a number of interesting issues which are worthy of discussion. Pupils can design, draw and make things without the use of computers. Indeed, many pupils (and teachers) have no experience of using computers and are able to realise designs without their use. Yet this is a technology that can enhance design and technology work in schools, and it is an excellent way of helping pupils to achieve a high-quality output from their work.

What added value does the use of CAD/CAM bring to design and technology?

Typically, a CAD/CAM system will comprise a means of representing a design component (usually with object-orientated line-drawing software such as AutoCAD, Pro/DESKTOP or Techsoft 2D Design) which has links to manufacturing equipment such as a lathe, sewing machine or milling machine. The design is drawn using the computer, viewed on the monitor screen, and possibly printed out for future use. While this may well result in a neater or more accurate drawing, the printed output hardly starts to exploit the full potential of using a CAD system. Greater advantage comes from its ability to allow the design to be modified and edited without the need to redraw the whole component, or to change the component's colour at the touch of a button. This will encourage a pupil to experiment with design modifications, to ask 'what if…?' and to revisit previous work – all of which are considered to be essential activities in the design and technology curriculum. Link the design drawing to computer-driven manufacturing equipment and the CAD drawing is exploited still further. If the CAD system can generate computer numerical control (CNC) code, then a CNC milling machine or lathe can cut the component to an accuracy of one hundredth of a millimetre. Similarly, it is possible to link drawings with CNC embroidery, sewing, knitting and rapid prototyping machines.

Such a 'draw it, then make it' system is a far cry from the original school-based systems which, for no good reason, emulated the line by line entry of CNC code which was typical of industrial equipment at that time. The manufacturers of CNC equipment were often surprised that teachers were less than enthusiastic about the product, perhaps not realising that the time required to learn and implement CNC programming far outweighed the benefits that CAM provides. Fortunately, both schools and industry now exploit this CAD to CAM approach, and so the cooperation between industry and school is another feature of design and technology education that can be enabled through the use of this technology.

But beware, the reasons for using CAD/CAM in schools are quite different to those for its use in industry, so teachers and suppliers need to be aware of the features which school-based CAD/CAM equipment requires, rather than relying on those systems which have been designed to support the needs of industry. Industrial users will exploit the use of a CAD model to integrate the many different functions of product development. By simultaneously working on the same CAD model, those responsible for marketing, manufacturing, costing and engineering are able to work more efficiently. The consequence is a significant reduction in the time taken to move from product concept to the marketplace. Design approaches in school do not usually reflect this concurrent approach. Designs and products are often very personal in nature, and are necessarily developed over long periods of time because of the demands of a packed curriculum and timetable. These issues should be considered when selecting appropriate CAD software. Some schools will opt for the industry-standard software, characterised by systems such as AutoCAD, Mechanical Desktop or MasterCAM.

There may be good reason for this with older pupils, or if collaboration with industry is a key objective, but this software is often difficult to learn and may require a full-time employee to devote months to acquiring sufficient capability. How will a young pupil, with only one hour per week timetabled for design and technology, be able to develop a reasonable capability? It is far better to work with software specifically designed for use in schools than that designed to serve the needs of industrial users with different priorities. School software will be characterised by fewer features, less capability and less flexibility than its industrial counterpart, but will focus on a simple, easily learnt user interface and robust delivery of the features required by schools. Typical of such software is a system called TABS which prints (or cuts) the net of a 3-D shape designed on the computer (see Figure 5.1).

Although pupils using TABS have only a few graphic tools at their disposal, they are able to draw 3-D objects in a manner that is entirely consistent with its more expensive and complicated industrial equivalents. The system works out what the net of an object is and prints it out so that pupils are able to assemble a 3-D model of the design – it even provides the 'tabs' which are used to glue the model together! Although the system has limitations, it is easy to learn and use,

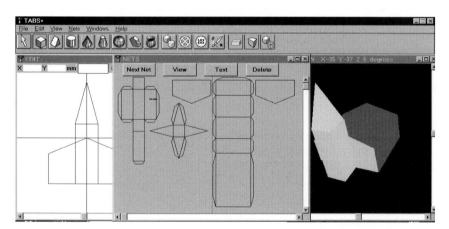

Figure 5.1   Solid model and net from TABS software. The church was modelled as part of a KS2 project about 'my village'. There is clear potential for packaging projects associated with many different projects and materials (www.aspexsoftware.com).

and it provides an introduction to CAD/CAM which is entirely appropriate for packaging, modelling and visualising design ideas. TABS was originally designed with help from an educational consortium that had design teaching objectives clearly in mind.

However, as we expose pupils to this technology and allow them to take advantage of the tools it can provide, it may be argued that we are undermining some of the skills we aim to develop. There is a need to consider which educational objectives we are addressing. In this case, are we teaching pupils how a net may be developed from a 3-D model, or are we bypassing the need to learn how to do this because the computer can achieve the same result more quickly? Similar questions arise from using other CAM equipment. For example, is it necessary to know how to use a conventional milling machine before using its CNC counterpart? It may be suggested that technology education should teach pupils the fundamental principles that underpin designing and making activities. In this context, that progression in the development of capability is characterised by moving from the more traditional, or conventional, approach to the use of more modern systems or equipment. Understanding the key learning objectives that are to be achieved through such activities, however, is vital to the teacher. By sequencing manufacturing operations so that CNC equipment will correctly cut, sew or build a product's part, it may also be argued that fundamental manufacturing capability is being effectively developed.

Whatever the CAD/CAM system or software selected by schools, there is a need to support pupils' learning using appropriate resources, tasks and project work, which help to develop capability in a progressive manner. It would seem appropriate that younger pupils will become aware of the technology and exploit some of its benefits during relatively structured work, thus enabling them to identify its potential to help them, probably on an individual basis, with more open-ended project work in later years. Unfortunately, early systems were characterised by software which was difficult to use (or took a long time to learn) and unreliable in operation. Only in more recent years has school-based CAD/CAM technology provided a 'turnkey' capability and combined it with the resources that enable pupils to exploit this capability in a manner that complements the aims of design and technology education.

Having achieved a greater awareness and understanding of the technology and its more reliable use in schools, some teachers are looking to exploit its use still further. Hitherto, CAD/CAM components were typically two-dimensional and cut from sheets of plastic or timber using machines with a 3-D cutting capability as simple profile cutters. Although 2-D components may be combined to produce a 3-D product (by stacking in layers or slotting together), the true 3-D manufacturing of industrial systems offers even greater potential. If this were possible in schools, then it would truly reflect the current technology as it is applied in industry. However, the move from 2-D to true 3-D CAD/CAM manufacturing requires a stepped change in capability and the careful consideration of teaching and learning issues. Generally speaking, it becomes necessary to model the whole component in 3-D, rather than represent part of the design in 2-D. Three-dimensional modelling systems used to be found exclusively on expensive computers and took many months of training to master, limiting them to industrial rather than educational users. Recent advances in low-cost and high-powered PCs, together with advances in the design of 3-D modelling software, means that schools can now have access to this capability. The CAD software has a simpler user interface and post-processors enable the necessary CNC code to be easily generated. However, there are still many barriers to the implementation of the 3-D CAD/ CAM systems in schools:

- Despite improved software, it still takes a long time to develop the skills needed to model even simple 3-D design ideas.
- Some shapes lend themselves to computer modelling more easily than others, and so the designed outcome is often compromised in terms of what is achievable rather than what is required or desired.
- The time taken to manufacture a 3-D model is much greater than that required for a 2-D shape. A CNC milling machine will take many hours to cut a 3-D mould the size of a computer mouse, whereas the 2-D profile of a mouse will take only a few minutes. The implication for a group of twenty pupils is clear.

Yet many schools will lust after the 3-D capability, as it may be considered relevant technology which provides an element of progression in a student's design and technology profile. Three-dimensional computer modelling brings with it many other benefits. The general approach is to use a 3-D model to provide data for many purposes, capitalising on the time and effort required to produce it. The generation of CNC manufacturing data is just one example; it may also be used to provide a rendered image and the 2-D working drawings and assembly views required to complete the manufacture. However, once again this raises some interesting dilemmas. If 2-D drawings can be extracted from 3-D models, why teach formal 2-D drawing at all? If it is possible to modify the lighting, colour and material properties of a computer model before printing out the result, then how should we balance the teaching of traditional drawing and sketching skills with computer-based skills? Older pupils and industrial users may have little difficulty in visualising their design ideas in 3-D and then representing them in a computer model, but are younger pupils able to do this? Resources may be developed to help the younger pupils to acquire the relevant skills, but is it desirable or even possible for them to do so?

Once again, there is the need to reflect upon the nature of design and technology in the curriculum. What are its aims, and what are our teaching and learning objectives? Interestingly, there have been significant advances in the ease of use and reliability of 3-D computer modelling software. These have arisen partly as a result of low-cost computing provision, but also as industrial users have identified the need to provide such software for a wider range of less specialised users. This software appears to be more attractive to educational users and, at the time of writing, is the focus of a national CAD/CAM initiative, involving the distribution of free 3-D CAD software to teachers who will commit to training and implementation in schools.

Despite such advances, the CAD tools that currently exist are not entirely appropriate for younger pupils or for developing certain shapes and products. Perhaps it is necessary to consider alternative ways of designing in 3-D with computer systems.

Representing a 3-D object on a flat piece of paper or on the flat computer screen is difficult, but even very young pupils (or older pupils with few computing skills) are able to create 3-D objects from sand, Plasticine, clay and foam. A more appropriate use of the technology would be the scannning of such objects into the computer as a rough model, which would then allow pupils to modify and edit their design models, rather than having to create them from scratch with CAD drawing tools. Once the model represented the object to be made, the system could be used to control a high-speed router, rather than a milling machine, as this would cut softer materials like foam and timber much more quickly, thus reducing manufacturing times to those which would be appropriate for groups of pupils in school. It is worth noting that in only a few years' time, 3-D printing systems will provide intricate, hollow 3-D products – a wax, starch or plastic outcome of the 'virtual' computer model – at a lower cost than conventional CNC manufacturing equipment. Examples of this type of output are illustrated in Figure 5.2.

Interestingly, these approaches have been adopted in industry for some time for reasons of efficiency, shorter product development times and improved management of design and manufacturing. The revised design and technology curriculum for schools, (DfEE: 1999) makes increased reference to the use of CAD/CAM, but provides little guidance about appropriate hardware and software. Educational users should look to the CAD/CAM technology of industry but adapt it in line with their students' needs.

Relevant electronics systems for school-based technology

Electronics is clearly an area of technology that is considered to be important in the school curriculum. Each description of technology in the National Curriculum highlights it, and virtually every technology curriculum and syllabus will make reference to 'systems', as a means of identifying and illustrating some particular function or purpose. The practice of breaking down a complex functional requirement into a series of sub-systems is well known as a means of exposing particular technological elements and providing a number of accessible blocks which describe it more clearly. By focusing on a particular part of the system it is easier to understand how it works or to consider alternative ways in which it might be provided.

It is the use of systems as a means of designing technological functions that has made them a popular feature of the curriculum. By designing individual parts of a system, typically inputs, processes and outputs, and then combining them into a whole, a complete system can be developed more easily. This approach also lends itself to clearly structured and managed teaching routes, which is another reason for its popularity.

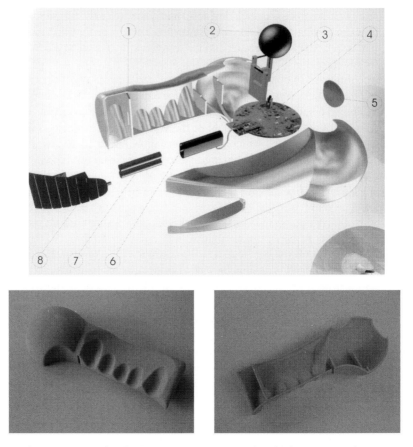

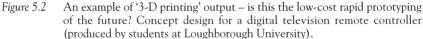

Figure 5.2   An example of '3-D printing' output – is this the low-cost rapid prototyping of the future? Concept design for a digital television remote controller (produced by students at Loughborough University).

Although many different technologies may be described in terms of systems, electronics in particular seems to lend itself to the systems approach. It is relatively easy to identify input and output elements, and, although process capability may be complex, it is often rationalised into an integrated circuit which is relatively easy to understand. The design of electronic systems is often supported by kits and resource packs that enable pupils to experiment with different system elements without any need to construct circuits from many discrete components. This leads to a situation in which pupils may understand how different system elements combine to perform the technological function they require but may not understand how each of those elements works in detail.

Is it important that pupils should have a detailed understanding of electronics if they are able to design and build a whole circuit by combining a series of sub-systems? This question is at the heart of debate about systems versus discrete components, and may never be fully resolved. There is a need to consider whether it is relevant to teach the fundamentals and principles of electronics or if the aim is to provide experience of systems. Indeed, it may be that the curriculum requires both, in which case, which comes first – the fundamental understanding or the development of a circuit through sub-systems? Issues raised in the remainder of this section will begin to address some of these questions.

Simple circuits, built from individual discrete components, tend to be preferred as a means of illustrating electronic principles. It is possible to measure current flow and voltage drop at different parts of the circuit and so start to build an understanding of how the technology works. In any event, it is argued, if pupils are ever to design their own sub-system elements, in addition to the system as a whole, they will have to understand electronics in detail. This issue is further highlighted as pupils progress through a course. Design and technology education will often require pupils to design and make an electronic product. Although their circuit may be modelled using a system kit, how is the circuit to be transferred to the final product? Clearly, the most appropriate way is to design and build the circuit on a printed circuit board, and this usually requires a deeper understanding of the electronics than the systems approach alone can provide. There have been a number of valiant attempts to overcome this dilemma, but it is still not fully resolved and teachers often polarise into the 'systems' and 'discrete' camps. Many pupils solve the problem by modelling with systems, then finding a circuit with similar functionality from books, magazines or data sheets. To what extent do pupils actually design their own circuits? Is this a relevant application of electronics in design and technology?

The National Curriculum, revised in 1999 (DfEE 1999), makes specific reference to the knowledge and understanding of systems and their control required at each Key Stage. Throughout the Key Stages, there is great emphasis placed on systems terminology and very little on detailed electronics requirements. Does this suggest that a detailed understanding is not required? I believe that this detailed understanding is implied, and that some pupils will progress to a point where they need to design electronic circuits that fulfil the requirements of their designed system. It is also worth considering the extent to which pupils are able to design electronics circuits which emulate the technology they experience every day. The game which causes a simple buzzer to sound, or LED (light-emitting diode) to flash, after a metal loop makes contact with a bent piece of wire is a far cry from the cheap electronic games in the market place. Is the electronics we are able to teach young pupils going to motivate them to design inspired products or provide an accurate reflection of the technology we wish to promote? If one of our aims in design and technology is to develop an understanding of electronics, are we destined to do it through mundane, boring or old-fashioned projects?

It is possible that a blend of the systems and the discrete approach may provide a solution. It is not difficult to find integrated circuits (ICs) that are designed to provide functions which pupils will find interesting and relevant. For example, radios, noise and music generators, and remote control devices, are always readily available. With a little thought these can provide the basis of an interesting product which pupils are capable of designing. Sometimes, just the successful inclusion of a functional electronic circuit is sufficient, allowing the learning to focus on the other elements of design and technology capability. At other times, these integrated circuits may form the process element of the system, allowing pupils to actually design the input and output elements for themselves – this provides an opportunity for the teaching of the electronics principles, circuit design and printed circuit board manufacture.

In a more general sense, the peripheral interface controller (PIC) chip may provide the stepped change required. While it must be remembered that it cannot provide full circuit functionality on its own, it is able to control different outputs, depending on the input signals it receives, provide timing and memory functions and convert analogue to digital signals. This is contained in an affordable package that is small enough to fit into a matchbox. More importantly, the detail of its operation can be designed, programmed and implemented using simple computer software tools. This opens the door to a whole host of electronic applications with a genuine design input which pupils may now achieve. Beware, however, this is not the panacea it may appear, as input and output circuits will still be required, and teachers will need to consider whether this requirement provides opportunities for learning about electronics or unreasonable barriers to the successful implementation of the system.

Using technology to teach technology

Having considered some of the issues concerned with *what* technology should be included in the curriculum, it is worth considering some of the difficulties concerned with *teaching* it. Three general problems appear to characterise the difficulties surrounding the management of teaching, particularly in the context of design and technology education.

First, technology is always moving. The rapid development of technological products in today's society challenges even the most expert to keep abreast of recent innovation and current systems, so schools, teachers and pupils cannot be expected to keep up. This leads to an ever-increasing gap between the technology that is taught in schools and the technology employed in everyday life. These difficulties will be increased by the National Curriculum guidelines and GCSE syllabuses (both of which tend to determine teaching subject matter) if they fail to reflect current technologies.

Second, design and technology teaching in schools is characterised by relatively large groups of pupils who are encouraged to develop individual solutions, products or outcomes. In some cases, this can lead to the need to learn about specific elements of technology on an individual pupil basis. This can be very difficult for a teacher to manage efficiently.

Third, despite attempts to standardise what is taught, and to record pupil attainment, there is still an alarming range in the background and experience of pupils as they move from one phase of education to one other. This is particularly true for teachers of design and technology because of the subject breadth and the need for individual schools to interpret the curriculum in their own way.

Fortunately, some of the technological development that makes it difficult to decide *what* technology should be taught may provide some solutions to the management of teaching and learning. Information technology heralds a whole new direction for teaching and learning resources. It is now able to help teachers provide learning that is appropriate for small groups or individuals and to provide tools for teaching and management that should help them to work more effectively.

School and home-based computing systems are now powerful enough to provide real-time simulations of technological activity. These can be used to illustrate principles or to prove design ideas. Pupils are able to see the effect of changing electronic component values, or moving a linkage pivot point, very accurately and quickly. There is no need to produce endless prototypes and model different systems in a laboratory or workshop, so a great deal of time can be saved without sacrificing the learning required. Similarly, the cutting path of a CNC milling machine can be rapidly simulated by computer, proving the manufacturing process before time-consuming or expensive machining takes place. As we move closer to the realms of virtual reality and systems which can be controlled more accurately in the computer than in reality, is it still necessary to design and make real products? Could it be that pupils could learn enough about technology through simulations that would allow them to ask 'what if...?', and then illustrate the outcome using further computer simulations?

The role of the teacher may be challenged still further by the introduction of on-line teaching and learning systems. Computer-aided learning (CAL) has, I think, broken free from the poor reputation it had many years ago. The behaviorists' 'drill and test' theories of early software have been replaced by cognitive thinking and software that provides more control for the learner and teacher than the computer. It is now possible for pupils to use a teaching or support package 'at the point of need', so that they can acquire particular information or learning when their project work or academic development requires it. This means of supporting individual needs within large groups would enable teachers to concentrate on pupils and issues that they previously had little time to address. It also means that learning at a distance is supported, providing much needed tutorial support outside conventional times for learning in schools.

The screen shots in Figure 5.3 illustrate two systems that support learning at the point of need. They are designed to support initial tutor teaching and run alongside commercial CAD software. Imagine how close to a teacher's role such software may become. It can ask questions of the pupil, appraise the level of understanding he or she already has, relate it to the task in hand and determine the most appropriate learning route for the individual concerned. These systems are much loved by administrators with tight budgets and large pupil numbers, but quite rightly challenged by teachers who see their role as far more than an instructor. But should teachers dismiss completely the potential of CAL to support and enhance their traditional teaching role?

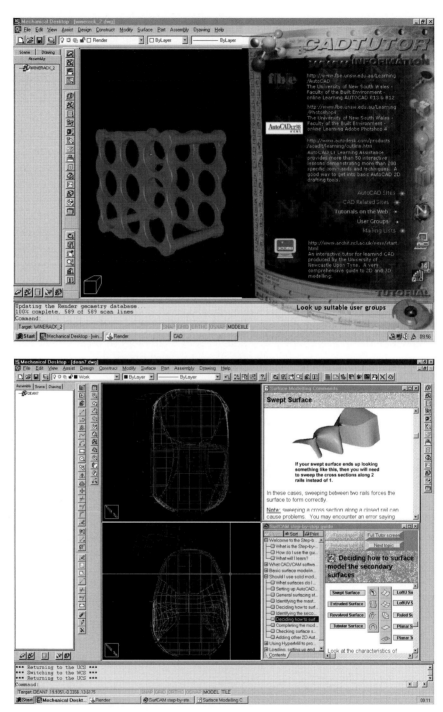

Figure 5.3   Systems that support learning at the point of need. Screen shots of SurfCAM and CADtutor, computer-aided learning (CAL) packages for computer-aided design (CAD). Designed by Tony Hodgson using Autodesk software.

Conclusion

There are no easy answers to many of the issues I have raised, or solutions to the problem of determining the role of technology in design and technology education. The extent to which it is possible to reflect current technologies in teaching and learning programmes or teach fundamental principles through relevant applications will always be contentious. However, it is clear that technology will have just as important a role in *how* we teach as in *what* we teach.

Questions to consider

This chapter has raised many questions already but, in addition, you may also wish to consider the following:

1   Why do curriculum guidance materials make increased reference to the use of CAD/CAM in design and technology, and what added value does it bring to a pupil's work and development?
2   Does the nature of design and technology in schools require pupils to have a detailed understanding of materials properties and fundamental principles of technology?

  •   If so, which ones should be overtly taught through more focused tasks?
  •   If not, which may be acquired through more open project work?

3   As increasing numbers of pupils have access to more sophisticated computer systems at home, should we exploit the use of IT, ICT (information and communications technology) and CAL to help with the development of technological capability, and what problems can this approach bring for both schools and their teachers?

References

Department of Education and Science (DES) and the Welsh Office (1988) *National Curriculum Design and Technology – Interim Report*, London: DES.
DfEE (1999) *National Curriculum for Design and Technology*, London: HMSO.

Further reading

It is difficult to suggest further reading in this area, as few texts address the issues directly. However, I would suggest that current journals (professional and academic) concerned with technology education will provide further information and alternative views. Those worth particular consideration are:

Educational Computing and Technology, Training Information Network Ltd.
Electronics Education, The Institution of Electrical Engineers.
Journal of Design and Technology Education, Design and Technology Association.

Some research papers and chapters discussing issues concerned with information technology are available in texts, but may be well out of date unless recent books are selected. I would suggest that the following would be a useful starting point for those wishing to pursue some of the issues raised here:

Passey, D. and Samways, B. (1997) (eds) *Information Technology – Supporting Change through Teacher Education*, London: Chapman & Hall.

Bridget Somekh's chapter 'Towards effective learning with new technology resources', pp. 269–77, and Toni Downes' chapter 'The computer as a toy and tool in the home', pp. 309–15, are particularly relevant, providing some useful discussion about the changes which CAL, in its widest sense, may bring to teaching and learning.

Underwood, J. and Underwood, G. (1990) *Computers and Learning*, Oxford: Blackwell Publishers.

This is a key text covering many issues concerned with computers, IT and learning. Chapters 1, 3 and 8 are particularly useful for those wishing to implement IT-based teaching and learning systems.

Design and Technology Association (DATA) (1999) *Teaching CAD/CAM*, Wellesbourne: Design and Technology Association.

This is particularly relevant for those wishing to implement CAD/CAM technologies in schools.

6 Information and communications technology

Supporting quality in design and technology?

Torben Steeg

ICT or IT?

Information and communications technology (ICT) is a term that embraces more than just computers. It includes a wide range of devices that interact with a computer, for example to send information to it (using equipment such as scanners or digital cameras) or to receive information from it (for example a plotter or robot arm). It also includes items that you might not at first consider, such as broadcast television, audiotapes, mobile telephones and computer networks. To keep your life interesting, innovation in this area is so rapid that the term ICT (itself recently coined) is likely to embrace new technologies at an increasing rate.

Despite the broad scope of the term ICT in principle, most people using it are referring to computers and their peripherals and networks, and it is this narrower use that this chapter focuses on.

What impact have computers in schools had on learning?

From the time that computers started to arrive in schools[1] to the present, as computer numbers have increased, claims for the improvements in teaching and learning that they can be expected to bring have been made. Papert (1980; 1993), for example, is well known as a passionate advocate for the potential of computers to transform education:

> The child programs the computer. And in teaching the computer how to think, children embark on an exploration about how they themselves think. The experience can be heady: Thinking about thinking turns the child into an epistemologist, an experience not even shared by most adults.
>
> (Papert 1980: 19)

Writing ten years later, Underwood and Underwood (1990) also focused on the role of computers in developing children's thinking skills, but noted both the importance, and lack, of proper evaluation:

> We cannot say whether any of the studies which we have reviewed would find any long-term changes in the cognitive development of the children who participated. The measures simply have not been taken.
>
> (Underwood and Underwood 1990: 58)

It is fair to say that there are, another ten years later, still too few serious studies that unequivocally demonstrate improvements in teaching and learning that can be attributed to the use of computers.

Others have gone even further in questioning the effect of computers on education by looking beyond technical and cognitive issues to discuss the impact of ICT both on the culture of teaching and on wider cultural issues:

> … what must now be established is a theoretical framework within which teachers can start to raise wider cultural issues concerning technology and its future relationship to the related acts of teaching and learning.
>
> (Benyon and Mackay 1993: 218)

There is also, and will continue to be, a strand of writing that warns, in no uncertain terms, of the outright dangers of using ICT in education. This generally takes the view that ICT is a dangerous development that will destroy the great strengths of traditional approaches to education (see also Cordes and Miller 2000):

> Yet the effects of this online obsession are already being felt. Elementary and high schools are being sold down the networked river. To keep up with this educational fad, school boards spend way too much on technical gimmicks that teachers don't want and students don't need – and look at the appalling state of our libraries' book acquisition programs!
>
> (Stoll 1995: 11)

How you react to writing such as the above will probably depend mainly on your own instincts about the effectiveness of ICT in education. Whatever your views are, it is worth at least listening to such authors if only because they provide a useful counterbalance to the unbridled enthusiasm that you will also undoubtedly meet; there is usually benefit in having your beliefs challenged and in being made to justify them.

Meanwhile governments, including those in the UK, have invested much faith and money in the ability of computers and, more recently, networks to raise standards in education:

> Standards, literacy, numeracy, subject knowledge – all will be enhanced by the National Grid for Learning.
>
> (Tony Blair, in DfEE 1997: Foreword)

> ICT is more than just another teaching tool. Its potential for improving the quality and standards of pupils' education is significant. Equally, its potential is considerable for supporting teachers, both in their everyday classroom role, for example by reducing the time occupied by the administration associated with it, and in their continuing training and development… The curriculum aims, in particular, to equip every newly qualified teacher with the knowledge,

skills and understanding to make sound decisions about when, when not, and how to use ICT effectively in teaching particular subjects.

(TTA 1998: 1)

It is important to notice in the above that the Teacher Training Agency (TTA) recognises that there are times when the use of ICT is *not* appropriate in teaching. One of the skills you will need to develop as a teacher is the ability to make good judgements about the appropriate use of ICT to support your teaching. This notion, that ICT is, in principle, a good thing but that there are good and less good ways of introducing computers into teaching, is developed further in a rather more practical strand of literature, the aim of which is to support teachers in implementing ICT in their classrooms. Some of these books are aimed at education generally. For example, Squires and McDougall (1994) discuss systems that can guide the choice of software for use in schools by helping teachers focus on how a program supports teaching and learning rather than on its technical capabilities. Collins *et al.* (1997), for their part, focus on a particular type of software (multimedia) to provide a critical overview of both practical and pedagogic issues surrounding its introduction and use in schools. Though their focus is on CD-ROMs, most of what they say is equally relevant to Internet use and they conclude that:

> [the skills that learners need to acquire]... include the ability to collaborate with colleagues, to access and select from large stores of information, to have insight into the ways in which new knowledge is acquired, to take responsibility for one's own learning, to understand how images can clarify and distort. These are precisely the skills that we believe are promoted by the type of guided exploration with multimedia for which we have argued.
>
> (Collins *et al.* 1997: 130)

Further specific advice for teachers of design and technology is also available, and you should use the references at the end of the chapter to widen your enquiry,[2] but remember that books about ICT tend to date very quickly as both the hardware and software available change. However, because the books listed here are concerned as much about pedagogy as technology, you should find that they continue to be useful general guides to the effectiveness of ICT even when the technological detail is no longer current.

It is worth noting in this context that, of all subjects, design and technology in secondary schools has, on average, the second highest number of computers permanently located in its study areas and workshops. Only business studies has more (DfEE 1998). However, the impact of computers on the practice of design and technology teaching and its curriculum has been rather variable:

> Availability of sufficient equipment on its own, however, is no guarantee that the progress of pupils in IT will be good.
>
> (Ofsted 1998)

An important point that Ofsted inspection and summary reports constantly make is that the quality of work with ICT depends less on the actual amount of ICT equipment that is available and more on teachers' ability to plan for effective use of the equipment.[3]

When you set out to consider the use of ICT to support your teaching in design and technology, the question you should be asking yourself is *not* 'How can I insert ICT into this activity?', but rather 'How (if at all) can ICT help the pupils learn better?', or 'How (if at all) can ICT help me teach this better?' You will be in a better position to answer such questions if you have a clear idea of the ways in which ICT is able to support learning and teaching and of the range of technologies that is available to you.

Your learning objectives in planning to teach design and technology will usually fall into one or more of three areas:

- learning and understanding design and technology knowledge content;
- quality designing;
- quality making.

The following sections explore some possible uses of ICT to support teaching and learning in each of these areas. In each area both software and hardware that is relevant are considered along with some of the issues that arise from their use. Note, however, that the boundaries between the areas are porous; you can expect to find software doing multiple jobs. However, to avoid repetition, types of software are described only once.

Can ICT support the learning and understanding of design and technology knowledge content?

Research and experience show that pupils will understand and learn new knowledge content more easily if they are able to interact with the content. This is particularly true when pupils are dealing with ideas that are abstract in some way and when explanation is usually provided in the form of diagrams or analogies.

It is now a almost a cliché to say that computers are particularly good at providing a working environment that is very visual and encourages interaction:

> We know that learners in general enjoy using computers and that they are motivated and engaged by multimedia materials. Research further suggests that multimedia (along with other IT) can widen learners' experiences by giving them access to activities which would be impossible or time consuming to organise in other ways. Finally, IT can provide opportunities for learners to take more control over their learning and accept more responsibility.
>
> (Collins *et al.* 1997: 27)

However, there are issues to be aware of in the use of multimedia software. For example, have the visuals and interactivity provided by an application become ends in themselves? Is pupils' engagement with the content or the surface features? The same authors also warn (picking up from Scaife and Wellington (1993)) that 'It's not what you use it's the way that you use it':

> … seemingly unattractive software can promote successful classroom activities. In the same vein, emancipatory software can be used for quite untaxing, mindless activities … [we can] value exploratory work done, say, with *Logo* on a BBC computer, above button pushing activities carried out using the latest all singing, all dancing CD-ROM.
>
> (Collins *et al.* 1997: 17)

There is a wide range of software available that is aimed at teaching specific content areas in design and technology. Very often this is sold as 'interactive multimedia CD-ROMs'. However the use of 'CD-ROM' as a specific marketing point is particularly vacuous; a CD is simply a medium for holding digital data and cannot, of itself, add to the quality of the materials being sold. If the most exciting thing a publisher can tell you about a product is that it comes on a CD, you should probably approach the product cautiously!

Schools are full of software that is used little or not at all, because it has turned out that the content or its presentation is in fact not suitable.[4] This lack of suitability can manifest itself in a number of ways, including:

- mismatch to the curriculum actually being taught;
- errors and inaccuracies;
- a poorly designed user interface that gets in the way of learning;
- slow operation that simply leads to frustration;
- weak advantage over a book (for example, a linear route through the materials with little use of interactivity, animations, hyperlinks, etc.).

It is important to remember that computers are most certainly not the only way to inject interactivity into your teaching; practical experience with real equipment also provides effective learning, especially in design and technology in which the ultimate aim of your teaching is capability in designing and making. The best teaching usually employs a mixture of resources including appropriate ICT.

Materials teaching specific content

These tend to concentrate on particular content areas of design and technology such as electronics, mechanisms, nutrition, health and safety or industrial manufacturing methods. In some cases the software aims to teach by presenting material in an interesting way, in others, devices such as simulations with which the pupil can interact are used. You need to take particular care to evaluate such software to ensure that it really does support your teaching and does so better than other approaches.

A development of software that is designed to teach specific content is an integrated learning system (ILS). An ILS goes a step beyond the provision of ordered content by including a management system that assesses and tracks an individual's learning over time and arranges for an appropriate level of content to be 'delivered' to each individual. ILSs are usually expensive because they incorporate a great deal of material as well as the management, assessment and tracking systems. To make the purchase cost-effective they are generally run across a network so that the learning of many individuals can be managed at once.

Currently, ILSs are mainly employed in the teaching of mathematics and English, and debate continues both about their effectiveness in promoting learning and about their cost-effectiveness, particularly, in the latter case, as research has shown that ILSs are most likely to be effective when a high level of teacher support is also present. Fortunately, unlike some other ICTs, their use in these subjects at least has been intensively researched and principles to maximise their effective use are beginning to emerge (Underwood and Brown 1997). For example, there are serious questions to be asked about whether a computer-based system like this can really manage and assess learning as effectively as a teacher. However, a significant strength lies in their ability to give the pupil undivided attention; this is something that pupils frequently say they appreciate but that teachers will always fail to do, even in the best classrooms. In addition, the best ILSs provide a great deal of detail about pupils' performance, which teachers can scrutinise, and the ability to control both the content and the level of materials to be presented to pupils.

There are other worries too:

> ... the majority of parents do not want their children to learn by sitting at a screen all day long. Most normal adult behaviour is interactive – and you get some strange people if they've been up in the attic staring a computer screen from the age of five to 16.
>
> (Ted Wragg, cited in Underwood and Brown 1997: 190)

So it is reassuring that research indicates that short (20–30 minutes) but frequent (daily) doses of the ILS medicine appear to maximise the likelihood of improving learning. As with other medicines, overdosing generally does more harm than good, in this case by increasing pupils disaffection.

ILSs to support teaching in design and technology also exist (Watson 1998). These have content largely focused on technical areas of the curriculum such as electronics. A difference with ILSs aimed at design and technology is that they include a hardware element that is also connected to the computer at which the pupil is working (Figure 6.1). For example, in a system teaching about digital electronics, the computer might instruct a pupil to construct a particular circuit on an attached circuit board and it can then test whether it has been correctly made. This certainly helps to deflect the criticism of over-reliance on screen-based work, but it raises a different concern: design and technology has as its focus capability in designing and making and a computer-based system like this is not able to develop such capability. Clearly, this is true of any curriculum based solely around the acquisition of knowledge, but design and technology departments that

Figure 6.1 ScanTEK 2000 ILS Robotics in use at Clough Hall High School, Kidsgrove, Stoke-on-Trent. Reproduced with permission from LJ Group (ljgroup.com)

have spent a great deal of money on this type of ILS equipment will need to resist pressures to make 'full' use of it that lead to distortion of their curricula.

Electronic reference sources

A popular product with publishers is the digital database of information.[5] These include general encyclopaedias and design and technology specific information including data on materials, picture libraries, health and safety information, data on nutrition, component catalogues and so on (Figure 6.2).

Generally speaking, electronic reference sources support learning in the same way as a reference book might. Whether or not they provide an advantage over paper-based materials depends on factors such as speed, ease of use, interactivity, the ability to view information in a range of ways and so forth, as discussed earlier. A significant difference between paper and digital sources of information is that it is usually possible to 'cut and paste' both textual and pictorial data out of a digital source. The information collected in this way can be incorporated seamlessly into a pupil's own computer-based work. This may be seen as a good or a bad thing; pupils who use the facility to improve the efficiency of their work, for example, to consult a wider range of sources or views, are likely to improve their understanding. Those who simply use electronic pasting to fill up their assignments with ill-considered and poorly synthesised text clearly will not benefit very much. However these are arguments neither for nor against the technology *per se*; it is the teacher's

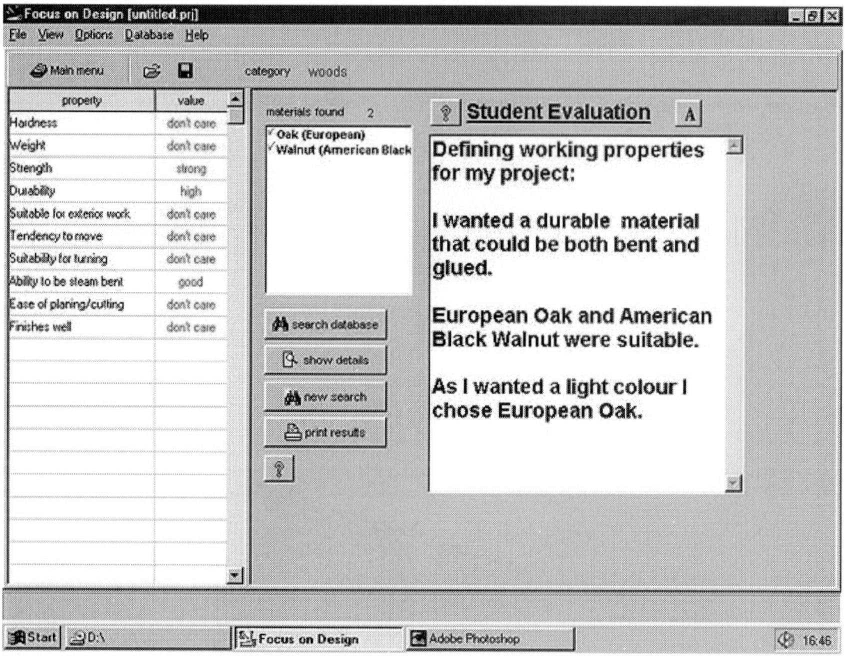

Figure 6.2 Focus on design (materials) database. Reproduced with permission from focuseducational.com.

responsibility to see that pupils are taught properly how to use ICTs to benefit their learning and to respond to poor-quality work in this realm as in any other. A concern often raised is that teachers will not be able to see the 'seams' in the way that they can when cutting and pasting has been done physically rather than electronically. Though this is true, teachers' knowledge of their pupils will generally alert them to surprisingly good work. Developing methods of getting under the skin of a pupil's work, such as the use of a friendly interview to establish what a pupil really understands, will become increasingly important, both for teachers and for examination boards (in both examining and moderation), as the use of ICT penetrates ever deeper into education.

Modelling

Computer modelling has quite a wide range of meanings and applications in education. Mellar *et al.* (1994) provide a comprehensive overview, describing models as 'artificial worlds' and detailing a range of approaches, with a particular emphasis on pupils learning through constructing their own computer models:

> The actual world in which we live is by no means easily predictable and understandable; we often know little of how things work or of what they can or will do. One human strategy to deal with this is to construct artificial worlds

made of entities whose behaviour we do know because we decided what it should be.

(Mellar *et al.* 1994: 12)

Currently this approach to computer modelling is not well supported in design and technology, though it mirrors common physical approaches to modelling such as the use of Lego or card to model physical objects. The former National Council for Educational Technology (NCET 1996) has provided examples of modelling activities using a wide range of types of software, from a simple wordprocessor to specialist design software, that support the development of pupils' design capability, from developing and clarifying ideas through developing, testing and communicating to evaluating these ideas.

Increasingly, a significant approach to computer modelling is through the use of ready-built 'artificial worlds' in which an area of design and technology can be explored (National Association of Advisors and Inspectors in Design and Technology 1994b). Usually this is a technical area such as electronics, mechanisms or structures. Most common in secondary and upper primary education is material focusing on the working of electrical and electronic circuits and on mechanical modelling, schools with software for modelling structures being more often found post-16. For example, in an electronic modelling environment a pupil can 'construct' a circuit on the computer screen by dragging components together, this circuit will then operate in a very similar way to one built with real components. The modelled circuit has the advantages that connecting components is relatively straightforward, poorly connected circuits can do no damage to virtual components and animations can be used both to aid understanding of abstract concepts, such as voltage and current, and to provide motivation to persevere with work (Figure 6.3).

There is little doubt that such environments do motivate pupils; however, to support learning a teacher cannot rely just on motivation – though it is a useful starting point. It is important that the computer-based work matches the teacher's aims for learning; for example, if the aim is improved practical capability then it is unlikely that work based only on virtual components will achieve that aim. A similar mismatch arises from the use of a component-based environment when a systems-based understanding of electronics is the aim. As ever, the lesson is to match your teaching tools to your objectives; it is particularly tempting to do the reverse when you have an exciting software tool in your hands.

Control

There is always a danger in education of assuming that 'control' equals 'computer control'. The ICT focus of this chapter could reinforce this notion. However, computer control is just one aspect of control, which also includes, in educational as well as industrial practice, electrical, electronic, mechanical, pneumatic and hydraulic control. That said, this chapter *is* about ICT, and computer control is the focus of this section. Computer-based control has a number of advantages that include:

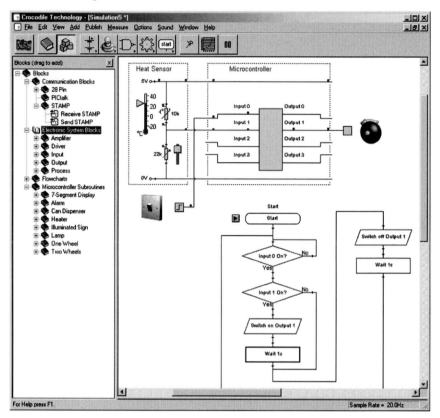

Figure 6.3 Crocodile Clips software (© 1993–2001 Crocodile Clips Ltd) (created using Crocodile Technology).

- the ability to simulate a control program before trying it out in 'real life';
- the ability to easily change a control program – this allows for flexible manufacturing systems to be created;
- the ability to copy and adapt an existing control program for a new situation;
- low-cost components – this is increasingly true as control programs are embedded in single-chip microcontrollers that cost just a few pounds;
- a highly graphical and easy to use development environment;
- the need to bring a wide range of technical aspects of design and technology together – even a computer-controlled system has to respond to real sensors and control real actuators (output devices).

At first glance control may not obviously be a 'knowledge content' area of design and technology. One common view of control is that pupils are first taught how to use a particular combination of control hardware and software and then required to use this knowledge to solve control problems. On the whole, formal teaching *about* control is rare.

A better approach is to accept that control is a content area of design and technology, like other aspects, and that the principles underlying it should be taught. This is certainly the view of the National Curriculum, which has a significant section on 'Systems and Control'. Once this view is accepted, it becomes apparent that the choice of hardware and software that pupils will use needs to be carefully chosen to support the teaching that is required. There are different types of both hardware and software available to schools for control and not all are compatible with each other or all computer platforms. In many ways it is the software that is the most important element because this is, effectively, the design medium within which pupils will be working. There are, broadly, three types of control software available to teachers:

1 Programming languages; here a simple computer language, usually based on LOGO or BASIC, is used to write programs that are then interpreted into control actions when the program is run.[6] Modern versions of such software have support built in to help the pupil write syntactically correct programs and may also support a degree of simulation (Figure 6.4).

2 Flowcharts; in this case a flowchart of a control solution is developed on screen.[7] This flowchart is 'run' to implement the control process. The development environments for such software are usually very graphic; for example, to test the working of a chart it can be run at a slow speed while each active element is highlighted in turn. It may also be possible to have multiple charts 'running' in parallel with, and independently of, each other (Figure 6.5).

3 System diagrams; this approach is visually very similar to a flowchart program, but in this case a system diagram is drawn, using graphical tools, to represent the control process required. Like the other approaches, simulation and graphic representations of actions will be provided[8] (Figure 6.6).

Modern software, of whatever type, will provide on-screen information about the states of the input and output lines. As described above, many also provide a simulation mode that allows a program to be tested without the need for external devices to be present.

The environment you choose should reflect your teaching aims; for example, if you base other areas of your curriculum, such as electronics, around a systems approach (as advocated by the National Curriculum and GCSE boards), you might decide that a systems diagram approach would best support this. On the other hand, you might decide that, say, a flowchart approach would provide a useful complementarity. Whatever your approach, your aim should be broader than simply teaching pupils how to use the software; they need to understand how the software relates to more general control ideas such as feedback. In addition, if you are using flowchart or system diagram software, you need to make sure that pupils understand what the graphic elements represent and the differences between the two types of diagram; if this is not made clear, pupils will usually confuse the two.

The other element of a control system is the hardware, which comprises an

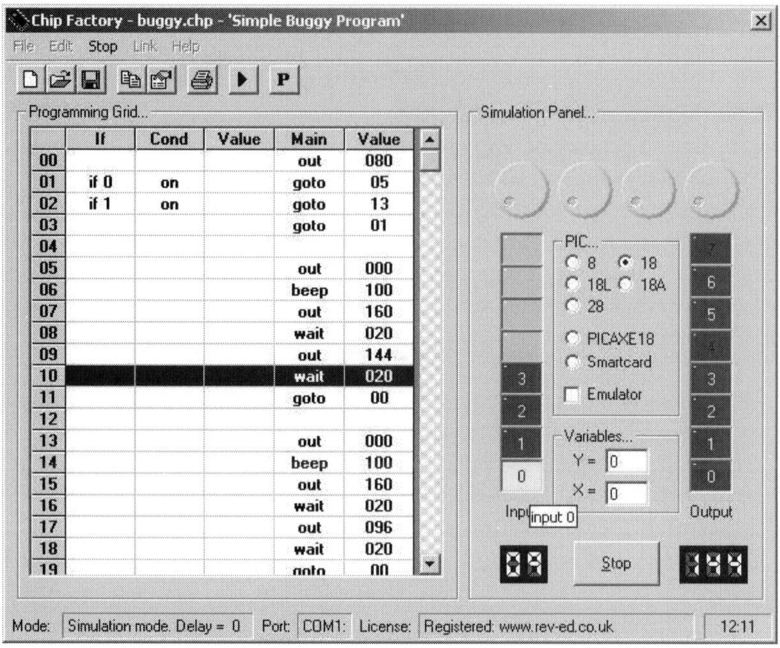

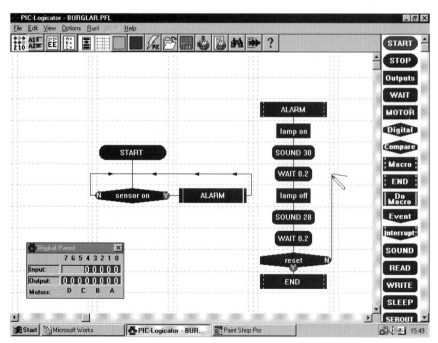

Figure 6.4 Chip Factory software for programming PIC chips. Reproduced with permission from Revolution Education Ltd (www.rev-ed.co.uk). © Revolution Education Ltd 2001.

Figure 6.5 Logicator software for programming PIC chips. Reproduced with permission from Economatics (Education) Ltd.

(a)

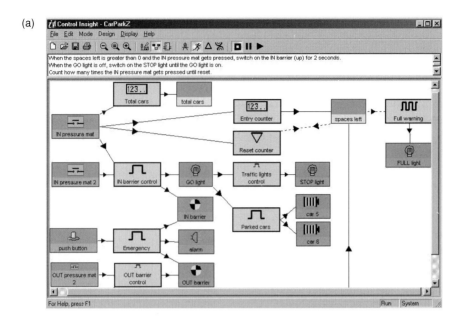

(b)

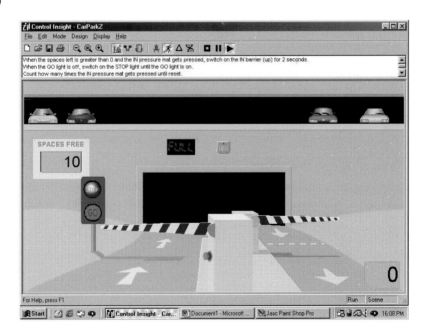

Figure 6.6   Control Insight software. (a) System view of design. (b) Simulation view of design. Reproduced with permission from Logotron Ltd (www.logo.com).

interface[9] and appropriate sensors and actuators. Sensor and actuator components are usually either matched to a particular interface or made of generally available components. In some cases the software is designed to automatically recognise the components attached.

Most modern software is able to communicate with a range of interfaces. A word of warning is in order here; there are computer control systems for schools on the market that pride themselves on working only in simulation mode without the 'need' for hardware. However, our aim as teachers of design and technology is to develop capability in designing *and* making. Real computer control is, of necessity, a messy business. It requires pupils to bring together their understandings of programming, electrical (and perhaps electronic, pneumatic, or hydraulic) control, structures and mechanisms to create an interactive product. Simulation of a situation can be useful in that it allows the pupil to concentrate on and validate programming aspects. It should not, however, be the end point of a control curriculum; pupils need the experience of designing and making fully working real systems if their capability is to develop.

In general the computer you use for control work does not need to be of the highest specification.[10] Quite useful control work can be done using palmtop computers such as the Psion PocketBook and Windows CE machines. Some 'interfaces' contain an internal microprocessor and are able to store and run downloaded control programs independently of the computer. These are akin to industrial 'programmable logic controllers' (PLCs). This type of interface requires control software that is able to compile appropriate code for the internal processor. A special case of this approach is the use of microcontroller chips. Microcontrollers are single ICs (integrated circuits) containing a processor, memory clock and input/output control – a computer on a single chip. They are sometimes called 'PIC' (peripheral interface controller) chips, after a particular make. These are extremely important devices to industry, being at the heart of most modern consumer electronics from microwaves to the current electronic toy of choice for young people (in recent years this has included such things as virtual pets and Furbys; Figure 6.7). There are now friendly systems for programming microcontrollers available to schools.

The reason that microcontrollers are so important is that they combine flexible control capabilities with very low cost; typically a PIC chip costs less than a pound and is thus a realistic component for school project work. So there is a real opportunity for pupils to develop complete products that incorporate computer control. Other applications of control found in schools include robots, assembly line control and process control (for example in food manufacture; Figure 6.8).

Datalogging

Datalogging using sensors linked to a computer allows measurements of physical signals (data) to be taken and recorded electronically. The resulting data set can be displayed as a table or graph on the computer screen. When displayed as a

Figure 6.7 Furby – controlled by computer. Reproduced with permission from Tiger Electronics (UK) Ltd.

graph, a range of measurements, such as gradients or readings at various places on the graph, may be made (Figure 6.9).

This is mainly an activity carried out in science laboratories, but it also has its place in design and technology. For example, when investigating the effect of a force on a material (resistant or compliant), the size of the force on the sample being tested and the amount it stretches or squashes can be measured and displayed graphically. This kind of measurement can be done by hand, but the end result is often disappointing or unclear. The precision of electronic measurement coupled with the speed at which the measurements can be taken means that the graphs obtained make the teaching point much more clearly. In addition, the graph can be observed being drawn as the force is applied so that the link between the graphical representation and the physical reality it represents is also clearer.[11]

Can ICT support high-quality designing?

The quality of design work in schools continues to be an issue of concern to many observers:

Figure 6.8 Armfield food process control: fermenting yoghurt. Reproduced with permission from Economatics (Education) Ltd.

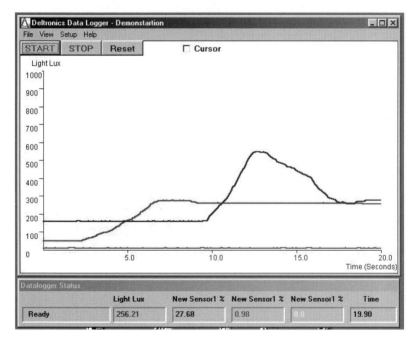

Figure 6.9 Datalogging software. Reproduced with permission from Deltronics (www.deltronics.co.uk).

In design and technology, skills in making remain stronger than those in designing.

(Ofsted 1999b)

A powerful use of ICT in design and technology is to support the development of effective designing skills and to allow children to apply those skills to produce high-quality designs. In some cases design and technology will be the ideal environment for pupils to learn the basic skills of using a program. Alternatively, pupils may come with the basic skills from elsewhere in the curriculum but will still need teaching how to apply these skills to a particular design and technology situation.

The use of ICT to support high-quality designing does raise a number of general issues:

- The development of pupils' manual design skills should not be neglected.
- For most pupils, it takes a great deal of skill, or advanced software, to produce work that matches the quality they can produce by hand.
- Pupils can waste a great deal of time using software for tasks that are either trivial or that would be more quickly done by hand; they may well hold a view that work done on a computer is, *per se*, better.
- Designs developed using ICT need at least as much validation as those developed using more traditional methods. Pupils may hold a view that if the design 'works' on the computer then it will be bound to work when realised; the limitations of computers need to be emphasised as well as their strengths.

Examples of uses of ICT to support designing include:

1   Wordprocessing and desktop publishing (DTP) software to support writing activities such as portfolio development and product user guides (Design and Technology Association (DATA) 1998a). As with many of the technologies described below, judicious use of wordprocessing or DTP can speed pupils' work and add greatly to its quality. Overuse and the neglect of hand-produced work bring the risk of pupils wasting time, producing work that is dull and flat and failing to develop hand-lettering skills.

2   The use of a database (strictly speaking, a 'database manager' – the organised collection of data is the 'database') to organise data gathered during pupils' research. DATA (1998b) provides a number of straightforward examples of this. Organised data can, for example, be sorted or displayed graphically and correlations can be sought. Where research data is numeric, a spreadsheet may be more useful than a database in its analysis. It is more likely that valid conclusions will be drawn from data that can be properly interrogated because it is well organised.

3   The use of spreadsheets to provide a data-handling tool. Again DATA (1998c) provides a number of straightforward examples of this. In particular, spreadsheets allow pupils to build and explore their own mathematical models.

This need not be as high-powered as it might sound; mathematical modelling includes things like exploring the consequences for cost or weight of using different materials or components, the effect on product price of mass-production, or investigating the nutritional consequences of varying ingredients. Because a spreadsheet takes the pain out of repeated arithmetic operations, pupils are more likely to engage in simple mathematical modelling to improve the quality and effectiveness of their designing.

4   Modelling the function (workings) of a proposed design is common in industry,[12] and can allow many design decisions to be made without the costs of materials. A spreadsheet can be regarded as a general tool for modelling; however, to build all but the simplest models will usually require a great deal of prior mathematical understanding. For this reason a range of dedicated functional modelling tools is available, particularly in technical areas such as electronics, mechanical or structural modelling. These tools are powerful provided they allow pupils to easily and rapidly try out ideas; when modelling with physical components a great deal of time can be absorbed simply assembling and disassembling the models, whereas well designed software will make this easy. On the whole though, it is not a good idea to allow pupils to go straight from virtual model to final artefact. Pupils' own visualisation skills tend not to be well developed and a real model, informed by the virtual modelling process, is usually a wise step in the design process.

5   Modelling form, that is, what the product or some aspect of it will look like. A wide range of graphic tools is available for modelling form, but broadly speaking, there are two types: bitmap graphics and vector graphics (see DATA 1998d). The difference between these is the way that they represent images. In bitmap software a solid circle of colour, for example, is described as a series of dots (called 'picture elements' or 'pixels'); this imitates the way that a circle on a piece of paper is, in effect, a series of blobs. In vector software the circle would be an object described mathematically in terms of its size, colour, position, the thickness of the encircling line and so on. The consequences of using these different approaches are profound. Bitmap software is most like working with paint or crayons and paper; once a mark is made on the 'paper' it can only be changed by drawing over it – even 'erasing' is effectively drawing over it in white. To move the circle, or even to change its colour, entails erasing it and redrawing it. The size of bitmap files tends to be large, and a completely blank file is the same size as a complex picture because the colour of each pixel is always recorded. Like a painting or photo, when a bitmap image is enlarged it becomes 'lumpy' as the pixels are simply made larger. Bitmap software allows pupils to work with very natural images. Scanners and digital cameras (still or video) can be used to capture images such as photos or artwork that has been created by hand. Graphic tablets are also useful both for creating original work and also to trace complex shapes such as maps. Vector image objects are similar to the words in a wordprocessor document. An object can be moved or resized, and its style (line thickness and colour, fill, etc.) can be changed simply. The file size of a vector image is

generally small as the size depends mainly on the number of objects in the image; a large circle will require just the same amount of description as a small one. Vector images lend themselves particularly to relatively simple images such as cartoons, line drawings and design drawings. Once again a graphic tablet will often be a better device for drawing than a mouse. When the size of a vector object is increased its quality is maintained. Pupils will need to be taught the appropriate uses of both types of drawing software. They will also need to learn when the use of ICT is appropriate and when they should use hand drawing. For example, pupils may well be tempted to spend hours using ICT to accomplish what should be done by hand in a few minutes or to use ICT fruitlessly to 'pretty up' initial sketches for a portfolio. The ability to create graphics by hand is one that will always need to be nurtured; the uses of ICT suggested here allow pupils to do things that are usually not possible by hand.

6 The use of CAD, a type of vector drawing, is of particular use in design. 'CAD' variously stands for computer-aided drawing/drafting/design. In modern software the distinctions between these have largely evaporated and 'design' is the usual term chosen. CAD software is used to create what might loosely be described as 'technical' drawings – properly scaled representations of either an existing or to-be-realised artefact. These may be executed in two or three dimensions; software may specialise in one or the other (Figure 6.10). Perhaps the most significant aspect of CAD, both in industry and schools, is the ability to link the software to manufacturing tools in computer-aided manufacture (CAM). These CAD/CAM systems are explored in the next section of this chapter.

7 The use of communication networks and software, from e-mail to video conferencing, to support designing. This is of increasing importance in industry, but at first glance the use of such technologies in schools may seem irrelevant since individual work by pupils is almost ubiquitous. However, the very fact of increasing reliance on group working in industry is leading to reconsideration of its role in education. Some interesting pioneering projects, linking schools in different phases or schools to industry, have shown that such work does have potential for motivating the development of capability in design and technology, though it requires careful planning. A pupil whose GCSE coursework involves designing for someone outside the school could use e-mail to discuss the progress of the design or to send sample design files. In other projects pupils have used CAD to design in school and sent their design files to industrial partners or further education colleges for manufacture, in some cases observing the manufacture via video conferencing. Projects including this kind of communications element should do so because it adds a demonstrable benefit in cost, or time or the development of pupil capability. The fact that a technology is novel does not of itself mean that it will bring benefit to learning. However, a degree of risk-taking with new technologies is inevitable as both benefits and problems can often only be seen with hindsight.

8 The use of control software. In the context of design it is important to realise

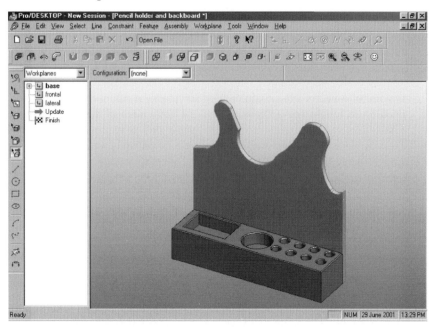

Figure 6.10   Image produced using Pro/DESKTOP™ 3-D modelling software. Reproduced with permission from Paul Clewes and Mike Brown, product line manager, Pro/DESKTOP™, PTC.

that control software is a design medium in which pupils design (as well as test and implement) control systems. The user interface presented to pupils by the software and its ability to support effective design (which implies, among other things, the ability to choose different approaches and move fluidly between ideas) should therefore be considered when selecting control software.

Can ICT support high-quality making?

Using ICT to support high-quality making depends on two things. First, you need to have available a range of computer-driven manufacturing hardware that provides flexibility in the kinds of things that pupils can make. CAM hardware tends to be expensive, so you should avoid equipment that only allows pupils to make a very limited range of artefacts. Second, you need software[13] that can create the instructions to drive the CAM hardware.

The usual ICT caveat needs to be emphasised again; pupils' need for a broad range of making experiences and opportunities to develop their own adroitness with a range of manual tools should not be neglected because such experiences cannot compete with the glamour of CAD/CAM. Schools that have invested heavily in CAD/CAM could become reluctant to 'waste' the expenditure by allowing pupils to spend too much time with hand tools (compare with ILSs earlier in this chapter).

However, realistically, it is going to be a rare school that has such a weight of CAM equipment that it is possible for pupils to avoid the use of hand tools. A more common scenario is that of teachers who are reluctant to allow pupils to use the limited CAM facilities that are available. This may happen because it simply seems too complex to organise the rotation of pupils' experience of the CAM, or it may be that the development of hand skills is seen as a priority, with CAM, perhaps, an opportunity for the more able. Organising the effective use of machinery whose availability is limited is always a challenge, however it is a challenge that most design and technology teachers have to tackle every day, as there are rarely sufficient hand or machine tools for every pupil. Not every pupil may, in the end, have their work produced by CAM, but every pupil can see both the process and products of CAM and compare them to hand produced items. Very often schools allow pupils to observe just one or two items being produced while the rest of a groups' designs are made either while pupils are doing other work or at another time (often with technicians' help). As for CAM being an 'extra' for more able or faster working pupils, because one of the strengths of CAM is its precision in machining, there is a strong argument for it being made available, in particular, to pupils whose making skills are limited, or who have other special needs, though not, of course, to the exclusion of work with hand tools.

Where possible, pupils should be able to choose between hand and machine working and this choice should be an informed one. This means that pupils need to be taught explicitly about the relative strengths and weaknesses of hand and machine working and be able to weigh such things as individuality and speed against precision and mass manufacture in their own work, and thus justify their chosen manufacturing methods.

Hardware

New CAM hardware is being created all the time, as are new uses for existing hardware. In all cases the hardware tends to fall into one of the categories below – though some sits in more than one:

1   Two-dimensional output. The most basic, but perhaps easily overlooked, CAM device is the humble printer[14], useful not only for printing design sheets, user guides and so forth on to paper but also printed circuit board (PCB) masks and presentation slides on to acetates and, using special transfers, images on to textiles.
2   Cutters are effectively 2-D devices that control a knife. They can be used to cut and score card, for example, to construct nets, backed vinyl sheet to produce sticky-backed lettering or other designs to stick on to artefacts or to cut fabric patterns. By using sticky-backed card, 3-D models can also be created: individual slices of the model are cut into the card and these slices are then assembled into the model by sticking the layers together. A hand-held cutter incorporating a scanner allows a design to be scanned and cut in a single process without the use of a computer at all.

3   Three-dimensional output for resistant materials. Almost overlapping with
    cutters are low relief millers. A miller contains a cutting head that can be
    moved in three dimensions: over the surface of a material (x- and y-axes) and
    into the material (z-axis). A low relief miller is only able to move the cutting
    head a few millimetres along the z-axis, this is sufficient to cut thin sheet
    materials and score their surface. Typical uses include making signs with
    laminate plastics by cutting through a surface layer to reveal a different
    coloured layer below.[15]

4   Full millers are able to shape materials to a considerable depth (typically
    100 mm or more). Usually a miller is material specific, though both wood and
    metal millers can usually also deal with plastics. Instead of using CAD software,
    the data to drive a miller can be obtained from a 3-D scanner; this device
    uses a sensor to collect data from an object. These data are then used to drive
    a miller to create replicas of the original, which can, if desired, be scaled up or
    down. An interesting possibility that this opens up is for pupils to create organic
    shapes with a mouldable material and then use a scanner and miller to mass-
    produce the shape, thus challenging a common notion that links CAD/CAM
    and mass-production to work with a lack of personality.

5   Three-dimensional 'printers'. This is a little more speculative as 3-D printing
    (or 'rapid prototyping') equipment, although relatively common in industry,
    is, at the time of writing, far too expensive for schools. However, it is likely
    that costs will fall during the next five years and that rapid prototyping tools
    will begin to appear in schools. There are various approaches to 3-D printing,
    but they all allow a reasonably robust prototype to be produced in a few hours
    from a model created in 3-D design software.

6   Three-dimensional output for textiles. CAD software can be used to drive
    knitting, sewing and embroidery machines from appropriate patterns produced
    by CAD; usually generic CAD software is unable to drive these machines
    because of the particular requirements of the hardware (Figure 6.11).

7   Process control. This tends to be expensive equipment, largely found in post-
    16 institutions or secondary schools that are technology colleges. There are
    broadly two groups of process control equipment available: those that mimic
    assembly lines with computer-controlled conveyor belts, hoppers, robot arms
    and so forth, and those that control the mass-production of foodstuffs, such
    as yoghurt, by careful control of the fermenting environment (see Figure 6.8).

Preparing to use ICT in design and technology

Being aware of the range of ICTs available to you and some of their possible
applications to support design and technology teaching is clearly an important
starting point, but this awareness, by itself, is not enough. You need to plan very
carefully how you are going to use ICT in your particular situation (TTA 1998),
and you need to do this as carefully as you would any other activity.

Figure 6.11 Textiles: CAD/CAM embroidery using a sewing machine, Key Stage 2.

Questions to consider

Details of planning are beyond the scope of this chapter, but it is appropriate to finish with an outline of some of the questions that you could ask yourself:

1 Are you fully familiar with the hardware and software that you are going to use?
2 Have you evaluated the suitability of the hardware and software for your teaching purpose?
3 Have you considered the limitations imposed by the actual equipment that is available to you?
4 Have you planned how the room will be organised and how pupil access to hardware and software will be arranged?
5 Are you aware of the ICT skills that are taught elsewhere in the school and how and when this happens?
6 Have you thought through the ways in which the ICT can support your teaching and learning objectives?
7 How will your assessment of pupils' learning be organised (how will you distinguish between design and technology and ICT capability)?
8 Have you planned for the use of ICT to support differentiated learning, which will include pupils with special needs and those who are particularly able?
9 Have you considered all appropriate legal and ethical issues such as health

and safety, data protection, preventing access to illegal or unsuitable material, copyright and acknowledging sources?

Notes

1 Computers started entering UK schools around thirty years ago. Since then, as elsewhere in society, their numbers and capability have increased to the point where in secondary schools the computer–pupil ratio is about 1:8 and in primary schools about 1:12 (DfEE 2000). The growth in provision seems to have become almost static at about this level; schools continue to buy new computers but they are largely replacing those that are outdated rather than providing new capacity (Jervis and Steeg 1998). However the development of new technologies, such as wireless networks and cheap portable devices that are Internet enabled, may change both our view of what 'a computer' is and schools' ability to improve the computer–pupil ratio.

2 McFarlane (1997) provides a clear general overview of some of the uses of ICT to support primary pupils' learning across all subjects as well as pointing to some of the possible pitfalls; most of what she has to say is of relevance to secondary teachers as well. Scaife and Wellington (1993) provide a comprehensive history covering the introduction of computers into schools, discuss some frameworks that teachers can use to help decide on the 'when/when not to' question and detail a wide range of uses in design and technology education. NAAIDT (1994a; 1995a; 1995b; 1998) and NCET (1994; 1995; 1996) provide materials with a wealth of practical, and, usually, tried and tested, advice for teachers of design and technology that in some cases includes workshop activities and example worksheets.

3 In a few departments teaching has been transformed for the better. These are generally in schools that have won extra government funding for computer equipment and have chosen to site at least some of this equipment in the design and technology department (see also Ofsted 1998; 1999a).

4 Increasingly, interactive multimedia software is also appearing on the Internet in the form of web-based materials (for example, Anglia Multimedia's secondary design and technology website http://www.angliacampus.co.uk/). A growing number of texts discuss the various practical uses for the Internet in education (Cunningham *et al.* 1997; de Cicco *et al.* 1998; Mailer and Dickson 1997; TEP (Technology Enhancement Programme) 1998a; 1998b). They suggest further issues of possible concern raised by the use of Internet based materials: undesirable materials; inappropriate or inaccurate materials; inability to find information on the topic in question; concerns from staff, parents and governors; chatlines and newsgroups; and the high cost of staff time (TEP 1998b: 4).

5 Databases are usually provided on CD though more and more useful information is appearing on the web. However, web-based information needs to be checked particularly carefully for accuracy, bias and the level of the language used. A teacher needs to check Internet-based resources before use; a CD designed for educational use will also need prior checking for suitability, of course, but this will usually be a less onerous task.

6 Such software is generally not very demanding of memory and computer power and can therefore be run on older computers. However it has the disadvantage, for at least some pupils, of being less intuitive to use than other types of software.

7 The highly graphic nature of such software does mean that the demands for computer power are higher, however the graphics are also very motivating and intuitive for most pupils. It is worth noting that both programming languages and flowcharts are very sequential in nature and lend themselves particularly to situations where the control solution is also naturally sequential.

8 This approach has similar graphic strengths to flowcharting programs although the

diagrams represent rather different things. Whereas a flowchart shows actions that the computer should take and defines the order in which these actions should occur, the focus of a systems diagram is on information, or signals, flowing between the input and output devices, and on the ways that these signals should be changed to achieve a control outcome. Systems diagrams can usually represent control solutions very economically and this is especially true in the case of continuous control (that is, where input devices are being constantly monitored to control output devices).

9 An interface connects the computer to external devices. As a minimum it must provide adequate 'buffering' to protect the computer's electronic circuits from damage caused by inappropriate voltages being applied or currents being drawn.

10 You may still meet BBC computers in design and technology departments; they remain perfectly useable for control work and may be worth keeping for this purpose if computer access is a problem. They are largely restricted to programming language software.

11 Investigations such as that described can be carried out using the generic datalogging equipment that a school science department will typically carry. Alternatively, equipment is available for design and technology departments that is dedicated to this type of investigation; for example, using a modified vice that has the sensors to measure stress and strain built in and is able to apply considerable loads to resistant materials and textile samples.

12 Mellar *et al.* (1994) discuss a wide range of approaches to modelling in the curriculum, whereas NAAIDT (1994b) and NCET (1996) provide a good range of practical ideas and materials to support computer-based modelling.

13 Some modern CAD software is able to drive a wide range of CAM devices, treating them effectively as alternative printers and thus hiding a series of complexities that the user used to have to deal with. In other cases an intermediary program may be needed that takes a CAD file and from it provides the instructions for the CAM device.

14 Plotters are useful when high-quality drawings are required – especially if they are required on paper larger than A3 or in colour; printing on larger paper remains prohibitively expensive as does colour laser printing, and inkjet printing may not provide adequate quality. With a little ingenuity other ends can be achieved with a plotter, such as drawing directly onto copper-backed board with an etch-resistant pen, thus eliminating the need for ultra-violet exposure and developing chemicals in PCB manufacture.

15 There is also available a system for milling the copper off copper-backed board to create a circuit board without the need for any etching; although this is not a method found in industry, it does eliminate slightly unpleasant chemical processes.

References

Benyon, J. and Mackay, H. (1993) (eds) *Computers into Classrooms: More Questions than Answers*, Lewes: Falmer.

Collins, J., Hammond, M. and Wellington, J. (1997) *Teaching and Learning with Multimedia*, London: Routledge.

Cordes, C. and Miller, E. (2000) (eds) *Fool's Gold: A Critical Look at Computers in Childhood*, College Park, MD: Alliance for Childhood, http://www.allianceforchildhood.net/projects/computers/computers reports.htm

Cunningham, M. (1997) *Schools in Cyberspace: A Practical Guide to using the Internet in Schools*, London: Hodder and Stoughton.

DATA (1998a) *Information Technology in Design and Technology: Using DTP in Design and Technology*, Wellesbourne: DATA.

DATA (Design and Technology Association) (1998b) *Information Technology in Design and Technology: Using Databases in Design and Technology*, Wellesbourne: DATA.

DATA (1998c) *Information Technology in Design and Technology: Using Spreadsheets in Design and Technology*, Wellesbourne: DATA.

DATA (1998d) *Information Technology in Design and Technology: Using Drawing Packages in Design and Technology*, Wellesbourne: DATA.

de Cicco, E., Farmer, M. and Hargrave, J. (1998) *Using the Internet in Secondary Schools*, London: Kogan Page.

DfEE (1997) *Connecting the Learning Society*, London: DfEE.

DfEE (1998) *DfEE Statistical Bulletin Issue 11/98: Survey of Information and Communications Technology in Schools 1998*, London: The Stationery Office.

DfEE (2000) *DfEE Statistical Bulletin Issue 07/00: Survey of Information and Communications Technology in Schools 2000*, London: The Stationery Office.

Jervis, A. and Steeg, T. (1998) *The Internet in Secondary Schools: Report of a Survey into Internet Provision and Use*, Manchester: University of Manchester.

Mailer, N. and Dickson, B. (1997) *UK School Internet Primer*, London: Koeksuster.

McFarlane, A. (1997) *Information Technology and Authentic Learning: Realising the Potential of Computers in the Primary Classroom*, London: Routledge.

Mellar, H., Bliss, J., Boohan, R., Ogborn, J. and Tompsett, C. (1994) (eds) *Learning with Artificial Worlds: Computer Based Modelling in the Curriculum*, London: Falmer.

NAAIDT (National Association of Advisors and Inspectors in Design and Technology) (1994a) *Guideline: Information Technology for Designing and Making at Key Stages 3 and 4*, NAAIDT (distributed by DATA, Wellesbourne).

NAAIDT (1994b) *Guideline: Modelling: Using IT as an Aid to Design and Technology*, NAAIDT.

NAAIDT (1995a) *Design and Technology at Key Stages 3 and 4: A Pupil's Entitlement for Information Technology*, NAAIDT.

NAAIDT (1995b) *Enhancing Design and Technology through the use of IT*, NAAIDT.

NAAIDT (1998) *Using Information Technology within Design and Technology: a Teachers' Guide for Key Stages 3 and 4,*: NAAIDT.

NCET (National Council for Educational Technology) (1994) *The DITT Pack: IT in Design and Technology*, Coventry: NCET.

NCET (1995) *Approaches to IT Capability; KS Design and Technology*, Coventry: NCET.

NCET (1996) *IT in Design and Technology: The Modelling Pack* , Coventry: NCET.

Ofsted (1998) *Secondary Education 1993–97: A Review of Secondary Schools in England*, London: The Stationery Office.

Ofsted (1999a) *Standards in Primary Information Technology*, London: Ofsted.

Ofsted (1999b) *The Annual Report of Her Majesty's Chief Inspector of Schools; Standards and Quality in Education 1997/98*, London: The Stationery Office.

Papert, S. (1980) *Mindstorms: Children, Computers and Powerful Ideas*, London and New York: Harvester Wheatsheaf.

Papert, S. (1993) *The Children's Machine: Rethinking School in the Age of the Computer*, London and New York: Harvester Wheatsheaf.

Scaife, J. and Wellington, J. (1993) *Information Technology in Science and Technology Education*, Buckingham: Open University Press.

Squires, D. and McDougall, A. (1994) *Choosing and Using Educational Software: a Teachers' Guide*, London: Falmer.

Stoll, C. (1995) *Silicon Snake Oil*, London: Macmillan.

TEP (Technology Enhancement Programme) (1998a) *Introducing the Internet (Pupil's Guide)*, London: TEP.

TEP (1998b) *Using the Internet (Teacher's Guide)*, London: TEP.

TTA (Teacher Training Agency) (1998) *Initial Teacher Training National Curriculum for the Use of Information and Communications*, London: TTA.

Underwood, J. and Brown, J. (1997) *Integrated Learning Systems; Potential into Practice*, London: Heinemann.

Underwood, J. and Underwood, D. M. (1990) *Computers and Learning: Helping Children Acquire Thinking Skills*, London: Blackwell.

Watson, J. (1998) *ScanTEK 2000: A Modular Technology Training Program*, London: Technology Colleges Trust.

Further reading

An important document for all teachers is the Teacher Training Agency's *Initial Teacher Training National Curriculum for the Use of Information and Communications* (TTA 1998). Despite the 'Initial Teacher Training' in its title, it is identical in (almost) all respects to a set of standards for the use of ICT in subject teaching that all teachers are expected to meet. These standards are not about personal capability with ICT software or hardware, rather their focus is on the use of ICT to support effective subject teaching. The document expands considerably the previous section of this chapter.

Seymour Papert's writings are a valuable antidote to the rather cautious and wooden prose of a government agency. *The Children's Machine: Rethinking School in the Age of the Computer* (Papert 1993) is a book to get you excited about the potential that computers have for transforming education.

Finally, to bring you back to the realities of classroom teaching in the UK, Angela McFarlane's *Information Technology and Authentic Learning: Realising the Potential of Computers in the Primary Classroom* (McFarlane 1997) provides well-written and -argued advice for teachers wanting to use computers to support high-quality learning. Despite the 'primary' in the title; this book is useful for and relevant to *all* teachers.

7 Issues in planning design and technology at Key Stages 1 and 2

Su Sayers

Introduction

This chapter discusses three current issues about planning to teach design and technology in primary classrooms that will concern both primary and secondary teachers:

- in full Key Stage 1 and 2 curricula, allowing children to obtain valid experience of designing and making;
- planning appropriate challenges to develop quality and progression in children's designing;
- transition between Key Stages in design and technology.

Teachers in primary schools face many pressures, some of which their peers in secondary can avoid. The generalist nature of most teaching at this level means that teachers need to be up to date with the complete diet of National Curriculum subjects. In addition, the introduction of new curriculum initiatives can make excessive demands on the teacher's time and energy. So, issues for primary teachers often concern making the most effective use of their own existing skills in design and technology, rather than investing time and energy in learning new ones. To stick with tried and tested ways of teaching design and technology (perhaps derived from the days when the subject was called 'craft'?) may be a safe haven in a changing world. However, Office for Standards in Education and Training (Ofsted) reports (1998–9) suggest that many Key Stage 1 and 2 teachers' lack of experience with resistant materials, or in technological areas, is to blame, and that lessons are sometimes less satisfactory 'because of teachers' weaker subject knowledge and experience'. But do primary teachers have access to adequate resources to extend beyond the familiar materials of paper and card in teaching design and technology? And is the curriculum so crowded that design and technology is incorporated into science or art lessons? This chapter rehearses the arguments for and against the concerns raised by this first issue.

The second issue relates to children's designing. Teachers seem unsure about how to engage different age groups in worthwhile design activity. Helping children make progess in designing may involve choosing appropriate strategies to support their designing at Key Stages 1 and 2. Various writers have considered the best way to go about doing this, and some of these are considered in this chapter. The third issue concerns transition between Key Stages 2 and 3 in design and technology. It may not be the first thing in the mind of Year 6 teachers who have other demands on their time, such as SATs (Standardised Assessment Tests) preparation in mathematics, science and English. However, the gap between pedagogical approaches in each Key Stage, drawn attention to by Kimbell *et al.* (1996), has revealed concerns about pupil progress in design and technology. The issue here involves insularity and compartmentalisation, which is not always in the best interests of children's smooth progress in design and technology, and also resources such as time for planning and managing the transition process effectively.

How can we fit design and technology in to an already full curriculum?

The response to the 'squeeze'

Is it possible to ensure that there is enough space in full Key Stage 1 and 2 curricula to allow children to obtain experience of making things, in the spirit of design and technology? One response to the 'squeeze' is not to do any design and technology at all. Indeed, after the introduction of the numeracy and literacy strategies (in 1998–9), the need to reduce the load on primary teachers was officially recognised, and the requirement to teach all of the programmes of study was temporarily removed (QCA 1998)[1]. However, as Herne (2000) has pointed out, the consequences of the two-year relaxation of the requirement to teach all the programmes of study may be longer term in some primary schools, despite the focus from September 2000 on teaching all the foundation subjects once again (ibid.: 217–23).

With an INSET (in-service education and training) emphasis on new curriculum initiatives, the monitoring of curriculum coverage in design and technology may have lost its priority. Design and technology may not be on the agenda unless a spokesperson or coordinator (or Ofsted inspector) raises the issue.[2]

The place in the curriculum

Some teachers remain apprehensive about design and technology and its management in the classroom, perhaps lacking appropriate equipment or anxious about children's safety when using saws and sharp tools. Teacher education has been subject to the squeeze on time in all the foundation subjects, leaving newly qualified teachers short of experience of design and technology in a practical context. The safety guidelines for science and technology may help to reassure teachers and inform good practice (CLEAPSS 1990; NAAIDT 1992). However, the perceived location of the knowledge base for design and technology in science (Layton 1993: 65) is an issue of concern for teachers who have had little experience with technology. It might be argued that a more overt emphasis on links with art would help to give some teachers a better grasp of the 'challenge' and the process of designing and making. Indeed, primary teachers' creative flair for design and construction using card and 'found' materials, highlighted by Ritchie (1995), could be a good basis for development of skills in other materials.

Could design and technology be taught as part of science?

Science is tested at the end of Key Stage 2, according it, in many people's view, higher status than design and technology. The relationship between the two subjects can be contentious, as each competes for its proportion of curriculum time. Some of the literature on primary design and technology argues that a subject knowledge base is crucial for teaching design and technology effectively. Usually, what is meant by 'knowledge' is scientific knowledge. This is the most powerful contributor to technological understanding, and indeed many teachers come to teach or coordinate design and technology in primary schools because they have a scientific background. Daniel (1997), in his study of the relationship between science and technology in the primary curriculum, provides useful insights into the variety of positions that people take (ibid.: 102).

What are the differences between science and design and technology?

A food project, on fruit salad or bread for instance, can be planned purely as a science lesson. However, designing and making with fruits and vegetables, though it certainly helps children to learn scientific concepts, also helps them learn about planning and using tools and equipment, and thinking about colour, texture, shape and the taste of fruit pieces. Most teachers would allow children to share in the excitement of designing, making, tasting and evaluating a food product, so the design and technology opportunities are not usually ignored in such topics. If bread is being used as the basis of a science lesson, experimenting with the chemical action of raising agents sometimes takes precedence over designing and making real bread. Similarly, topics on energy, such as levers and mechanisms, incorporate scientific concepts, and can be design and technology and/or science. Is there a difference between a scientific approach and a design and technology approach?

The working party for the original National Curriculum proposals pointed to distinct differences between science and technology:

> Technology and Science are closely linked and many teachers have come to Technology through activities they regard as practical Science. There are however distinct differences. Because Science is enquiry led and discovery is for its own sake, the conclusions drawn from the evidence and data are as objective as possible. Technology, on the other hand, essentially involves meeting a need or solving a problem. The best solution will often involve a subjective judgement, and will be arrived at after taking a wide range of factors into account.
>
> (*Technology 5–11*, cited in Tickle 1990: 122)

A sound knowledge base, for Tickle, is fundamental, allowing trainee teachers to gain practical know-how. He sees the knowledge base being developed through a series of practical experiences, and very tightly focused examples are given in his book to illustrate a series of focused practical tasks. Exercises and practical experiments form the basis of many of his examples (for example, the experiments on structures), and these appear like scientific experiments. 'Practical knowledge of CDT [sic] content and teaching strategies can grow through an accretion of experience' (Tickle 1990: 29). It is clear that in his approach to design and technology precedence is given to understanding scientific concepts rather than the holistic design and technology processes, which involve more difficult evaluative tasks. Problem solving like this has the danger of not always being located in the context of real problems that children can empathise with. While appreciating the value of gradually refining skills and teaching new concepts through focused tasks, it is also important to remember the value to pupils of a broader focus. The National Curriculum calls for holistic designing and making assignments (DMAs) to also form part of the diet towards capability in the subject.

Tickle admits that he takes risks in advocating a division between subject content and teaching activities, but is adamant that a full understanding of the nature of design and technology and its principles can only come through experiencing problem solving at first hand in this controlled way. However, the shortcomings of a curriculum in which priority is given to imposing knowledge on pupils, a content-led approach, are exemplified below.

What are the shortcomings of an approach to design and technology that prioritises scientific methods and content?

Approaches to design and technology teaching, as in the example above, emphasising key scientific concepts and methodology, perhaps do this at the expense of holistic designing and making activities. Dwyer's case study of a Years 3 and 4 project on bridge building is an example (Dwyer 1999: 50). The scientific approach (linking science/geography with design and technology) led most groups to build a 'successful' bridge, (one that was strong enough to hold the required weight and did not wobble). However, the majority of solutions did not permit access for a vehicle. Dwyer points out that only one group actually constructed a ramp by which a vehicle could get on to the bridge to cross the river. Thus, there is evidence that children, presented with a decontextualised problem, might direct their problem-solving energy towards engineering a holistic solution, despite the planned focus on a narrow concept. Year 1 children show a similar need to contextualise when working on vehicle projects. For example, those who choose to make a 'Cinderella coach' as their vehicle also want to make the horse (see Figure 7.1).

When planning tasks for children, it pays to remember that in design and technology they should be engaged in real tasks, and that the setting often gives the task meaning and motivates the learner, giving 'starting points for action' (Kimbell *et al.* 1996: 16). Effective planning involves using focused practical tasks, not in isolation, but to support the knowledge and skills for a holistic activity.

Figure 7.1 Vehicle projects with Year 1 pupils.

Scientific approaches can lead to oversimplification of the problems, resulting in rather hollow and oversimplified solutions, in the interests of teaching scientific concepts and knowledge thoroughly. Real problems, however, are 'wicked problems' involving many discrete factors which are difficult to reconcile. The conflict and compromise that is inherent in many design and technology problems has to be balanced when working out a solution.

Layton (1993) offers some good advice on the way science can be 're-worked' to afford some help to design and technology projects: 'to articulate effectively with design parameters in specific practical tasks' (ibid.: 58). He recommends that teachers:

1   adjust the level of abstraction, so that a hypothesis is presented in concrete terms;
2   repackage the knowledge to make it apply to pupils' needs and experiences;
3   reconstruct the knowledge, so that it draws on examples from the real world;
4   contextualise the project to make a real solution possible.

His advice provides ideas for organising knowledge, in terms of the concepts in the science programmes of study, so that the knowledge is made appropriate to children's needs when they are designing and making. He provides an analysis that links content from science with the processes of design and technology.

The importance of process

In an analysis of the contribution of process and content, McCormick (1998) drew attention to the difficulties of combining process and content in design and technology. He pointed out that curriculum developments in design and technology (and in science as well, certainly in the 1980s) often neglected the role of knowledge in concentrating on process. He contrasts the sorts of knowledge that we use, with knowledge that is held in our heads, and makes use of the term 'qualitative knowledge' to cover propositional knowledge that is made available to be used in a problem-solving situation. He also shows that we cannot assume that things we teach in science and mathematics can be transferred easily to pupils' work in design and technology. He uses examples to show how conceptual knowledge is dependent on the context in which it is learnt, and argues that explicit links need to be forged that will help learners move the concepts and ideas to a foreign context. His message to teachers seems to be good practice: articulate your qualitative reasoning, especially when you are trying to help pupils understand how to get things to work:

> When pupils are investigating or dismantling products they can develop ways of reasoning about the operation of these products… Any experienced teacher will reason qualitatively quite naturally, and all they need to do is make this more explicit, and to support pupils in developing this kind of reasoning.
>
> (McCormick 1998: 12)

Other research has begun to provide ideas for how to move pupils forward while at the same time utilising their inbuilt personal resources. Some work focuses on the process rather than the content of design and technology. In her study of Key Stage 1 children, who were working in groups on typical design and technology activities, Roden (1999) examined the intuitive problem-solving strategies they used in order to characterise them and produce a taxonomy of group strategies. She then charted these naturally occurring strategies in relation to children's age, looking for things that changed over time. Starting with an Early Years group, she found strategies that evolved, ones that emerged at a later stage, those that did not change, and those that by Year 2 had declined. This work stresses the value of teaching approaches that reinforce the active learning that is taking place, in contrast to the imposition of knowledge, which might often be the priority in a science lesson:

> Asking young children questions about what they are doing and what they will do next, and encouraging children to question, is valuable teacher intervention. Also, consciously encouraging peer questioning and evaluation, requiring children to assess and monitor their own progress, should help them become aware of what they are doing and why.
>
> (ibid.: 27)

Her approach shows the value of putting children's needs and stage of development at the forefront of planning in design and technology. The drawback of a scientific approach that prioritises knowledge is that it may overlook these developing strategies.

In summary, therefore, it has been shown that, although there are those who equate science with design and technology, there are clear distinctions between the two subjects. There are ways in which learning in one subject can illuminate another: the National Curriculum (DfEE/QCA 1999) draws attention to cross-curricular links in the programmes of study for each subject. Experience in design and technology allows children to explore solutions to tricky problems to which there may be no clear-cut scientific answers. To allow children to make progress teachers need to be aware of both content and process.

Could design and technology be taught as part of art and design? What differences are there?

The issue of overlap and cross-curricular links between art and design and design and technology has been less contentious, despite the fact that 'design' is part of both subjects. In the literature it is generally acknowledged that the skills needed to design are common to National Curriculum design and technology and art and design. Activities might run into each other at Key Stages 1 and 2: does this matter? Daniel (2000), in his interesting résumé of the last decade in design and technology, has commented on the 'lobby groups that claimed an ownership of the new subject of design and technology'. In relation to art and design, he concludes that art teachers were quite happy to have their own subject, so there was no real rivalry or political manoeuvring for priority. Thus, it has not provided an overt impetus for research and nor, probably more significantly, has there been any recent funding to support research in this area.

For Jarvis, art is seen as a resource for design and technology '… learning in art makes significant contributions to design and technology capability by assisting in developing children's critical skills and judgements about the aesthetic dimension' (Jarvis 1993: 36). She gives details of elements of visual language and principles of design, showing how these 'provide a structure for children's observation and design'.

For Ritchie (1995), it is the area of communicating ideas through designs that provide the 'most obvious' link between art and designing in design and technology:

> Through art, children learn to use drawing and other means of communication for a range of purposes: recording from observation, exploring ideas and responses, visualising, generating and refining ideas in visual form.
>
> (ibid.: 82)

He goes on to state that 'Art is about personal, emotional, imaginative and affective responses and therefore has a vital contribution to make to design and technology' (ibid.: 83).

It is important to note that here there is an opportunity to redress an overemphasis on technical aspects of technology that might come from an emphasis on science. (Consider, in Chapter 12 of this book, Pacey's definition of a limited view of technology.) By focusing on the personal, the affective and perhaps also the social context, a teacher can help children out of a minimalist and reductionist view of learning design and technology. Indeed, Jarvis links values with the aesthetic dimension of design and technology very closely, and it is clear that she believes that art reinforces the evaluative element of the subject.

The case studies used by Ritchie (1995) provide some useful examples of ways of running design and technology projects to enhance pupils' capabilities in a holistic way. He has a constructivist view, in which the central tenet is to build on prior learning. The pupil is at the centre of his model of design and technology. Knowledge, concepts, skills and strategies are secondary. Might this be a key to the differences observed when design and technology is taught and studied as an adjunct of a science curriculum rather than an art-biased curriculum? The art approach accords more closely with Ritchie's constructivist approach.

The danger here, however, lies in the association with only art materials, for example graphics and malleable materials; it is important for children to experience designing and making with resistant materials, electronic components, textiles and food, as well as with card and paper.

Is it possible to ensure that high-quality design activity takes place in primary classrooms?

The notion that this is a key factor derives from the belief that designing is at the heart of the rationale for what that which is transferable, and therefore useful to pupils in other situations. One of the concerns expressed by Johnsey (1995), in his analysis of how to teach pupils to become better designers, is about progression and how to achieve high-quality design work at this age. By doing this it may be possible to enhance skills later on.

In classrooms where designing is not a focus in children's design and technology work, children might produce stereotyped copies of products thought up by someone else. The teacher wants to make sure that the children achieve a successful outcome. However, the children do not experience taking ownership of an idea; they also miss out on trying out ideas and reflecting on ways forward. (Chapter 3 of this book discusses designing in more detail.)

How can teachers plan to support children's progress in designing?

Johnsey (1998) has criticised the way in which the National Curriculum programmes of study for designing were separated from making in the 1995 post-Dearing revisions. He has put them both together into his 'toolbox' model, developed as a result of extensive observations of primary children as they carried out design and make tasks in a classroom setting:

> There is evidence to show that the making skills stimulate the designing skills, especially in young children who learn through practical experiences.
>
> (ibid.: 2)

The latest curriculum revision follows Johnsey's lead, in putting the two attainment targets – designing and making – together (QCA 1999). His 'toolbox' approach has some value in helping non-specialists to become familiar with what is involved in designing, as it can be seen as a direct extension of National Curriculum programmes of study. The elements included are:

- investigating
- identifying/clarifying
- specifying
- researching
- generating ideas
- modelling
- planning/organising
- making
- evaluating.

He acknowledges the active characteristics of the categories by using 'doing' words, for example 'researching' rather than 'research'. He also shows, by including this wide range of process skills, that designing is more than drawing. However, the formality and compartmentalising of skills in his toolbox may distract from and contradict a creative approach. There is little reference, for instance, to 'imaging' in Johnsey's categories, and where is 'communicating'? The compartments are headed by concepts that owe more to science than to art.

In contrast to this approach, Ritchie focuses on the designer's interface with materials in reinforcing the idea that '… designing does not always involve drawing before making and that a variety of means and media can be used when designing' (Ritchie 1995: 95). He goes on to conclude:

> The interaction between thought and action is at the heart of good designing: cognitive activities such as imaging and concrete modelling are two linked and essential dimensions to this. Children need to be taught the benefits of imaging and offered a variety of ways of developing their imaged possibilities. Designing should not be… a chore to get out of the way before the real job of making can be started.
>
> (ibid.: 96)

The emphasis on 'imaging' is in contrast to the emphasis on the 'toolbox'. It could be said that this highlights the difference in approach between the viewpoints of science and art.

The activities and strategies that might usefully be part of children's design and technology activity often overlook the wide variety of approaches to designing that exist. As Kimbell *et al.* point out:

> One of the most common and most serious misconceptions in Design and Technology [is] that design development can only happen on paper with a pencil… The concreteness of Design and Technology is a major part of its appeal and the source of its power to support children's learning.
>
> (Kimbell *et al.* 1996: 97)

They go on to remind us that ideas can be developed in any number of ways, through verbal discussion (very useful with Key Stage 1 and Early Years), modelling using Plasticine, Lego or paper, and taking photographs, as well as through drawing.

Benson too, considering how to develop the design work of young children, summarises what, besides drawing, could be included under the heading of 'designing' activities:

> There is still a very narrow view of the nature of design and frequently children are asked to draw a picture of what they want to make without being given opportunities, for example, to research using a variety of sources, to develop drawing skills, to examine a range of made products, to disassemble them to gain an understanding of how they work, to investigate the properties of the materials that have been used and how the parts have been assembled.
>
> (Benson 1998: 11)

Her list however has an emphasis on the cognitive dimensions of designing. The empirical dimension, which includes making prototypes, modelling and trying things against each other for size and shape, provides other opportunities for children to make progress in designing.

In a study of children's design work, Barlex *et al.* (2000) found that pupils move straight to three-dimensional modelling when this is possible: 'They do not view sketching as a mediating instrument between mind and hand, between thinking and doing' (ibid.: 12). And in a survey of reception class children, Egan drew attention to the concern of many teachers, throughout the primary-age range, that when asked to draw what they want to make, children become disillusioned: ' "They can never make what they draw" is a common worry' (Egan 1995: 14).

Design and Technology Association (DATA) guidance material clarified that drawing can be used more appropriately as a task or activity in which children draw what they have made (DATA 1995). In this way they are also being encouraged to evaluate their products, by reviewing the overall effect and reflecting on successes and possibilities for refining or improving what they have made. As Kimbell *et al.* point out, in relation to Key Stage 1 children:

> Pupils respond to problems as they arise but see less need to make summative evaluations of their finished product. To begin to develop this aspect, teachers need to help pupils develop design criteria at the start of the activity, and then allow time for discussion at the end which focuses on the degree to which these criteria have been intentionally modified or met as originally stated.
>
> (ibid.: 72)

An issue for teacher's planning, therefore, is how to build in strategies for evaluating outcomes of design activity, and thereby help children progress in their design skills.

Is sufficient emphasis given to progression towards high-quality designing?

The unresolved issue in primary education, which for Ofsted has become a major focus of its comments, has been the whole area of designing:

> Standards achieved by pupils in specific lessons at Key Stages 1 and 2 are generally satisfactory, but overall standards of achievement in primary schools in design and technology are often low.
>
> (Ofsted 1995: 3)

The emphasis, or rather the lack of emphasis, placed on designing in terms of moving children's design skills forward has also been highlighted by HMI (Her Majesty's Inspectorate) in its summary reports. Using the techniques and refining pupils' capabilities as designers is not given as much weight/time/curriculum emphasis as making. The problem is often ascribed to deficiencies in teachers or their teacher training, but increasingly it has been recognised as generic to the subject, and a lack of basic research on pedagogy in 'design methods' is a contributory factor:

> Teachers are very skilful at deconstructing sensory motor skills and cognitive concepts related to established school subjects, so that their pupils can identify those components which form the building blocks of the concepts and skills they are attempting to enhance. In 'designing' this understanding is not so refined.
>
> (Chalkley and Shield 1995: 53)

Meaningless making is often in evidence as a result, with children unable to capitalise on time for reflection and evaluation of their ideas. In a small-scale curriculum development project, Chalkley and Shield suggested a strategy that could be used by teachers working with Key Stage 2 children to support the development of pupils' design capabilities:

> If the design and technological capability of children (and of their teachers) is to be improved, and not become either a subset of science or of art and craft, specific strategies must be developed to identify appropriate design sub-processes so that techniques can be used by 'designers' but also as the first stage in the development of a pedagogy which is suitable for teachers in the subject area.
>
> (ibid: 53)

Similarly, Hope has raised the concern, in relation to drawing, that there is still much for educationalists to learn about the development of design capability at Key Stages 1 and 2:

> If making explicit, modelling and developing ideas through drawing are considered desirable and to be promoted in schools, then we need a clear understanding of the ways in which young children can begin to develop these skills.
>
> (Hope 2000: 113)

Clearly, further research will be needed to resolve these issues, and perhaps provide a taxonomy of design skills and processes which can be used effectively by teachers. In this way planning for the primary curriculum will take account not just of the subject but also of children's needs.

The gap in approach to design and technology between Key Stages 2 and 3

Cross has pointed out that most primary teachers are very skilled at linking the design and technology that pupils engage in with other curriculum subjects (Cross 1998: 8). Contrast this with the situation in secondary schools, where knowledge tends to be compartmentalised as the province of the subject specialist and cross-curricular links are less in evidence.

Evidence of a gap between pedagogical approaches to design and technology at Key Stages 1, 2 and 3 is reported by Kimbell *et al.* (1996: 86) in an overview of the Understanding Technological Approaches Project:

> Primary teachers appear to be concerned to allow their pupils to experience technology and to capitalise on their tacit understandings... Secondary teachers, by contrast, are constantly seeking to make these understandings explicit – so much so that they spend a lot of time instructing pupils about them.
>
> (ibid.: 108)

The case studies reported in this study show huge differences in practice across the age range, but the crucial stage is the Year 6 and 7 boundary, at which there was 'a very stark contrast' between the amount of time children spent *listening to the teacher* as opposed to *discussing* work among themselves. The authors conclude that although, in each case, children enjoyed what they were doing and teachers felt that the projects were successful, nonetheless, Key Stage 2 project work was 'typified by uncertainty and the need to work things out for themselves', whereas Key Stage 3 project work was 'typified by certainty and predictability, under the tight control of the teacher' (ibid.: 110). The concern expressed here is not about which approach is best (indeed it is argued that both have their place), it is about the issue of pupil progression and how progress in understanding and in doing design and technology can be hindered by such glaring differences in approach.

Comments from Ofsted (1996) have pointed to general concern about continuity and coherence between Key Stages, especially between primary and secondary education, because of the effect on children's progress. It has been expressed as a problem that teachers are responsible for, especially with regard to their planning in design and technology:

> ... [they] need to plan progression from Key Stage 2 to Key Stage 3 and Key Stage 3 to Key Stage 4 more carefully. Secondary teachers often undervalue and discount what pupils have done in their primary schools. Often they will have developed particular autonomy in selecting appropriate materials. However they may not have a broad range of experiences in using the tools, materials and equipment commonly used in secondary schools. Greater liaison is essential if transfer is not to retard pupils' development. Similarly transfer from Key Stage 3 to Key Stage 4 must be carefully planned, otherwise pupils may find themselves with unaccustomed freedom which they are unable to use effectively in less structured circumstances.
>
> (ibid.)

Ofsted's recognition of the problem in general terms (across the whole curriculum) has resulted in proposals that might help to narrow the gap (QCA 1996). Policy changes have resulted in some schools and local education authorities appointing liaison officers between feeder primary schools and their high schools. It has been important to do this to avert crisis management and avoid the after effects of alienation of pupils in the early years of secondary education. Whether or not this has had an effect on the disparity in the curriculum for design and technology is not so clear. Gorwood (1991) is sceptical of a bureaucratic approach; he believes that liaison on a departmental/subject basis has more potential. Kimbell *et al.* (1996) suggest that modifications are needed to the curriculum at both Key Stage 3 and Key Stage 2: 'We would suggest that this should be a double-ended modification, with changes to both such that the interface at Year 6–7 is less traumatic' (ibid.: 115).

Should design and technology at Key Stage 2 be more like Key Stage 3: taught by a specialist, in a specialist workshop? Design and technology lessons at Key Stage 3 are usually the first occasion when children have worked in a specialist workshop. Hopton (1998: 137), considering whether the primary teacher should be a specialist or a generalist, argues a convincing case for the continuation of generalist teaching at least until Year 5 or 6. Her main arguments centre round the value of integration between subjects. She admits, however, that 'the case for specialist teaching becomes stronger in a school that has little or no design and technology expertise and/or teachers who are unwilling or unable to take the subject on board' (ibid.: 139). Benson has commented on some of the stumbling blocks that impede progress towards full articulation between key stages. She claims that it resides in teachers' concern for their pupils' current, rather than future, development: 'With all the pressures on teachers' time, individuals whose main concern is for their year group will not see it as a priority' (Benson 1998: 6).

Whose responsibility should it be? In considering the role of the primary design and technology coordinator, Cross (1998) does not give readers any guidance on transition issues across the Key Stages 1 and 2 boundary, except within the school. Kimbell *et al.* (1996: 109) seek to break down this self-contained approach to pupils' development in their appeal to teachers to look at the 'big picture' and then see how the bits of that picture might contribute to the whole: 'This means cross-phase dialogue and planning. Infant, junior and secondary teachers need opportunities to talk to each other to agree priorities and practices'.

Recent suggestions (from student teacher feedback following school experience) indicate that some design and technology teachers in secondary schools are running successful curriculum projects with children from feeder primary schools, starting in their familiar setting and then later moving to the secondary school workshop. The resource issues embodied here need to be prioritised, so that teachers have time to plan effective ways to promote transition.

Conclusion

Despite the areas for development in design and technology in the primary school that still concern educationalists, the general flavour is optimistic. Benson has drawn attention to comments made by Ofsted in 1994–5 and points out:

> Design and technology was the only subject about which inspectors commented that 'pupils are almost always enthusiastic about design and technology and find the work enjoyable and interesting'. Talk with any INSET provider and it is almost certain they will support the notion of enthusiastic teachers and children.
>
> (Benson 1998: 6)

Issues that face the teacher are thus to be set in the context of a highly successful 'new' subject. The temptation to conflate design and technology with other subjects, such as science or art, and the resulting loss of its identity, is an issue with potentially serious consequences. Its position relative to science and to art and design in the curriculum deserves careful analysis by teachers when they are planning for each key stage, but especially for Early Years and Key Stages 1 and 2 in which demands on the curriculum from the core subjects are so strong.

Planning for activities using card, in the form of recycled packaging, as a construction material and a basic material for modelling, is popular, but a conservative and unadventurous approach to design and technology might limit pupils' design competences. Does it compromise their achievements at the end of Key Stage 2, in terms of designing and making? And what might the effect be on their transition to secondary school? The contrast between a safe, constrained approach to teaching and the ambition and eagerness to experiment, which many children show when engaging in a design and technology activity, is sharp. It is important to value what children will get out of using whatever materials are provided and to utilise concepts and ideas from science and/or art and design. And, whilst making 'models' has a place in the design and technology curriculum, most writers on the subject agree that pupils ought to be engaged in designing, modelling and, most importantly, making 'real' products.

Children's design and technology experience needs to build in opportunities to design and model solutions to problems that challenge them. The use of a variety of accessible materials, including electronic components, wood, food and textiles, is built into the statutory requirements for design and technology. These points have implications for resource provision. The Design and Technology Association (DATA 2000b: 13) has argued for changes to enable a more appropriate resourcing framework for primary teachers, and this has to be a major factor in curriculum enhancement.

By devising appropriate challenges, resourcing them effectively, and teaching skills in the context of understanding of materials, equipment and processes, teachers create opportunities to develop their pupils' capability in design and technology further. In relation to short- and medium-term planning and the success of DMAs, FPTs (focused practical tasks) and IDEAs (now Product Analysis), different kinds of design and technology activity can be used judiciously to plan

Introduction

This unit gives children an opportunity to use their knowledge of electric circuits and switches to produce a motorised vehicle, which has been geared down (slowed up) by use of a simple pulley system. With appropriate cladding the vehicle can become anything from a carnival float to a moon buggy.

Componenents from construction kits can be used with other materials

Let the children investigate controllable vehicles. These can either be manufactured toys or alternatively made up from construction kit parts. Focus on how the vehicle is powered and how movement is transmitted from the motor to the wheels. Ask the children to sketch the vehicle from different angles or make an exploded diagram showing the details of the mechanism used.

Investigate a range of different switches which could be used to control their vehicles. (This could be done in sience sessions)

Switches

paper clip
wire
paper fastener *paper fasteners*
wire *card*
fold in card *wire*
wire
wire *foil* *wire*

Use construction kit parts to explore how simple vehicles can be motorised by the use of pulley systems. Experiment with different sized pulleys. How does this influence the speed of the vehicle?

Ask the children to make a range of switches and show them ideas for making a simple reversing switch.

Demonstrate the safe use of the tools needed for this activity and show ideas for making the chassis for their vehicle.

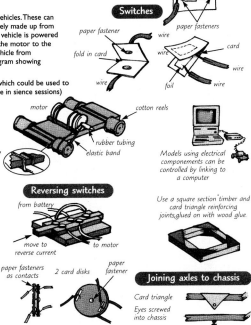

motor
cotton reels
rubber tubing
elastic band

Models using electrical componenents can be controlled by linking to a computer

Reversing switches

from battery
move to reverse current *to motor*

Use a square section timber and card triangle reinforcing joints, glued on with wood glue.

motor *belt* *card disk*
B *A*

The small pulley (B) rotates much more quickly than the large pulley (A) but has less turning force (torque)

paper fasteners as contacts *2 card disks*
paper fastener

Joining axles to chassis

Card triangle
Eyes screwed into chassis
Holes drilled into chassis
PVC tube glued to chassis
Cable clips to hold axle
Clothes peg to hold axle

very fast *standard* *slow*

Pulley wheels connected in a pulley train can be used to give a greater increase or decrease in speed

Chassis

cardboard box *plastic bottle*
card or corrugated plastic *wooden block*

Figure 7.2 DATA Helpsheet for Key Stage 2: Unit 6D Vehicles/Key Stage 2. Reproduced with permission from DATA.

effective work at Key Stages 1 and 2. Planning schemes of work for primary pupils may involve adapting QCA schemes to suit the curriculum in the school, using the DATA guidance for support in detailed planning (DATA 2000a)[3] (see Figure 7.2). The teacher-led developments of the Nuffield Primary Project (Barlex 2001) are also building a resource of useful ideas to offer teachers some further support in venturing from 'safe havens' into design and technology for the twenty-first century.

Questions to consider

1   How do you view design and technology?

- as part of science?
- as a 3-D adjunct to art and design activities?
- as an independent field of study in its own right?

Further reading: Layton (1993), Ritchie (1995), Daniel (2000), Tickle (1990).

2   In what ways can you structure design activities to help children develop key skills and make progress in designing?
Further reading: Johnsey (1995), NAAIDT (1998), Bold (1999).

3   To what extent will your future projects take account of the prior learning that pupils bring to the activity, and also build in some new challenges to your teaching?
Further reading: Roden (1999), DATA (2000a).
Further information: Staffordshire Learning Net (www.sln.org.uk), QCA Exemplar Schemes of Work for Design and Technology, Science, Art (www.standards.gov.uk/schemes), Nuffield Primary Website (www.nuffield.org.uk/primary).

4   Who needs to be involved in planning across Key Stage boundaries? How will the design and technology activities you have planned help to prepare children for what lies in store for them at the next Key Stage?
Further reading: Kimbell *et al.* (1996).

Notes

1   OFSTED claimed: 'There is little inspection evidence to support the concern that the literacy and numeracy strategies are undermining standards in other subjects. Most primary schools continue to provide a broad balanced curriculum.' (Annual Report of HMI of Schools 1998–9).
   The number of good or very good lessons in design and technology in primary was found to be very low – only 20% of lessons, with, on average, 14% poor or unsatisfactory. The subject specific comments are set out below:
   'Design and technology remains weaker than most other subjects in all aspects of provision and response, mainly because of teachers' weaker subject knowledge and experience. Despite this, there are signs that there has been a marked drop in the incidence of poor teaching. Where in-service training opportunities are taken up, improvements are quickly apparent. The reduction in the National Curriculum

requirements has led to a reduction of the amount of time for the subject in some schools, particularly where teachers have been uncertain what to do in design and technology. Despite reduction in time, pupils' making skills continue to be better than their designing skills. Pupils do particularly well when they are engaged in designing and making 'real' products, such as musical instruments for specific composition, rather than just models.'

2   Staffordshire Local Education Authority survey is an example of an attempt to keep the spotlight on design and technology within one LEA (see 'Quality learning systems' in *Staffordshire Newsletter* (DATA 2000c)).

3   The QCA Exemplar Schemes of Work (QCA 2000) provide a helpful guide to both time and management of design and technology projects. DATA guidance is available to support these schemes with input on the knowledge-based elements that teachers might be unfamiliar with. Visual help is also provided in the schemes of work in the form of diagrams, and there is advice on materials and skills in the form of tips for making strategies (DATA 2000a; www.data.org.uk). All of this guidance goes some way towards putting scientific knowledge in context, thereby making it possible for teachers with limited design and technology experience to move forward from only using card modelling to a fuller engagement with resistant materials, food and textiles.

References

Barlex, D. (2000) 'Preparing D&T for 2005: moving beyond the rhetoric', *Journal of Design and Technology Education*, **5** (1): 5–15.

Barlex, D. (2001) *Primary Solutions in Design and Technology*, London: Nuffield Foundation.

Barlex, D., Lim, H. and Welch, M. (2000) 'Sketching: friend or foe to the novice designer?', *International Journal of Design and Technology Education*, **11** (2): 125–48.

Benson, C. (1998) 'Primary design and technology for the 21st century: The Maurice Brown Memorial Lecture', *Journal of Design and Technology Education*, **3** (1): 11.

Bold, C. (1999) *Progression in Primary Design and Technology*, London: David Fulton.

Chalkley, C. and Shield, G. (1995) 'Supermodelling! Developing designing skills at Key Stage 2', *Journal of Design and Technology Education*, **1** (1): 50–3.

CLEAPSS (Consortium of Local Education Authorities for the Provision of Science Services) (1990) *Health and Safety in Primary Schools*, Uxbridge: CLEAPSS.

Cross, A. (1998) *Co-ordinating Design and Technology across the Primary School*, London: Falmer.

Daniel, D. (1997) 'The relationship between science and technology in the primary curriculum – alternative perspectives', *Journal of Design and Technology Education*, **2** (2): 101–11.

Daniel, D. (2000) 'Ten years of universal primary technology education in England and Wales – what have we learnt?', *Journal of Design and Technology Education*, **5** (1): 26–35.

DATA (Design and Technology Association) (1995) *Primary Guidance Sheets*, Wellesbourne: DATA.

DATA (2000a) *Design and Technology Guidance Material for Key Stage 1 and 2,* Wellesbourne: DATA.

DATA (2000b) 'Classrooms in urgent need of modification', *Datanews*, **15**: 12–15.

DATA (2000c) 'Quality learning systems', *Staffordshire Newsletter*, 24 August (www.data.org.uk).

DfEE/QCA (Qualifications and Curriculum Authority) (1999) *Design and Technology: The National Curriculum for England*, London: HMSO.

Dwyer, J. (1999) 'Building bridges', *Journal of Design and Technology Education*, **4** (1): 50–4.

Herne, S. (2000) 'Breadth and balance? The impact of national literacy and numeracy startegies on art in the primary school', *Journal of Art and design Education (JADE)* **19**: 217–23.

Hope, G. (2000) 'Beyond their capability? Drawing, designing and the young child', *Journal of Design and Technology Education,* **5** (2): 113.

Hopton, A. (1998) 'The merits of class teachers teaching design and technology against the use of the specialist teacher (Winnie the Pooh or Christopher Robin… Who is right?)', in *Journal of Design and Technology Education,* **3** (2): 137–9.

Jarvis, T.(1993) *Teaching Design and Technology in the Primary School* , London, Routledge.

Johnsey, R. (1998) *Exploring Primary Design and Technology,* London: Cassell Academic Press.

Kimbell, R., Stables, K. and Green, R. (1996) *Understanding Practice in Design and Technology,* Buckingham: Open University Press.

Layton, D. (1993) *Technology's Challenge to Science Education: Cathedral, Quarry or Company Store?* Buckingham: Open University Press.

McCormick, R. (1998) 'Capability lost and found – the 10th Maurice Brown Memorial Lecture', *Journal of Design and Technology Education,* **4** (1): 5–14.

NAAIDT (National Association of Advisors and Inspectors in Design and Technology) (1992) *Make it Safe!* Eastleigh: NAAIDT.

NAAIDT (1998) *Quality through Progression,* Eastleigh: NAAIDT.

Office for Standards in Education and Training (Ofsted) and DfEE (1996) *Issues for School Development arising from Ofsted Inspection Findings 1994/5 Key Stages 1 and 2,* London: HMSO.

Ofsted (1998) *Standards in Design and Technology 1996–1997,* London: Ofsted.

Ofsted (1999) *Standards in Design and Technology 1997–1998,* London: Ofsted.

QCA (Qualifications and Curriculum Authority) (1996) *Promoting Continuity,* London: DfEE (Department for Education and Employment).

QCA (1998) *Design and Technology: A Scheme of Work for Key Stages 1 and 2,* London: DfEE.

QCA (2000) *Exemplar Schemes of Work,* London: DfEE (Department for Education and Employment).

Roden, C. (1999) 'How children's problem solving strategies develop at Key Stage 1', *Journal of Design and Technology Education,* **4** (1): 21–7.

Ritchie, R. (1995) *Primary Design and Technology,* London: David Fulton.

Tickle, L. (1990) *Design and Technology in Primary Classrooms: Developing Teachers' Perspectives and Practices,* London: Falmer.

Further reading

Nuffield Primary Design and Technology Project: www.primarydandt.org.uk

Ofsted and DfEE (1996) *Characteristics of Good Practice in Food Technology Key Stages 1–4,* London: HMSO.

Ofsted and DfEE (1996) *Characteristics of Good Practice in Design and Technology Key Stages 1–4,* London: HMSO.

Staffordshire Learning Net: www.slu.org.uk

8 Assessment in design and technology
Authenticity and management issues

Kay Stables

Introduction

Assessment is a term that throws most of us into some kind of turmoil – from a mild feeling of apprehension for some, to a real sense of panic in others. At an emotional level, assessment is felt to be about being tested, having to 'come up with the goods'. So, if it has such unpleasant connotations, why do it at all? There are several answers to this question, and what an individual wants to accomplish through the assessment process will depend on where he or she stands. This chapter explores the issues surrounding the value and purposes of assessment through a discussion of the following key questions:

*   Why assess in the first place?
*   What should be assessed in design and technology?
*   How can you make assessment useful?
*   How can you make assessment manageable?

In doing so, it aspires to help in the process of understanding how assessment can support the development of capability in design and technology and how assessment processes can be managed in the learning and teaching environment.

Why assess in the first place?

The overall purpose of assessment is to provide information; who or what the information is for will place it into a different category. It may be that information is sought about the achievement or attainment of an individual learner, in order that he or she and the teacher can take this into account and so move the learner forward in his/her development. In this instance, the purpose could be described as *educational*. On the other hand, it may be that information is for a future employer to decide whether the person being assessed is suitable for employment. Assessment of this type is seen as being *instrumental*.

In the classroom, deriving immediate and ongoing information about learning that is taking place enables the teacher to support learning effectively. This type of assessment is called *formative* and is the type of assessment that can take place throughout the normal course of learning and teaching. It is sometimes also *diagnostic*, in that it helps the teacher to diagnose a learner's strengths and areas for development. A further type defines where the aim is to 'take stock' – checking what has been attained through a particular course of study, such as GCSE. This assessment is referred to as *summative*: it provides summary information such as the grade awarded for an examination. In addition, assessment can be used to check on the effectiveness of the learning experience: have pupils learnt well because they have been engaged in an appropriate course of study? Here the assessment can be seen to have an *evaluative* purpose.

Each of the above purposes brings with it a complexity of issues and priorities that will impact in different ways on teaching and learning. These purposes have assumed differing priorities in the development of assessment in design and technology, from the testing of knowledge and practical skill that characterises the approaches of the late nineteenth and early twentieth centuries, to the focus on the assessment of design and technology capability that has been fundamental since the introduction of National Curriculum Assessment (NCA).

The move from testing knowledge and skill to assessing process and capability

It was through the elementary schools that the early developments in assessment in the craft subjects (arguably the precursors of design and technology) took place. The early focus was on demonstrating technical skills through set 'practice' pieces. At a later date, theory tests requiring factual recall of knowledge were introduced, and this basic structure of testing was maintained for more than half of the twentieth century. Richard Kimbell, writing on the development of assessment in design and technology, reflected on his own experience of this system:

> When I took my O- and A-level examinations in the 1960s, I was required to engage in two kinds of activity. In one I was required to sit with rows of other candidates in the heavy silence of examination halls, busily writing 'answers' to test questions. In the other I was permitted to use a carefully defined set of tools and materials to mark out, cut, join and finish a practical test-piece of craftsmanship. I was one of the countless candidates processed through the tried and tested routine of 'theory' and 'practical' tests... I was always fascinated by the fact that there was absolutely no connection between these two kinds of examination. Whilst in everyday life... I was expected to operate as an integrated whole, as soon as it came to examinations I could be neatly parcelled up into two entirely separate packages.
>
> (Kimbell 1997: 5–6)

In the 1960s we had an assessment system based on externally set tests, such as 11 plus and O level GCSE, providing information for external agencies to decide on an individual's appropriateness for particular education or career opportunities. At this point the assessment was largely *instrumental*. The aim of the assessment was to provide *summative* information on the attainment of skill or the recall of factual knowledge. This status quo had existed for more than a century, but a shift in emphasis was on the horizon that prioritised the development of the learner, moving assessment into an era where the major thrust was *educational*. The history of the developments in the 1970s and 1980s can be found elsewhere,[1] but some key milestones in this shift include:

- the introduction of the Certificate of Secondary Education (CSE) with its emphasis on coursework assessment;
- the criterion-based assessment of the General Certificate of Secondary Education (GCSE);
- the introduction of the National Curriculum (NC) as an entitlement for all children aged five to sixteen; and
- the emphasis on key skills and transferability highlighted through the developments in vocational education leading to the General National Vocational Qualification (GNVQ).

Each of these developments had an impact on the education system. The next section explores in more detail how the shift affected principles and practices in teaching, learning and assessing design and technology.

What should be assessed in design and technology?

The significant change in design and technology was a growing belief, starting in the late 1960s, that central to the 'practical' subjects was the importance of *process*. This saw the move away from valuing knowledge and skills for their own sake to seeing the importance of being able to draw on them as a means to an end. This view was first articulated through two key research projects: Project Technology and the Design and Craft Education Project (the 'Keele' Project; Penfold 1988). Both identified process at the centre of learning activities, the Keele Project defining this as the 'design process'. This was a watershed for assessment practices, as the project took the important step of constructing both an examination and an assessment system with the design process at their core. This was a brave and pioneering step, years ahead of developments in other areas of the curriculum. As Kimbell points out:

> While science, language, maths and the rest of the curriculum are now recognised as having important process elements that need to be assessed, it is in technology that we have been trail-blazing models of process-centred assessment for the last twenty years.
>
> (Kimbell 1997: xi)

What is the design process?

The early developments of the Keele Project identified a simple, linear 'design and development process'. In turn, this became the structure of the mark scheme for a new CSE examination, developed jointly with the North Western Secondary School Examination Board (NWSEB). Pupils undertaking the course worked through design 'briefs' and were assessed, on a scale of 0–5, under the headings of 'situation and brief', 'investigation', 'solution', 'realisation' and 'testing'. Whereas with hindsight the approach may seem a little naive, it broke completely new ground in assessment and had a major influence on all ensuing developments in design and technology. Much of this influence has been helpful, for example, in the provision of a rationale that freed the syllabus writers from prescribing a fixed set of knowledge and skills to be taught and examined because it was:

> … not… possible to itemise a syllabus for practical work under the headings of specific knowledge or motor skills because these may vary according to the individual needs of candidates and the requirements of different design problems.
>
> (NWSEB 1970: 2)

It also helped teachers to focus their teaching on process rather than on the knowledge and skills paramount in previous (and virtually all concurrent) examination courses.

On the downside (and as is always a danger when assessment is driving the system), the 'process', as specified, became a straitjacket. The 'process' became a set of 'hoops' to be jumped through in order to provide enough evidence at each stage to get as many marks as possible in the assessment. The somewhat simplistic, linear process that was utilised became labelled not 'a' design process, but 'the' design process. The result was that a prescriptive model of both teaching and assessing processes became enshrined in the vast majority of public examinations in design and technology-related subjects. During the 1980s both the notions of linearity and of the single 'design process' came under challenge (Kelly *et al.* 1987; Margolin and Buchanan 1995). The over-riding problem was that, though it was clear that each of the 'stages' in the process were present in design and technology activity, the tight, linear prescription did not match reality. The classic example that illustrates this mismatch focuses on the 'stage' of evaluation, which simplistic logic places at the end of the process. But such positioning is problematic because in order to make any rational progress through a process, it is necessary to evaluate at every point at which a decision needs to be taken. Even at the very start of designing, when a vague design idea is being considered, an evaluative decision has to be taken over the quality and appropriateness of the idea before further action can be taken. Evaluating and decision making occur continually as the idea takes shape and becomes a working reality. To assume that all evaluation takes place at the end of the process and, furthermore, awards marks only to that phase presents a damaging model of designing and an unfair way to make assessments. Lawler (1999), in exploring the roots of both linear and iterative models, points to the fact that the first is a *management* model of design, whereas the second both allows for and facilitates individual designing *styles*.

During the 1980s the Department of Education and Science (DES)[2] funded a major research project into the assessment of performance in design and technology. The Assessment of Performance Unit Design and Technology Project (APU Design and Technology Project)[3] was at the forefront of challenging the linear model of both design and technology activity and its assessment. Through the research undertaken a model of process was formulated that saw designing as an activity in which steps were governed by responding to the developmental needs in the activity, rather than being prescribed in advance. The driving force of the activity was the iteration of thought and action: the interaction of the 'mind' and the 'hand'. Through this iteration an idea could be taken from its hazy beginnings to a tried, tested and detailed outcome (Figure 8.1).

As was explained in later development and use of this model:

> The approach… is built on a profoundly different model which views designing as an interaction between mind and hand (inside and outside the head) and the activity as being best described as iterative as ideas are bounced back and forth; formulated, tested against the hard reality of the world and then reformulated. We coined the phrase 'thought in action' to summarise the idea.
>
> (Stables and Kimbell 2000: 195–6)

The model and the research underscored the point that an iterative process is at the core of design and technology activity and that being able to operate

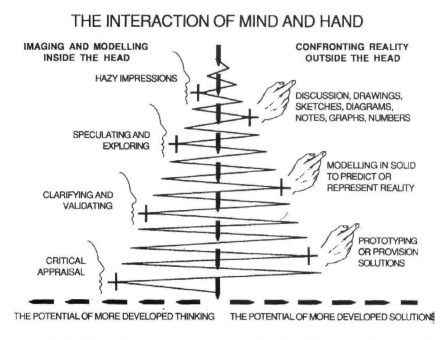

THE INTERACTION OF MIND AND HAND

IMAGING AND MODELLING
INSIDE THE HEAD

CONFRONTING REALITY
OUTSIDE THE HEAD

HAZY IMPRESSIONS

DISCUSSION, DRAWINGS, SKETCHES, DIAGRAMS, NOTES, GRAPHS, NUMBERS

SPECULATING AND EXPLORING

MODELLING IN SOLID TO PREDICT OR REPRESENT REALITY

CLARIFYING AND VALIDATING

PROTOTYPING OR PROVISION SOLUTIONS

CRITICAL APPRAISAL

THE POTENTIAL OF MORE DEVELOPED THINKING   THE POTENTIAL OF MORE DEVELOPED SOLUTIONS

Figure 8.1 The APU model of interaction between mind and hand. Reproduced from Kimbell *et al.* (1991: 20) with permission from HMSO.

procedurally is the key to capability. This holds implications for both pedagogy and assessment if both are to support the development of capability.

How can you make assessment useful?

Assessment can achieve different purposes and for the classroom teacher the priority has to be how it can directly support learning and teaching. Within this there are a number of issues.

Validity and reliability

First and foremost, if assessment is to be useful, it is fundamental that the information produced is a genuine reflection of the learning that has taken place and can be used to support development. In some situations, achieving this is easy. For example, if you want to know whether pupils have understood and can apply knowledge about how to use a piece of equipment safely, you can provide them with the opportunity to demonstrate their knowledge by both telling you and showing you what they know. The 'answer' they provide will have limited leeway: there are 'right' (safe) and wrong (unsafe) ways of doing things. It will be possible to assess the pupil *reliably*. Knowing that pupils can use equipment safely, or being able to modify their understanding and practice if they cannot, is important for the teacher and learners. Its *validity* in terms of teaching, learning and assessment is clear. In other situations, things are less clear cut. Take, for example, the desire to know whether pupils can respond creatively to a design and technology situation. First, the 'answer' cannot be defined in simple terms of right or wrong. The situation itself may affect their response: did they find it stimulating enough to respond creatively? Could they have responded more creatively in a different situation? What constituents of creative responses can be measured?

This leaves the teacher in a difficult situation: it is important to help pupils develop the ability to respond creatively – equally, but in a different way, it is important that they are able to use tools safely. It is *valid* in terms of teaching and learning and therefore it is *valid* to attempt to assess such learning. But assessing creative response *reliably* is a different ballgame. The danger inherent in this situation is that if it is difficult to assess it will not be assessed. And not assessing something is a slippery slope to not focusing on it in the course of teaching and learning. Being able to assess something reliably makes a person feel both comfortable and confident. But, if assessment only focuses on things that can be assessed reliably, there is a danger that the learning experience provided is reduced to the lowest common denominator. This is a particular problem for the design and technology teacher because at the heart of developing capability is the need to be able to operate *procedurally*, and process is inherently more difficult to assess than knowledge and skill, because there are fewer 'right' and wrong' answers.

With formative assessment, the stakes (in terms of judging incorrectly) are low, because the assessment can be revisited and modified again and again. No 'grade' is required, just that the teacher has enough of a handle on the learner's understanding to move their learning forward. In terms of creative response, it may be enough to say 'Jane appears to be hindered by her desire to stick to safe options', and then to set up situations in which Jane is supported to take risks, or 'John doesn't seem to be able to get beyond stereotypical responses', and then provide stimulus to encourage John to think more laterally. Setting up diagnostic or summative assessments may require a more detailed approach, and we will come to this later.

Achievement, attainment, norms and criteria

Two further sets of issues surround how assessments are measured: first, is it achievement or attainment that is being measured and, second, what reference points or 'benchmarks' are being applied to make judgments?

Achievement and attainment are terms that tend to be used interchangeably, but in fact are quite different. As a novice volleyball player I may never *attain* scoring a point, but in trying I may *achieve* a successful serve, a good attempt at a return and a basic understanding of the rules. Where assessment in design and technology is concerned, this differentiation is important, not least because the National Curriculum level descriptors provide general statements which may only show progress in *attainment* every two years. Also, where areas such as evaluation or creativity are being assessed, unambiguous attainment levels may be difficult to define. Whereas attainment has its place in summative assessment and where specific learning targets are set, the notion of achievement is more helpful in the day-to-day business of supporting learning in design and technology.

Whether one is concerned with achievement or attainment, in order to make an assessment it is necessary to decide what constitutes progress. What reference point demonstrates that one performance is better than another? Literature on assessment tends to highlight two approaches: *norm* referencing and *criterion* referencing. In simple terms, norm referencing means assessing performance against the standard expected of a particular cohort. Learners are measured against each other. Criterion referencing takes an ostensibly more objective stance; criteria of good, indifferent and weak performance are defined and performance is then measured against these criteria. In the UK, before the developments that led to the introduction of GCSEs and subsequently NCA, norm referencing was typical. With GCSEs came the shift to 'grade descriptors'. With NCA we had 'Statements of Attainment' (SoA) and then 'Level Descriptors'. All of these were criterion-referencing systems. When this shift took place, many educationalists and government officials took an overtly judgemental stance: norm referencing was 'bad' because it had negative overtones (someone always had to be at the bottom, however good they were), and criterion referencing was 'good' because, in theory, all could potentially gain top grades. The experience of operating these two systems leaves us somewhat wiser. Black suggests that we should view the two types of criterion as 'two different sets of properties possessed by every test and/or... possible interpretations of its results' (Black 1998: 62). He illustrates this with an example from athletics:

Thus a qualifying test for a competitor in an athletics event may well be that they can surpass two metres in a high jump – a very clear criterion. But this criterion has only been chosen in the light of normative data showing that there are enough athletes, and not too many, who can achieve this level.

(Black 1998: 62–3)

Kimbell elaborates on this issue, particularly with reference to the confusion caused in both developing and applying the original National Curriculum Order for Design and Technology (Kimbell 1997). He cites the example of the carefully honed and polished SoA for Level 10 (a level that only the most accomplished of all sixteen-year-olds could be expected to achieve) that primary school teachers felt the learners in their classrooms to be capable of – because they were 'normatively' interpreting it as excellent performance by a ten-year-old.

A third form of referencing that gains depressingly little attention in the literature on assessment is *ipsative* assessment – in which learners are referenced against themselves. Is the level of performance demonstrated by this pupil today an improvement on his or her performance yesterday, last week, last month or last year?

Ipsative assessment is assessment of a pupil not against norms (based on the performance of his/her peers) or against criteria (derived from particular conceptions of subjects and/or of education) but against his/her own previous levels of attainment and performance. In short, it is linked to a view of education as individual development.

(Kelly 1992: 12)

Ipsative assessment may be the most common form of assessment used in the classroom, as it is informal, non-threatening, supports formative judgments and is directly valuable to both the teacher and the learner. For the design and technology teacher, ipsative assessment allows for the gradual building up of a broad and detailed profile of an individual learner, taking into consideration strengths and areas for development across practical skills, conceptual understanding, procedural know-how and interpersonal skills. Such a profile can ultimately inform judgments against norms and criteria, should more summative statements be required. Ipsative assessment is also valuable where individual learning targets are set, making it especially appropriate for children with special educational needs.

Authenticity

Much of the discussion so far has explored the desire to make a comprehensive and fair assessment of the learner's capability. This places an inevitable priority on validity. First, is the activity through which the assessment takes place valid? Is the assessment instrument valid? Are the criteria or reference points for making judgements valid? For many, the key issue in validity is authenticity; in short, if you want to know if someone can do something, get them to do it 'for real'.

A different view has informed the assessment, not of capability, but of potential (for instance in intelligence testing; Gardner 1999). Here testing is explicitly decontextualised in order to gauge raw 'talent' or aptitude:

> There is within the testing profession considerable belief in 'raw', possibly genetically based potential (Eysenck 1967; Jensen 1980)... [F]or tests that purport to measure raw ability or potential, it is important that the performance cannot be readily improved by instruction; otherwise, the test would not be a valid indicator of ability.
>
> (Gardner 1999: 92)

Some might argue that the approach described here is anti-educational; others may see it as a fair and objective way to decide who might benefit from a particular experience, such as a higher education degree programme. The experience of conducting the research for the APU Design and Technology Project left us in no doubt about our own belief: ask pupils to demonstrate their learning 'on task' (that is, in context and for real) and they will surprise even their own teachers. Two good examples of this came in the testing of the assessment activities we were to use, which were short design activities derived from the iterative model described earlier. In the first example, we tested the activity with a mixed ability cohort of Year 10 pupils. Following the activity, the teacher of a boy who had a reading age of an eight-year-old exclaimed that the boy had written more for us in two hours than for her in the space of a whole term's work. The second trial was with a group of pupils who were studying for their GCSE in craft, design and technology (CDT): thus a specialist cohort. In this example, the teacher became exasperated as he watched a boy make more evaluatory comments in the short activity (in which the iterative model prompted the inclusion of evaluation throughout the activity) than he had made in the whole of his major project portfolio.

The APU Design and Technology Project was founded on a basis of assessment 'on task', or what is referred to variously as 'performance assessment' or 'authentic assessment'. For the APU project, 'on task' meant predominantly 'on short, focused, assessment activities'. Authenticity, however, can be viewed much more broadly in terms of utilising a whole range of assessments to build a profile of a learner, with the overarching criterion that each assessment is 'authentic'. The statement below, taken from a curriculum guidance document issued to teachers in New York State, USA, exemplifies this broader view:

> Assessment should: be as authentic as possible, representing real-world tasks and situations requiring 'higher order' thinking and complex, integrated performance; provide multiple ways for students to demonstrate their skill, knowledge, and understanding, including written & oral examinations, performance tasks, projects, portfolios, & structured observations by teachers; enable teachers to assess student growth in cumulative, longitudinal fashion using many kinds of evidence; communicate expectations and support student motivation, self-assessment, and continual growth; inform instruction and

encourage reflective practice; be valid and accurate for identifying students‘ strengths, abilities, and progress, opening up possibilities for encouraging further growth rather than precluding access to future, advanced instruction.
(New York State Curriculum and Assessment Council 1994: 11)

The above guidance is somewhat awesome: at the same time both wonderfully inclusive and asking the impossible. The APU Design and Technology Project provides a useful case study for considering some of the ideas and issues embedded in it. The project developed an approach to making summative assessment of design and technology capability. Whilst this initially underpinned the project, it soon became evident that the approach taken also fostered pupil performance, and helped teachers to understand both design and technology and the assessment of process in new ways. Keen to break free of a linear model, the research team developed an assessment instrument in the shape of a scripted activity and portfolio response booklet, derived from the iterative model outlined earlier. Pupils were presented with a short video exposing issues that could be resolved through design activity: for example helping the elderly prepare food. The response booklet provided a sequence of alternately active and reflective sub-tasks: identifying starting points for ideas; thinking about potential clients; identifying key issues for product success; developing the ideas and so on. Each stage was presented as a manageable next step – drawing students forward through the process. The booklet had the benefit of allowing 'real time' performance to be developed, and be displayed, in its entirety, captured for summative assessment. It took a single sheet of A2 paper, which unfolded in such a way that each new sub-task was progressively revealed. Figure 8.2 shows the structure of one test booklet that focused on 'Early Ideas'.

The features that created authenticity were:

1   the activity was set into a 'real' context, presented vicariously through a video, with encouragement for pupils to draw also on their own related experience;
2   theory and practice were not artificially divided;
3   the activity was choreographed through a responsive, iterative process rather than a prescriptive linear one.

The research showed that the activities enabled pupils to respond well, while allowing assessors to discriminate between levels of performance. In making their assessments, the assessors were required to make both holistic judgements (that is, taking into account all that the students had considered and integrated into their ideas and solutions), and more detailed judgements about dimensions of students' capability (for example, grip on issues, exploring and developing ideas, ability to appraise for value and consequences) (Kimbell *et al.* 1991: Appendix 11.2). Assessors were required to draw on evidence wherever it appeared within the students' responses, not to expect it to appear in a linear sequence. In this way, the assessment approach complemented the authenticity of the activity.

However, the research also raised concerns over the potential for bias (in terms of gender and ability) in assessment. These concerns arose from the variable

The booklet cover provides gives a first clue to the focus of the activity and space to record adminstrative information.

The main task and step 1 (first thoughts) are recorded on the lower flap.

Whilst still viewing the task and their first thoughts, the student can open the upper flap to reveal space for the development of their ideas and prompts for ongoing evaluation.

The lower flap is then unfolded to reveal space for further idea development and prompts to begin to think through planning issues.

The upper flap is then folded down to provide space for more detailed planning to be projected.

Finally the booklet is closed and the student turns to the back to record thoughts about what they would now need to research to successfully complete the task and how they might approach this research.

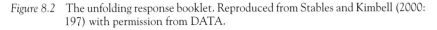

Figure 8.2   The unfolding response booklet. Reproduced from Stables and Kimbell (2000: 197) with permission from DATA.

performance that was found between groups of different gender or ability, depending on the way the task had been structured, or on the context into which it had been placed. The total matrix of the assessments presented a range of structures and contexts and, broadly speaking, five aspects of 'test design' were identified as providing differential support or suppression. These five were:

- the tightness of the structure of sub-tasks;
- the predominance of 'active' or 'reflective' dimensions;
- the breadth of the starting point;
- the support 'features' of the tasks (that is, instructions, opportunity for discussion and the use of modelling materials);
- the context in which the activity was located.

The full details of these findings are provided in the final report. It is worth noting here however, that the differences in performance, which could be created by structuring tests differently, provoked enough cynicism in the research team to cause it to comment:

> One is led to the somewhat sinister conclusion that it would be possible – given an understanding of the nature of these effects – to design activities deliberately to favour any particular nominated group.
>
> (Kimbell *et al.* 1991: 208)

From the perspective of learning, teaching and formative assessment, awareness of these issues has a particularly positive value, as they raise awareness of how the teacher may need to provide extra support and encouragement to enable certain groups of pupils to overcome difficulties. But it is important to be aware of the ominous implications of differential performance deriving not just from the capability of the learner but also from the structure of the test. This issue is not specific to the APU project, it potentially pervades all assessment and testing. Murphy and Gipps (1996) draw attention to the wide range of ways in which the structure and context of tests can be 'unfair' to one group or another across a range of curriculum areas. More specifically to design and technology, Spendlove (2000) highlights ways in which GCSE assessment may have a negative impact by creating boys' underachievement, and Atkinson (1995) indicates that differential performance between boys and girls may even be provoked by particular coursework assessment regimes.

The importance of evidence

Whatever the approach to assessment, making judgments requires evidence. The APU response booklet exemplifies how the production of *tangible evidence* can be promoted; a crucial ingredient if the level of performance is to be demonstrated to a third party, for example another examiner or parent. For the APU project, the evidence was in the form of writing, drawing and 3-D models of ideas. In regular classroom activity this can be supplemented by photographs and audio and video tapes. But not all evidence is of this kind. Sometimes evidence is *ephemeral*, disappearing without a trace, such as actions and talk. For formative assessment, the critical thing is not whether the evidence is tangible or ephemeral, but that teachers have seen (or heard) enough evidence to be confident in their assessments and that they are not relying on assumptions:

> Before we can assess the effectiveness of any piece of behaviour we need to know the intention that the pupil has in doing it. Without that, our assessment must of necessity be based on guesswork – and that will not do.
>
> (Kimbell *et al.* 1991: 23)

Being able to make a valid assessment is therefore dependent on having enough evidence to avoid assumptions and, within this, knowing why a pupil has taken the actions he or she has.

How can you make assessment manageable?

In the days when assessments were only explicitly carried out through written or practical tests that assessed specific knowledge or skills, manageability was not much of an issue for the teacher. The assessment process was neither complex nor unwieldy enough to require 'managing'. Growth in coursework assessment was the thin end of the wedge in changing this situation. The introduction of NCA, with its formal requirements for recording and reporting assessments, teachers' awareness of the value of assessment in supporting progress and differentiation and, for design and technology teachers, the growing emphasis on assessing process, have added further complexity. If the teacher is not to drown in this complexity, assessment must be manageable.

Managing evidence

'Managing' both the production and collection of evidence demands clear priorities. Seen as a bureaucratic necessity, it can become at best a meaningless chore, at worst a waste of time that detracts from teaching and learning. Lawler's description of linear models as management models explains why their dominance in assessment has been so strong: it is easier (even if less valid) to assess evidence that is neatly packaged into 'stages' than the messy free-flow that emerges from an iterative process (Lawler 1999). So, what is crucial is that evidence is created as a genuine element within the development of a project, not as an afterthought merely to meet assessment requirements.

Within this process, ephemeral evidence should not be discounted, and indeed it can be made tangible through the use of observation, photography, audio taping and so on. But in design and technology the production of tangible evidence is a critical part of the thinking process:

> It is not uncommon for pupils to believe that, almost from the start of an activity, they have a complete solution in their mind and this often leads them to try to short-circuit the process of development... In fact we know that they cannot, in their minds alone, have sorted out all the issues and difficulties in the task – let alone reconciled them into a successful solution... to enable the idea to develop, it is necessary to drag it out of the mind and express it in real form.
>
> (Kimbell *et al.* 1991: 20)

As teachers, we need to be able to 'see' a pupil's thinking if we are to help them to identify the strengths and weaknesses of an idea, target what they need to find out to move forwards or consider alternative ideas for development:

> The second reason for dragging the idea out of our mind and expressing it in some way is that by doing so we make it possible for others to share our idea... [and] as teachers, [it] is one of our major responsibilities, to act as a catalyst

by providing helpful, critical but supportive comments on pupils' developing ideas.

(Kimbell *et al.* 1991: 21)

Encouraging pupils to externalise and record the progress of their project enables two vital components: reflection and projection. Reflection allows them the 'pause for thought' to consider the effectiveness of what they have done; projection encourages them to 'think forward', to visualise new possibilities. There is a range of ways teachers can 'manage' this aspect of the work into some form of portfolio of evidence, from sketch books to diaries to logs. The APU design and technology response booklet was a short, targeted version of this. A second development exemplifying a related approach was a system of 'Reviews', introduced into project work in trials for the development of the original SATs for Key Stage 3 Design and Technology NCA. This system identified three review points: one early in the project, one in the middle and one at the end. At each point, pupils focused on sets of questions under the headings of 'research', 'having ideas', 'planning', 'making' and 'evaluating'. Considering a full range of design intentions at each stage encouraged a break with a linear model, and served, first, to create a reflective pause for the pupils and, second, to provide the teacher with additional evidence of their thinking (Consortium for Assessment and Testing 1990; 1991; Kimbell 1997). A third example is the use of 'process diaries'. Rogers and Clare (1994) explored the use of these in a range of settings, working with children from Year 1 to Year 11 and those with special educational needs. To build their diaries, learners were encouraged to record and reflect on their design and technology experience using a broad range of techniques including photography and video and audio tapes, alongside writing and drawing.

When the evidence for assessment is derived directly from encouraging the learner to be explicit about their design intentions and ideas, both learner and teacher can gain from the process. Developing skills in communicating (writing, drawing, modelling and presenting) or in selecting and documenting work creates further 'added value'. But there are also dangers lurking: if evidence of the process becomes just another product, then the activity can be distorted as pupils jump through record-keeping hoops:

> … investigation as an *activity* becomes an investigation *folder* and active design *thinking* becomes a folio of *drawings*. The evaluation *report* at the end of the exercise is the only direct evidence of evaluative *activity* and therefore becomes synonymous with it. The process has become a series of products.
>
> (Kimbell 1991: 142)

Developing and using criteria

In making assessment judgements, it helps if you know what you are looking at and what you are looking for. Good assessment criteria play a very important part in doing this. The huge number of SoAs created to assess design and technology in the original order were an example of criteria that were, individually, largely unhelpful because they were difficult to manage. Taking a single statement, it was difficult to see how it related to the whole picture of a learner's achievement: a bit like trying to place a piece of sky in a jigsaw when you have not even found the corners, let alone the edges. Criteria, like pieces of a jigsaw, need to be located before they can make any real sense.

In attempting to manage the SoAs, it became apparent that they were more useful if seen, not as atomistic statements that *defined* capability, but as collective descriptors that *characterised* it. Each National Curriculum level had a cluster of SoAs attached to it that collectively had some coherence. The phrase 'basket of descriptors' became common parlance, and not just in design and technology. Thus a teacher could look at all of the statements for Levels 3, 4 and 5 and see which cluster provided the best match to a learner's performance. Seeing the SoAs in this way soon led to the development of the level descriptors for 'designing' and 'making' of the 1995 order and, with National Curriculum 2000, a single attainment target from which nine level descriptors emerged, thus providing us with a version of 'holistic' criteria. Such overarching criteria are important and useful in establishing summative judgments. But teachers need more detailed guidance in making ongoing judgements, and these they can create for themselves. This is particularly important in respect of the National Curriculum 2000 for design and technology, as tracking progress against the summative level descriptors can be achieved more effectively if teachers have built up detailed profiles of a learner's individual achievements.

Three linked tactics are useful, both to make assessments, and to develop and share understanding among groups of teachers:

- the development of progressive criteria that form benchmarks or rubrics;
- the collection of exemplars of work at different levels of capability;
- the use of *agreement* meetings in which teachers discuss, debate and agree criteria and levels.

The development of assessment criteria, which form a progressive *rubric* or set of *benchmarks*, can be helpful to assess understanding of cases in which there is no 'right' or 'wrong' answer. Table 8.1 shows two examples developed by elementary school teachers (equivalent to teachers of primary school children) in a workshop on authentic assessment with the author. Both look at the application of knowledge, in one case of structures and in the other of gears. The teachers worked to a simple framework, identifying an assessment target and then four levels of performance, working from 'novice' to 'excellent'.

The assessment target provides a reference point from which to look at the children's work: the descriptors provide not definitions, but characteristics of the way the learner has performed. The teachers created criteria from their knowledge of the pupils they teach (normative) and the aspect targeted for assessment (criterion). They worked in groups, and there was a good deal of heated discussion before the criteria were agreed. Taking the criteria back into the classroom, using

Table 8.1 Rubrics for assessing application of knowledge in elementary (primary) schools

Assessment target	Novice performance	Average performance	Good performance	Excellent performance
Gears: use gears; identify movement; clockwise, counterclockwise	For example: gears move; cannot identify direction of movement	For example: gears move; can identify direction of movement using adequate vocabulary	For example: gears move; can identify direction of movement using formal vocabulary; can show movement in pictorial form	For example: gears move; can identify direction of movement using formal vocabulary; shows in pictorial form with detail; can give examples of other uses
Structures: types; design strengths and weaknesses; forces on structures	For example: shows no understanding of structures or how they can be reinforced or strengthened	For example: shows limited knowledge of structures; demonstrates an awareness that structures may be strengthened through alteration	For example: shows knowledge of a variety of structures and identifies a range of structural modifications	For example: shows detailed knowledge of structures and creates new modifications for reinforcing and strengthening

them in design and technology activities and collecting examples of pupils' work at each level, were the next steps to hone the criteria and provide a resource to be shared and discussed to support teachers' development of their understanding of assessment.

A fourth tactic is to involve the pupils themselves. Asking the pupils, for example, how *you* will know that they have planned their work carefully, helps them clarify what planning means and set their own expectations for what constitutes good work. Class discussion to create the criteria further clarifies the activity and its assessment for all pupils, as they gain insight from each other, as does class involvement in the assessment. Clarke (1998) outlines how this approach may be used even in the early years of the nursery class. She provides an example of a class making Christmas cards, whose teacher used the opportunity to assess whether the children had learnt to use glue properly. The teacher asked the children how she would know if they had learnt this, and they gave criteria such as 'There will be no glue on our hands' and 'The glue won't be in blobs.' After the activity, she asked each of the children to display their hands while their classmates passed judgement. What is critical in all this:

> … is that children need to know what success might look like. If they don't achieve success in all aspects, the plenary provides a supportive environment for modelling ways in which they could have achieved success.
>
> (Clarke 1998: 60)

Using the assessments: feedback and feedforward

There is no point in making assessments if they are not going to be put to good use. The Task Group on Assessment and Testing (TGAT) Report (DES 1988) coined the phrase 'feedback and feedforward' to describe the ways in which assessment information may be used. In the above example, Clarke completes the learning and teaching circle of assessment when she comments:

> The teacher, at this point, is also made aware of the needs and achievements of the children, possibly providing a way forward for the creation of criteria for individual targets.
>
> (Clarke 1998: 60)

Having an understanding of the level at which pupils are working enables us to plan learning activities that will stretch the pupils just beyond their 'comfort zone' – to use the words of Vygotsky (1978) – to plan activities in their 'zone of proximal development'. A process is then set in motion in which learning outcomes or intentions can be identified, criteria for success can be established, learning experiences can be planned, achievements can be checked and targets can be set for consolidating and extending learning. At first glance, this might seem like another logical, linear sequence but, as with all such processes, the teachers need to be 'on their toes', adapting and modifying the learning and assessment to meet the needs of individual learners and any changes occurring as the learning situation evolves. We have yet another iterative model! The fundamental task for the design and technology teacher in all this is to edge forward the development of each child:

> It is vital that pupils are engaged in designing and making that is just within or just beyond their reach. This challenges them constantly to extend into new understandings in order to achieve success.
>
> (Kimbell *et al.* 1996: 76)

Conclusion

This chapter has highlighted the important role that assessment plays in teaching and learning processes in design and technology. In doing this, it has taken a stance that places the development of the learner at the centre of the process, seeing this development as the primary function of the assessment. Inherent in this is a view of development in which capability in design and technology is seen as being able to operate procedurally, drawing on knowledge and skills as a means to an end, rather than as an end in themselves. Taking this stance has highlighted the tensions and complexities presented when assessment is drawn into an integral role in teaching and learning, in which judgements are made 'on task', in authentic settings, rather than being presented as 'after the event' tests.

The importance of evidence, and issues of manageability in both creating and making judgments in ways that maintain the integrity of authenticity have been discussed. The chapter has stressed the particular developmental importance in design and technology of making thinking explicit in some tangible form through an iteration of thought and action during the process of designing and making. This is contrasted with the unhelpful practice of producing evidence retrospectively, purely to make pupils jump through assessment hoops.

Questions to consider

Meaningful assessment in design and technology is clearly a critical but complex activity. The following questions are suggested to help the reader to follow up the issues, further informing and developing principles and practice:

1   What assessment strategies are truly helpful to the learner?
2   Reflect on your own personal experience as a 'pupil' in an assessment relationship. What genuinely helped you to learn and develop? What negative or unhelpful experiences have you had? Share your reflections with colleagues and use the experience to construct your own 'shoulds' and 'should nots' of assessment.
3   How can teachers ensure that assessment approaches are equally fair, appropriate and helpful to all learners in their classroom and support the teacher to provide differentiated learning opportunities?

4   Consider the issues raised in this chapter and review the texts that develop these issues further. Discuss with colleagues practical approaches to using assessment and teaching strategies to support different learning needs and learning styles.

5   How can teachers develop and share assessment approaches that become embedded in practice in a sustainable way, supporting progression and continuity in teaching and learning?

6   Consider ways in which shared understandings of principles and practices in design and technology assessment can be evolved and how these can be built coherently into teaching and learning programmes without becoming ritualised 'hoops' through which to jump.

Notes

1   See, for example, Black 1998 (Chapter 1), Kimbell 1997 (Chapters 1–6), Penfold 1988 and Eggleston 1996 (Chapter 1).
2   Subsequently, this has become the Department for Education and Employment (DfEE).
3   The APU was the research arm of DES. It operated from 1978 to 1991, contracting research projects in science, mathematics, English, modern foreign languages and design and technology. The APU Design and Technology Project is reported in full in Kimbell *et al.* 1991.

References

Atkinson, S. (1995) 'Approaches to designing at Key Stage 4', in Smith, J. (ed.), *IDATER 95: International Conference on Design and Technology Educational Research and Curriculum Development*, Loughborough University of Technology, Loughborough, pp. 36–47.

Black, P. (1998) *Testing: Friend or Foe? Theory and Practice of Assessment and Testing*, London: Falmer Press.

Consortium for Assessment and Testing in Schools (1990) *Design and Technology Trial 1990 – Interim Report*, London: CATS and Hodder and Stoughton.

Consortium for Assessment and Testing in Schools (1991) *Technology KS3: Pilot 1991 – Report*, London: CATS and Hodder and Stoughton.

DES (Department of Education and Science) (1988) *Task Group on Assessment and Testing – A Report*, London: DES.

Eggleston, J. (1996) *Teaching Design and Technology*, Buckingham: Open University Press.

Eysenck, H.J. (1967) 'Intelligence assessment: A theoretical and experimental approach', *British Journal of Educational Psychology*, 37: 81–9.

Gardner, H. (1999) 'Assessment in context', in Murphy, P. (ed.), *Learners, Learning and Assessment*, London: The Open University.

Jensen, A.R. (1980) *Bias in Mental Testing*, New York: Basic Books.

Kelly, A.V. (1992) 'Concepts of assessment: an overview', in Blenkin, G.M. & Kelly, A.V. (eds) *Assessment in Early Childhood Education*, London: Paul Chapman Publishing

Kelly, A.V., Kimbell, R., Patterson, V.J., Saxton, J. and Stables, K. (1987) *Design and Technological Activity: A Framework for Assessment*, London: HMSO.

Kimbell, R. (1991) 'Tackling technological tasks', in Woolnough, B. (ed.), *Practical Science*, Buckingham: Open University Press.

Kimbell, R. (1997) *Assessing Technology: International Trends in Curriculum and Assessment*, Buckingham: Open University Press.

Kimbell, R., Stables, K. and Green, R. (1996) *Understanding Practice in Design and Technology*, Buckingham: Open University Press.

Kimbell, R., Stables, K., Wheeler, A.D., Wozniak, A.V. and Kelly, A.V. (1991) *The Assessment of Performance in Design and Technology*, London: Schools Examinations and Assessment Council and HMSO.

Lawler, T. (1999) 'Exposing the gender effects of design and technology project work by comparing strategies for presenting and managing pupils' work', in Roberts, P.H. and Norman, E.W.L. (eds), *IDATER 99: International Conference on Design and Technology Educational Research and Curriculum Development*, Loughborough University of Technology, Loughborough, pp. 130–7.

Margolin, V. and Buchanan, R. (1995) *The Idea of Design*, Cambridge, MA: MIT Press.

Murphy, P. and Gipps, C. (1996) *Equity in the Classroom: Towards Effective Pedagogy for Girls and Boys*, London: Falmer Press.

New York State Curriculum and Assessment Council (1994) *Learning-Central Curriculum and Assessment for New York State: Report of the New York State Curriculum and Assessment Council to the Commissioner of Education and the Board of Regents*, Albany, NY: University of the State of New York, the State Education Department.

NWSEB (North Western Secondary School Examinations Board) (1970) *A Course of Studies in Design*, Manchester: NWSEB.

Penfold, J. (1988) *Craft Design and Technology: Past Present and Future*, Stoke on Trent: Trentham Books.

Rogers, M. and Clare, D.J. (1994) 'The process diary: developing capability within National Curriculum design and technology – some initial findings', in Smith, J.S. (ed.), *IDATER 94: International Conference on Design and Technology Educational Research and Curriculum Development*, Loughborough University of Technology, Loughborough, pp. 22–8.

Spendlove, D. (2000) 'Gender issues – raising the attainment of boys in design and technology', in Kimbell, R. (ed.), *Design and Technology International Millennium Conference*, Wellesbourne: DATA (Design and Technology Association).

Stables, K. and Kimbell, R. (2000) 'The unpickled portfolio: pioneering performance assessment', in Kimbell, R. (ed.), *Design and Technology International Millennium Conference*, Wellesbourne: DATA (Design and Technology Association).

Vygotsky, I.S. (1978) *Mind in Society: the Development of Higher Psychological Processes*, Cambridge, MA: Harvard University Press.

Further reading

Black, P. (1998) *Testing: Friend or Foe? Theory and Practice of Assessment and Testing*, London: Falmer Press.

This text provides an extremely useful background to the whole area of assessment (not specifically design and technology) and how practices have developed, both in the UK and elsewhere. Its scope covers the history of assessment, purposes, issues and approaches and deals with the role of both teachers and pupils. As is indicated in the title, it highlights both the positive and the negative implications in assessment, providing the reader with alternative views to inform the development of his or her own teaching practice.

Kimbell, R. (1997) *Assessing Technology: International Trends in Curriculum and Assessment*, Buckingham: Open University Press.

This text takes a comparative look at the way assessment in technology education has developed in four different settings: the UK, the USA, Germany and Taiwan. This backcloth is used to explore quite different practices and approaches in order to highlight issues, such as validity and reliability, that impact on any assessment regime. It provides the reader with an opportunity to explore assessment matters through a broader context, supporting reflection on the ways in which principles and practices have evolved in their own setting.

Kimbell, R., Stables, K., Wheeler, A., Wozniak, A. and Kelly, A.V. (1991) *The Assessment of Performance in Design and Technology*, London: Schools Examinations and Assessment Council and HMSO.

This text is the final report of a major research project on assessment and design and technology. Although it was conducted more than a decade ago, it is still the largest and most influential study of its kind, internationally as well as in the UK. The report provides a rationale for the use of performance-based assessment, including the adoption of an iterative model of designing. It provides an account of the approach to the research, how the assessments were conducted and the findings. Within this, it provides a broad range of examples of assessed design and technology work and highlights the issues the assessment findings raised, particularly in relation to gender and ability groups. There are insights into principles, practices and implications of assessment in design and technology.

Part 3

Issues in the school context

9 Boys' performance in design and technology

The context and the issues

David Spendlove

Introduction

The relatively short history of design and technology has been closely linked with gender issues in response to the differential participation of girls and the changing examination success of girls and boys. Harding identified that '... all 3 antecedents of Technology have been sex differentiated in the past. They have been the most strongly gendered of all curriculum areas' (Harding 1997: 20). The subject of design and technology has, however, continued to evolve from what were predominantly male-dominated activities to its current position in which it continues to exist uncomfortably alongside the 1944 Educational Act philosophy of 'equality of opportunity'.

Many initiatives were introduced during the 1980s, some of which have some connection with the continuing gendered evolution of design and technology. These included the TVEI (Technical Vocational Educational Initiative), Women into Science and Engineering (WISE), Girls and Technology Education (GATE) and Girls into Science and Technology (GIST). Each maintained an equal opportunities philosophy. These projects were primarily designed to encourage access for and participation of girls into the traditionally male-dominated subjects of science and technology, with the object of increasing female participation in secondary education, undergraduate-level courses and, subsequently, in careers in these areas. The success of these interventionist programmes was variable. However, the outcomes of government legislation (Education Reform Act 1988) in establishing GCSEs, Ofsted and National Curriculum technology have had a much more profound effect in increasing female participation and success in the subject.

With the establishment of compulsory design and technology at Key Stages 1, 2, 3 and 4 in 1994, and again in 1996, one of the outcomes is that girls' participation in design and technology has increased to the point of complete dominance of the subject, as measured by end of Key Stage teacher assessments and GCSE examinations. This pattern of success in design and technology is now replicated in virtually all GCSE subjects and has led to serious concerns within schools, with boys being labelled as 'underachievers' (Ofsted 1997: 9). Politically and educationally, the subject of boys' perceived underachievement has become a major concern, and many equal opportunity and gender issues that were once on the agenda for the 'girl intervention programmes' are now, paradoxically, being re-examined from a boys' perspective. Biological, psychological and sociological factors need to be examined. In addition, the changing nature of the subject matter, out-of-school experience and expectations, the changing role of the male in society and the nature of teaching, learning and assessment have to be re-examined.

The context of the design and technology gender gap

One conventional method (there are many methods giving different results each time) of measuring school and pupil performance at GCSE level has been to count the number of students achieving five or more A–C grades in GCSE public examinations. This measure is used to inform the public, schools and politicians, via 'league tables', of the relative success of schools. Since this system was adopted in the late 1980s (which coincided with the introduction of GCSE), there has always been a gap in performance outcome in favour of girls over boys. However, what is now noticeable is that the gap is widening. Furthermore, in design and technology, with schools legally obliged to provide the subject to all pupils in England at Key Stages 3 and 4, the gap is increasing significantly in favour of girls.

Prior to the Education Reform Act (1988), there was a completely different pattern of assessment. Examination was in two tiers – CSE (Certificate of Secondary Education) and GCE (General Certificate of Education) O level – and what is now recognised as design and technology was made up of a diverse range of individual subjects. Participation was clearly divided by the sexes and comparison of attainment was difficult. The extent of the gender–subject division at the start of the 1980s can be seen by examining Figure 9.1, which illustrates the clear gender divide in subject participation at CSE level. From this, it can be seen that those subjects which were to contribute to the establishment of design and technology (metalwork, woodwork, technical drawing, needlework and domestic subjects) occupy the extremes of the table. The CSE examination was specifically for lower ability pupils and the higher number of entries for these subjects (compared with GCE design and technology type subjects) at this level reflects the low academic status that these subjects had. The results for GCE level (Figure 9.2) indicate a lower number of entries for the more demanding examination. In addition, the difference in academic expectations of teachers does not appear to transcend the gender issue. There remained a clear division between the sexes at the higher GCE O level:

> All 3 antecedents of technology have been sex differentiated in the past...
> Entries at 'O' and 'A' Level in Engineering Science, Electronics and Modular
> Technology in the 1980s were overwhelmingly from boys, until the TVEI
> programme required that efforts should be made to avoid sex-stereotyping
> where these subjects were included in the TVEI programme. Statistics for
> 1992 showed only 2.7% of CSE and 1.6% of 'O' Level Woodwork entrants
> were girls, for Metalwork the figures were 1.2% and 0.9% and for Technical
> Drawing 5.1% and 5.3%.
>
> (Harding 1997: 20).

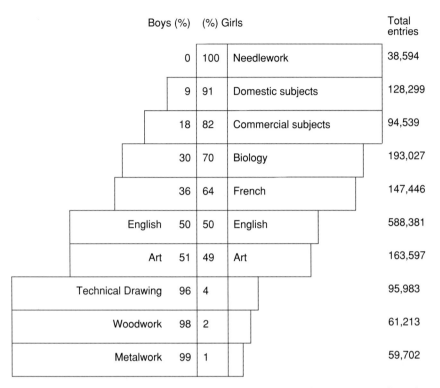

Figure 9.1 The GATE (1981) project: distribution of boys and girls in CSE (all modes) entries.

Through the establishment of a common system of examining (GCSE) and the introduction of National Curriculum technology (later followed by design and technology in 1995), the formal legislation for addressing equal participation was put in place. Participation of girls increased significantly at all key stages.

The GCSE course (introduced in 1988) was designed to tap a wider range of skills and attainment and employ a wider range of teaching styles, skills and assessment techniques. There was an increasing emphasis to be placed upon the application of knowledge through the enhanced role of coursework and a movement away from memorising facts in response to 'concerns about the validity of the context of terminal examination assessment' (Gipps and Murphy 1994 : 217):

> Cresswell (1990) analysed the results from the 1989 AEB GCSE examinations in English, mathematics and science… A clear pattern emerged from the data: girls' average coursework marks were higher than boys' in every case. In mathematics and combined science boys' marks on the other (non-coursework) components were, on average, higher than girls' marks; in English

Boys (%)			(%) Girls		Total entries
	0	100	Needlework		18,594
	3	97	Domestic subjects		52,696
	27	73	Sociology		46,210
Eng. Lit	42	58	English literature		250,493
Art	44	56	Art		121,200
Eng. Lang	46	54	English language		500,564
History	49	51	History		134,977
Technical Drawing	96	4			95,983
Design and Technology*	97	3			9,208
Woodwork	99	1			15,182
Metalwork	99	1			13,015

*This early use (1980) of the title 'Design and Technology' should not be confused with the generic title used today that now represents all variants of the subject

Figure 9.2 The GATE project: distributionof boys and girls in GCE O level entries, 1981.

the girls' average written paper marks remained higher than the boys' average marks, although the difference was less for the coursework.

(Arnot and Weiner 1998: 37)

A consistent pattern of success for girls began to emerge during the early 1990s, although initially, through the tiered examination approach (ironically a reason for moving away from the previous system), girls were generally being entered for the middle (safer ground) tier and were consequently restricted by an attainment ceiling. 'The researchers were particularly concerned about the potential underestimation of girls' ability evidenced by their overrepresentation in the intermediate tier' (Gipps and Murphy 1994: 224). It could therefore be argued that girls' increased success at GCSE level is due to teachers gaining confidence in the placing of pupils in the correct tiers, and that girls' progress in the past has merely been restricted by the lack of equal opportunities in schools. If this is true, then perhaps we are now seeing a pattern that more accurately reflects the performance of both sexes.

The establishment of Ofsted and the legislative requirements of a four-year 'quality assurance' inspection cycle have allowed for monitoring of equal opportunities and required increased accountability. Schools and departments are expected to have equal opportunities policies in action:

> There is an increasing consciousness of differences in the educational performance of boys and girls, but in one third of schools the monitoring of progress of boys and girls is weak. Where differences of performance are identified, this information is not adequately used to review practice and inform such planning.
>
> (Ofsted 1996: 8)

The inspection service, although recognising the higher standards of achievement of girls, does little to advise on how to respond to this changing performance, and merely uses it as another indicator to quantify a department's achievements or weaknesses:

> In both key stages, more girls than boys achieve higher standards when working with resistant materials, textiles and food, although the boys tend to do better with systems and control activities.
>
> (Ofsted 1996: 10)

The 1996 report was compounded by the 1997 Ofsted report, which reviewed inspections from 1993 onwards:

> Girls have increasingly made better progress and achieved higher levels of attainment than boys in all areas of design and technology except systems and control. In general, girls manage their work more effectively, meet deadlines and take greater care over the quality of presentation. They frequently write at greater length, but not necessarily more analytically or creatively than boys. Few design and technology departments analyse the reasons for such differences in performance, and so they have no strategies for raising standards overall.
>
> (Ofsted 1997: 138)

Ofsted Chief Inspector, Chris Woodhead, further commented on the overall issue of boys' performance '... the failure of boys and in particular white working class boys is one of the most disturbing problems we face within the whole education system' (Ofsted 1997). It is interesting that Woodhead clearly sees the issue as 'the failure of boys' and not the success of girls or as a consequence of the interventionist programmes of the 1980s.

The role of Ofsted in quality assessment can be considered to be one of deriving information from subjective observations, as the criteria for examining standards in education are not sufficiently articulated or quantifiable. National Curriculum and GCSE assessments do, however, provide a quantifiable and measured outcome through testing and assessment at the end of Key Stages 3 and 4. The National Curriculum arrangements for design and technology at Key Stage 3 in 1997 and 1998 were based upon teacher assessment. Table 9.1 highlights the gap in performance, based upon National Curriculum criteria at Key Stage 3. As the teacher assessments are based upon assessments over a three-year period which focused upon projects created by teachers, the question arises whether the teacher assessments are biased or whether the combination of teacher assessments, focused practical tasks (FPTs), design and make assignments (DMAs) and identification, disassembly, evaluation of artefacts (IDEAs) is gender biased? Additionally, is the National Curriculum gender biased or balanced?

The Consortium for Assessment and Testing in Schools (CATS) suggested that 'boys appear to be slightly under-predicted in TA (teacher assessment)' (CATS 1991: 57). This has a significant impact upon boys' attainment as there has been a movement away from Standard Attainment Tests (SATs) which tended to appeal more to boys' abilities. '… it was acknowledged that some of the SATs key features rendered the assessment tasks more accessible, and therefore more fair.' (Gipps and Murphy 1994: 208). The implication is that the National Curriculum assessment evolved from a system based upon teacher assessment and formal SATs. Unfortunately, as a result of the difficulties in administering the testing, the SATs were dropped (with the exception of mathematics, English and science). Subsequently, teacher assessments remained which generally favour girls. Although this is not sufficient to explain the considerable gap in performance at Key Stage 3, it must be considered to be an important factor and must be examined before further groups of boys are labelled as failures and underachievers.

If the progress of the 1997 cohort (Table 9.1) is monitored through to the 1999 GCSE results (Table 9.2), it can be seen that the gap in attainment between girls and boys remains consistent. In addition, the issue of a stereotypical gender division by entry (as in 1980) is still remarkably prevalent (Table 9.3). This suggests that design and technology may not have been successful in addressing gendered perceptions within the subject. There is clearly a division by gender within subjects within the broad remit of design and technology, notably in food, textiles, electronics, systems and control, and resistant materials.

Discussion

From the information presented above, interesting questions arise which can help to raise awareness of the complex range of inter-related issues involved in an examination of boys' performance in design and technology.

Table 9.1 Teacher assessment for Key Stage 3 National Curriculum
(Design and Technology 1997)

Subject	Assessment Key Stage 3	Level 5 and above	Boys	Girls
Design and technology	Teacher assessment	56%	49%	64%

Table 9.2 GCSE passes at grade A–C in design and technology in 1999

Boys	Girls	Difference
43%	58%	15%

Table 9.3 1999 (1997 National Curriculum cohort) design and technology by gender entry
and subject residuals

Design and technology subject	Entry	Overall residual[a]	Boys entry (%)	Boys residual	Girls entry (%)	Girls residual
Electronic products	17,051	–0.32	91	–0.31	9	–0.36
Engineering	3,885	–0.29	90	–0.25	10	–0.67
Systems and control	14,768	–0.41	88	–0.41	12	–0.42
Resistant materials	105,540	0.04	76	0.05	24	–0.01
Graphic products	88,582	–0.22	58	–0.31	42	–0.11
Design and technology	3,265	0.11	51	0.02	49	0.22
Food technology	101,115	0.14	26	–0.16	74	0.24
Textiles technology	41,122	0.10	5	–0.28	95	0.12

Note
a   Residuals are used to indicate the relative difficulty of one examination compared with
another. For example, in the subject of electronic products pupils are, on average, likely to
obtain a grade that is 0.32 less than in subject with a residual of 0.

Is the gender gap a fair reflection of ability in design and technology?

If our examination and assessment systems are sufficiently sophisticated and our
teaching and learning environments free from stereotyped reinforcement and the
political agenda so gender neutral, then perhaps the current apparent gender gap
is a genuine gap, with girls simply being better at design and technology activities.
However, even if the above were true, we would remain unable to make comparative

judgements because we continue to have a gendered entry pattern within design and technology; there are subjects which, although they have the same generic titles, are in essence different subjects with different teaching, learning and assessment styles.

When considering the consistency of the gap we also must consider the nature of what is design and technology. Its evolution has meant it is a 'constantly changing mosaic', without any real opportunity to reflect upon its impact on different groups of children. The design and technology identity remains uncharacterised, which makes it difficult to predict the effects of current and future changes on the existing gender gap. The most important feature of any educational gap, however, is that it must be a genuine gap. Unfortunately, we are not yet in a position to confirm that the gap is a genuine one.

Is the National Curriculum/GCSE flawed?

Although the National Curriculum is occasionally referred to as a 'straitjacket', it is remarkably flexible. This flexibility therefore creates the opportunity to slant a curriculum to suit any group (consciously or subconsciously). Teachers may unknowingly be reinforcing the underachievement of boys throughout the key stages by their selection of projects, tasks or contexts. It may be not that the National Curriculum is flawed but that its interpretation and implementation could be. The establishment and adoption of national schemes of work may in some ways address this issue; however, the interpretation and application remain open to bias.

At GCSE level we have the situation illustrated by Table 9.3, which clearly highlights a gendered entry pattern. When considering the massive changes within education and society over the last twenty years, the equal opportunities and interventionist programmes, the establishment of the National Curriculum, and the changes in assessment patterns, it is astonishing to discover that design and technology subjects continue to occupy the extremities of gender-divided subject tables. Why is this? In addition, GCSE design and technology is predominantly coursework orientated and girls have consistently been shown to be better at handling and managing coursework (Arnot and Weiner 1998: 37). Is the GCSE assessment mechanism loaded against boys from the start?

Are teacher assessments open to bias?

One of the over-riding reasons for not relying solely upon the use of teacher assessments, which currently underpins government reforms and provides comparative data, is concern about the degree of objectivity within assessments. Assessments should be systematic, objective and based solely upon the subject criteria. However:

> ... within this discourse it has been shown that subjective and erroneous evaluations of pupils [sic] abilities that teachers make, often informally, can

go on to produce a reality that reflects those original evaluations'. This resulted in 'the academically differentiated outcomes for children (which) lay in the working out of self-fulfilling prophecies in the classroom.

(Hutchinson and Schagen 1994: 50)

In view of the nature of project work being used as the basis for assessments within design and technology, it is appreciated that teacher assessment is currently the best way of assessing pupils' work. The weakness in the current system of assessment is that there is too little emphasis on consistency, moderation and consensus. The assessment mechanism could immediately be made more rigorous, valid and reliable by insisting upon consensus moderation – department to department, school to school and educational authority to educational authority:

I believe that teacher assessment is bound to be richer, more varied and more comprehensive – in short, more valid than any kind of externally set task or test... above all I would argue for the power of consensus moderation across schools in enhancing teachers' understanding of the curriculum, in widening their horizons of teaching approaches, teaching materials and assessment approaches, and in bringing them to a common shared understanding of levels or grades. Consensus moderation is a very powerful form of professional development.

(Murphy *et al.* 1995: 239)

Ensuring consistency, however, is only one feature of the assessment process. Ensuring the removal of gender bias in assessments and the use of gender analysis is a further issue.

The stereotypical labelling, and the use of teachers' day-to-day assessment as a means of disciplining pupils, in particular boys, provides a further contributory factor in boys' underachievement:

Some teachers view a low grade as a short, sharp spur to better effort, but it is not always perceived that way by pupils whose self-confidence is more brittle than we think... there is a danger that some boys will regard them as a sign of 'street cred' with their peers.

(Bleach 1998: 45)

The accuracy of and approach used in teacher assessments is further open to scrutiny. Gipps *et al.* (1998) found that teachers preferred the best-fit model of assessment, compared to the previous use of statements of attainment for the first National Curriculum, as the former provided a more manageable assessment system. However, the accuracy of the approach is variable:

The notion of 'best fit' is a consciously loose one. Because of this, teachers are taking a variety of approaches to making Teacher Assessment judgements. Some teachers will make quantitative judgements (to attain a level individuals must meet all the elements of a level description, 50%, or some other proportion); some will take a hurdle approach (individuals must be able to do x, y and z in order to reach Level 5); others will take an intuitive approach (this one feels like a good Level 4). Although not addressed in this study we know that some teachers will make ranking judgements (this individual is a clear Level 7, and this is a clear Level 6; less clear performances are then slotted in, in relation to these fixed points). Because of the lack of clarity of 'best fit', the differences in interpretation mean that, at times, there will have been a difference of one level awarded to pupils and this is not acceptable in a 'high stakes' programme.

(Gipps *et al.* 1998: 5)

In situations where a combination of test and teacher assessments is made (mathematics, science and English) the test result is considered more reliable and valid, with teacher assessments being used merely as a back-up. Hence, because of the combination of the boycott of tests in 1993 and the changing orders for design and technology, the current assessment system is firmly based upon teacher assessment. Optional standard attainment tests were available for the 1997 assessments but have since been discontinued.

Within design and technology the assessment arrangements are open to even greater manipulation and creativity. The end of Key Stage 3 National Curriculum results are based upon teacher assessments that are not open to scrutiny, even though the outcomes are published nationally. With the exception of the 'Exemplification of Standards' publication (School Curriculum and Assessment Authority 1995), there are no mechanisms for ensuring day-to-day consistency of moderation from school to school or department to department within the same school. This situation is unchallenged even though the TGAT (Task Group on Assessment and Testing) suggested that 'a complex process of group moderation through which teachers' assessments could be brought into line around a common standard was necessary' (DES 1989).

The statutory advice for determining a pupil's level of achievement is further limited as it uses the notion of 'best fit'. This is:

… based on knowledge of how the pupil performs across a range of contexts, takes into account strengths and weaknesses of the pupil's performance and is checked against adjacent level descriptions to ensure that the level awarded is the closest match to the child's performance in each attainment target.

(QCA and DfEE 1998)

This provides an interesting dilemma for teachers based upon the 'value added' approach now advocated by the government, which measures the movement from Key Stage 3 to Key Stage 4. A possible scenario could lead to the end of Key Stage 3 results being inflated (either consciously or subconsciously), creating the impression of a successful department. Alternatively, the Key Stage 3 results could be underestimated giving the appearance of an unsuccessful department.

Without any form of moderation from school to school, this is an undesirable outcome. Schools may, in addition, subscribe to a particular organisation that provides value-added data. Interestingly, these value-added scores can project GCSE targets based upon key stage assessment data. However, some organisations use value-added targets for boys that are lower (based upon previous statistical evidence) than those used for girls based upon the same key stage scores. Therefore, a variety of forces are also acting upon boys, which include 'self-fulfilling prophecies' and lower teacher expectations.

The system is further devalued because, in addition to there being little consistency in teacher assessment methods, there is no mechanism to ensure consistency of content. Although the programmes of study are prescribed, they are sufficiently flexible to encompass a vast range of activities. Teacher assessments can be focused upon any number of tasks, which ultimately have to be transposed to a single National Curriculum level (NC 2000) of attainment. However, the level descriptions are currently too global to be useful as assessment criteria, and if teachers are to use them for assessment purposes in anything more than a 'rough and intuitive' way, then they may need to break them down. Clear exemplification of levels is necessary in order to help classroom teachers make accurate assessments against level descriptions.

The most demoralising aspect of this series of inconsistencies is that pupils, predominantly boys, are being labelled as failures at an early age by an ultimately limited and weak assessment system.

Are Key Stage 3 and 4 projects gender biased?

With teacher assessments being used to inform value-added and target-setting processes through Key Stage 3 and GCSE results, the choice of design and technology projects has to be considered carefully. Projects must therefore not reinforce 'laddish cultures', 'tribalism' or stereotypical responses. Labour-intensive projects that support gendered behaviour patterns may inadvertently encourage boys to help girls through demonstration of strength and power, while 'macho' design projects can encourage 'laddish' anti-social behaviour. This topic relates directly to teachers' expectations and gender perceptions.

The balance of projects over a key stage must also be carefully considered. Passive reflective exercises, which are people focused, can be uninspiring to boys. However, loosely defined projects (APU 1991) can also contribute to a lack of appeal for boys. Projects need to be balanced over a key stage with opportunities to identify weaknesses and build upon strengths for both sexes.

At GCSE the nature of pupil projects is developed through negotiation with a teacher or through adoption of projects set by the examination board. The balance of projects can clearly be open to a gender bias in favour of either boys or girls. Kimbell suggests that 'one is led to the somewhat sinister conclusion that it would be possible – given an understanding of these effects – to design activities deliberately to favour any particular nominated group' (Kimbell 1996: 96). The APU (1991) study found that with reflective activities within design and technology, boys were more able to get to grips with these aspects of capability when they were practically engaged in developing solutions. Conversely, with aesthetics and people contexts, girls showed more understanding than boys in almost all tests. With energy systems, 'the complete dominance of boys in this conceptual area is the most straightforward of all our findings… boys demonstrate more understanding than girls in every instance' (APU 1991: 221). With respect to communication ability, the APU concluded that 'the difference between girls' communication and boys' communication is strongly contrasted and the girls outperform boys in all areas' (APU 1991: 219).

The difficulty for teachers is to develop projects which are gender neutral (environmentally orientated projects were consistently found to be gender neutral), or to recognise bias and act upon it. This may mean ensuring balance over a range of projects and ensuring that there is an awareness of likely weaknesses for either sex, with compensatory programmes being developed to overcome these weaknesses. Adding to the complexity of the issue is that findings are not consistent over all ability ranges, with low-ability girls' performance being found to be 'particularly fragile'.

Are social factors playing a greater role at Key Stages 3 and 4?

Social factors includes the development of gender-specific behaviour through reinforcement by socialisation and education. Children observe these gendered behaviours modelled by peers, parents and teachers, which are then reinforced by the media. Ofsted reported that 'there is evidence that teachers' gender values and expectations play an important role in shaping pupils perception's [sic] and reactions to school' (Ofsted 1990: 61). This involves teacher bias during interactions with pupils, the marking of examination papers, the setting of tasks, and guidance on subject options and career choices. The process of socialisation, however, starts at birth with the adoption (by parents) of gendered colours (blue for boy and pink for girl), carries on through early childhood with choice of toys and forms of communication, and is further reinforced at every stage of education, resulting in a stereotyped choice of subjects and career:

> At school, these attitudes are reinforced in a number of ways. First teachers clearly differentiate subject areas along gender lines, and in some cases curriculum's [sic] still channel males and females into distinctive subject choices. For example while heads were quick to assure that males and females had equal access to all subjects, this rarely included woodwork and home nutrition which were strictly organised along gender lines. I was told that 'the girls aren't encouraged to go into workshops' and asked 'well why would a boy want to do food and nutrition?' Subjects like technical drawing were felt to be 'inappropriate' for female pupils despite the fact that the skills acquired in technical drawing advantaged students entering physics. Furthermore certain skills were described by respondents as more feminine than others. English language and literature in particular clearly fell into this category. Consequently

reading and writing are dismissed by male students as 'girlish', 'nerdish' and 'effeminate'.

(Parry 1996: 12)

Research by Arnot and Weiner (1987) showed that there were differences in gender interaction between teachers and pupils in craft, design and technology lessons. Through observational studies, they found that girls interacted with the class teacher significantly more than boys did. The teacher was also more likely to intervene with girls' projects, using 'hands-on' demonstrations to show processes, whereas with boys intervention was provided in the form of 'let me explain'. The length of verbal interactions with pupils was also in favour of girls, lasting on average sixteen seconds compared with eleven seconds for boys' (that is, girls received 32% more verbal interaction with the teacher). Within the same study, girls' questioning technique of the teacher was also shown to differ from that of boys. Girls were more likely to ask questions and the questions would be more directly about influencing the quality of their work and 'what to do' next.

The stereotyping of pupils can be seen to link directly with teaching style and the teacher's perceptions and labelling processes. Much of this occurs so rapidly within a technology lesson that the opportunity to reflect is difficult. Equally, in encouraging pupils to be independent, teachers may be inadvertently contributing to boys' failure, as the monitoring of their work is limited because of boys' reluctance to seek assurances, whereas girls' ability to question and seek reassurance and the teacher's willingness for 'hands-on' intervention has contributed to girls' superiority in the subject.

The teacher who is aware of forms of stereotyping that could be present or reinforced in his or her classroom is in a position to intervene by changing his or her responses so that potentially harmful stereotypes and patterns of interaction are not reinforced. For example, if a lack of self-confidence were suspected in some pupils (say, low-ability boys), the teacher could look for ways to build up their self-confidence rather than accepting their dependence on him or her (Arnot and Weiner 1987: 171).

How does teaching and learning style interact with attainment?

Preferred learning styles and assessment procedures can reinforce or challenge students' beliefs, values and understandings concerning appropriate gender behaviours. Teachers, therefore, need to recognise that gendered experiences and understandings often shape 'learning styles' or preferred ways of learning.

Harding's (1997) research identified that many girls prefer to think laterally, interpreting new information from a variety of perspectives and making connections between new knowledge and prior experiences in the outside world, whereas many boys prefer to learn independently and focus on 'right answer/wrong answer' outcomes rather than thinking laterally and imaginatively when trying to solve problems. This research is useful in identifying gendered patterns of learning and assessment and in drawing attention to differences in starting points for particular groups of girls and boys. However, too much focus on identifying 'preferred learning styles' or preferred assessment processes of girls, or of boys, can 'naturalise' differences, making them appear unchangeable.

As gender is a complex relational process, we need to remember that there are significant differences in preferred learning styles to be found among different groups of girls and different groups of boys. Rather than conceptualising these differences as 'masculine' learning styles (for example, independent, logical, factual) and 'feminine' learning styles (for example, cooperative, emotive, imaginative), it is more accurate to understand that behaviour is an independent process. It is shaped by individuals (such as teachers and parents) and society (such as the media) and therefore different learning and gendered experiences must be anticipated.

Each of these preferred learning styles might be viewed along a continuum in which the learning styles of different groups of girls and boys will range from 'commonly used' to 'rarely used'. By identifying the point from which students are starting in their learning processes, teachers and students can acknowledge the skills evident in particular areas and identify other skills needing further development.

Conclusion

The current differentiated position of boys and girls within design and technology can be considered as an outstanding success for equal opportunities organisations. However, the overarching feature of any initiative aimed at ameliorating the incidence of gaps in achievement must be high achievement for all – both boys and girls. It is essential that policies aimed at raising the achievement of boys are not introduced at the expense of girls, whose improvement over recent years has been a tremendous success story.

Boys have now become the new focus and are now being labelled as 'underachievers' as part of a media-led 'male crisis'. They should not expect, as of 'right', success in any subject, but the extent of their lack of success has to be a concern, not least because they often enjoy the subject (research indicates that design and technology remains a favourite subject with boys) and they appear to have the same equal opportunities to achieve success as do girls. What is clear however, is that a range of inter-related factors has come into force – factors which have not always been sufficiently considered or their effects thought through. Of more concern is that 'quick-fix solutions' (neologisms – programmes introduced specifically for boys), as opposed to a considered approach, appear to be high on the agenda of every school concerned by a widening gap in achievement. Often these initiatives work in the short term merely because of the fact that their adoption has increased gender awareness temporarily. Ultimately, a pattern of attainment now exists which needs to be re-examined, not at the expense of girls' success but in the interests of equity for all pupils.

Literally millions of pounds have been spent upon design and technology within the last decade, updating and resourcing workshops and laboratories. This has been part of the essential growth of the subject. However, comparatively little has been spent on researching and developing the teaching and assessment processes within the subject. This lack of research has meant that the crucial debates about boys' underachievment, assessment issues and the effects of legislative implementation irrespective of gender have only taken place at a low level.

Questions to consider

From this chapter further questions arise which those involved in design and technology must be prepared to research and debate if the subject is to continue to evolve and achieve equality at its core:

1 Is the current gender gap in design and technology a function of an approach that is not well founded, and how desirable is it to have such a gap?
2 Do National Curriculum teacher assessments need to be standardised to ensure greater accuracy of the data produced and, if so, how can this be achieved?
3 Are more flexible approaches in the assessment of design and technology needed to avoid gender bias? If so, what form would these take?
4 Is design and technological capability currently assessed by the National Curriculum and GCSE?
5 How should schools analyse the data collected from National Curriculum assessments and how should this information be reported? In addition, how should the information be used to inform teaching methods?
6 How do new educational initiatives (for example, the literacy hour, the National Curriculum) impact upon the existing gender gap and the progress of particular groups of pupils?
7 Is the use of extended projects in design and technology the most effective way of gathering evidence for assessing ability and does this method favour particular groups of pupils?
8 Do self-fulfilling prophecies established through the labelling process at Key Stage 3 impact upon and transcend GCSE achievement?
9 Is the existing gender entry pattern within design and technology subject areas desirable?
10 Do we now possess a narrower perception of ability?

References

APU (Assessment of Performance Unit) (1991) *The Assessment of Performance in Design and Technology*, London: HMSO.

Arnot, M. and Weiner, G. (1987) *Gender Under Scrutiny: New Enquiries in Education*, London: Open University Press.

Arnot, M. and Weiner, G. (1997) *Gender and Politics of Schooling*, London: Open University Press.

Arnot, M. and Weiner, G. (1998) *Recent Research on Gender and Educational Performance*, London: Open University Press.

Bleach, K. (1998) *Raising Boys' Achievement in Schools*, London: Trentham Books.

CATS (Consortium for assessment and testing in Schools) (1991) Key Stage 3 Technology, London: School Examination and Assessment Council.

DES (Department of Education and Science) (1989) *Task Group on Assessment and Testing – A Report*, London: DES.

Equal Opportunities Commission (1996) *The Gender Divide*, London: HMSO.

GATE (Girls and Technology Education) (1981) *Objectives of Design and Technology Courses: as Expressed in Public Examination Syllabuses and Assessment*, London: Chelsea College Centre for Science and Mathematics Education.

Gipps, C. and Murphy, P. (1994) *A Fair Test: Assessment, Achievement and Equity*, Buckingham: Open University Press.

Gipps, C., Clarke, S. and McCallum, B. (1998) 'The role of teachers in national assessment in England', *American Educational Research Association Conference Symposium*, Leeds: Leeds University.

Grant, M. (1983) *The What, Why and How of GATE (Girls and Technology Education)*, London: Chelsea College Centre for Science and Mathematics Education.

Harding, J. (1997) 'Gender and design and technology education', *Journal of Design and Technology Education,* **2** (1): 20–6.

Hutchinson, D. and Schagen, I. (1994) *How Reliable is National Curriculum Assessment?*, Slough: National Foundation for Education Research.

Kimbell, R. Stables, K. and Green, R. (1996) *Understanding Practice in Design and Technology*, Buckingham: Open University Press.

Murphy, R. and Broadfoot, P. (1995) *Effective Assessment and the Improvement of Education – A Tribute to Desmond Nuttall*, London: Falmer Press.

Ofsted (1997) *Secondary Education 1993–1997. A Review of Secondary Schools in England*, London: HMSO.

Ofsted (1996) *Subject and Standards. Issues for School Development Arising from OFSTED Inspections 1994–1995*, London: HMSO.

QCA andDfEE (1998) *Teacher Assessment*, London: HMSO.

SCAA (1996) *Exemplification of Standards in Design and Technology: Key Stage 3*, London: HMSO.

Internet source

Parry, O. (1996) In one ear and out the other: unmasking masculinities in the Caribbean classroom, http://www.socresonline.org.uk/socresnline/1/2/2.html, 1996.

10 Is gender still on the agenda as an issue for design and technology?

Su Sayers

Introduction

The principle of gender equality should now be firmly embedded in design and technology, in contrast to the subject's traditional origins in the distinctly differentiated male and female crafts. During the 1980s, research into gender in design and technology was funded and hotly debated. Gender issues in education continue to be debated, but research evidence (from papers published in design and technology journals and IDATER (International Design and Technology Educational Research) conference reports) does not show gender to be a current issue in design and technology.[1] So, have the gender issues identified prior to the 1980s, and tackled by GIST (Girls into Science and Technology) and WISE (Women into Science and Engineering) projects (Whyte 1986), been resolved? Or is it complacent to make such an assumption?

This chapter starts by examining basic principles: the nature–nurture debate; some definitions of sex and gender; and the masculine–feminine continuum. These principles, as will be shown, are themselves not universally agreed, but they provide a framework to the area of gender for the design and technology specialist. The next section identifies some perspectives and positions on gender in design and technology, examining contrasting views so the reader can identify where his or her sympathies lie. The final section then applies the principles to curriculum organisation in design and technology, including workshop environment, option choice, teachers as role models, learning styles and career aspirations.

The 'gender' agenda: some basic principles

As sex defines the biological reference point for an individual at birth, it has been popular for scientists to categorise boys' and girls' performances in relation to this single variable factor. Kelly (1987) discusses the way in which biological factors, such as differences in spatial ability, have often been cited as factors affecting the lack of popularity of and achievement in science and technology for girls. Is biological difference one of the issues that needs to concern design and technology teachers? If biological determinism – the belief that the only determining factor in differences between boys and girls is their sex – is too simplistic an answer, then what are the issues?

The 'nature–nurture' debate: relevance for design and technology?

In Year 8, girls may have greater dexterity than boys because the bones in their wrists develop earlier in the adolescent growth spurt. Boys in Year 11, when their body frame and muscles have formed, may be stronger and taller than girls of the same age. Are these physiological factors so important? If physical skill were the main or only goal of education in design and technology, then physical differences would be very important. Does it matter that the Year 8 boys' design work is not as neat as the girls, that the Year 11 girl is not strong enough to tighten up the bolts on her GCSE major project? Surely, the good-quality design ideas and 'designerly' thinking are evident despite the untidy presentation, and not being tall or strong enough is only a minor handicap.

Paechter and Head (1996), while discussing differential treatment of the gendered body in PE (physical education) teaching, point out that both PE and design and technology are concerned with the body: '… although gender is primarily a social construct, it is attributed on the basis of physical signs and forms' (ibid.: 23):

> Given that physical working with the hands is bound up with hegemonic masculinity… it is tempting to suggest that, for some of the male CDT teachers, taking their woodwork and metalwork home had once acted as a symbolic claim to parental recognition of their manhood.
>
> (ibid.: 26)

The fact that girls and boys are physiologically different is less of an issue than the values placed by pupils, teachers and society at large on boys *relative to* girls, and the meanings constructed about them. The real issue is people's attitudes, beliefs about and expectations of girls and boys, attitudes that often remain hidden and unstated. An undetected prejudice or a biased attitude is likely to hinder equal access to a fair participation in the design and technology curriculum, equal opportunity to perform well at designing and making, and have equal achievements recognised.

These are not physiological or visible differences, therefore they can easily be overlooked. It is not dexterity that is the issue in boys' underachievement in design and technology coursework, nor is it necessarily physiological factors that affect their low performance in evaluation activities (Kimbell *et al.* 1991). It is not strength that stops girls getting on with modelling and making soon enough (ibid.), or choosing electronics as a GCSE option. Physiological differences have become less important than they were twenty-five years ago, when curricula were still very different, and, depending on whether you were a girl or a boy, you would do either boys' crafts or girls' crafts, not both (Penfold 1988).

As Scaife (1998: 63) points out in a review of science education and gender, there is 'little support' in the APU findings for biological explanations for differences in performance between boys and girls'. Thus, in terms of pupils' progress in design and technology, their biological sex ('nature', or the 'input') is less relevant. It is the experiences that the pupils encounter during the educational 'process' (as they are 'nurtured') that affect their opportunity to learn.

Definitions of sex and gender

Biological sex does matter when there is evidence of overt discrimination in favour of one sex or another, as Acker demonstrates in her analysis of Morrish (Acker 1994: 36). Whereas sex defines the biological reference point for an individual at birth, gender is the adopted societal identity of the individual and, by implication, acceptance of the identity by others. Gender, seen as a social construct, allows us to examine typical gender characteristics and even stereotypes. Curriculum developers have recognised that social differences, such as gender, are a product of conditioning, and are 'learnt' behaviours, and are an important factor to be considered at every level in education.[2]

Gender: a more relevant concept

The history of design and technology is gendered in its development, from traditionally male manufacturing crafts and materials, to traditionally female domestic crafts and materials (Penfold 1988; Paechter and Head 1996; Harding 1997). Research in primary classrooms (Rogers 1986; Walkerdine 1986) has confirmed that stereotypical, culturally defined behaviour is learnt very early in the family and in school.

In the DATA (Design and Technology Association) Handbook (DATA 1997: 3.3), the word 'gender' is used only twice in the section on equal opportunities, except in quotations from 'Genderwatch!'. Perhaps this is significant, reflecting coyness about terminology, and an emphasis on individual 'differences' (for example, special needs, ethnicity, etc., as well as gender)? Using a general 'equal opportunities' perspective masks (some might say, 'fudges') the specifics of gender issues, which means that problems do not get addressed.

Biological sex and gender identity are the same, in most cases, and Paechter (1993) has drawn attention to the inscription of gender roles and its importance to power relations within design and technology. Male domination of departments since the merger of CDT (craft, design and technology) and home economics, and also the way in which male pupils demand more attention from the teacher, are quoted as evidence. However, it is interesting that girls are able to adopt a masculine identity without much question: they can wear 'male' styles of clothing and adopt 'masculine' hobbies and interests. There are even issues about denying girls the opportunity to wear trousers for school uniform, which have been the subject of legal proceedings. There is nothing similar suggesting that boys should be allowed to wear skirts. It is much more cause for comment if a boy adopts a 'female' gender identity by his clothing choice (boys are usually limited by convention to certain colours and styles in clothes and shoes) or if a boy adopts 'feminine' hobbies and interests. Are design and technology teachers uncomfortable even thinking about this, so it only gets mentioned as a joke? Challenges to accepted values, and subjects that are taboo, tend to remain outside the provenance of mainstream design and technology.[3]

The masculine–feminine continuum: how important are these distinctions for design and technology?

In the 1980s, feminist writing in the UK became more insistent about the extent to which boys (sometimes aided by male teachers) oppress, demean and harass girls (and sometimes women teachers) (Mahony 1985; Weiner 1985). Masculine behaviour is associated with this sort of aggression, with power; feminine with submission, with compliance. The reference here is to attributes and behaviours rather than biological certainties; the social dimension is therefore influential. There is an element of some flexibility along a continuum of what people identify as typically feminine or masculine. Is metalwork seen as more 'masculine' than work in plastics or wood? Is catering less 'feminine' than nutrition within the 'feminine' area of food technology? We study 'attribute analysis' as part of product design in design and technology, but how often do we apply this process to our own assumptions and perceptions?

Many writers (see, for example, Acker 1994; Delamont 1996) have pointed to the danger of ascribing rigidly to expectations of masculine and feminine behaviour. Rigid stereotyping can impose a straitjacket to behave in a conformist way, and can be used as an element of control: 'Washing-up is girl's work'; 'Boys don't become nurses'; 'Girls can't do computing'. Parker (1984) makes the point that confining 'masculine' pursuits to men sanctions oppression of the female gender. So, in design and technology, any sense in which curricular experiences are confined to one or the other gender is to be abhorred:

> The conviction that feminine is natural to women (and unnatural to men) is tenacious. It is a crucial aspect of patriarchal ideology, sanctioning a rigid and oppressive division of labour.
>
> (ibid.: 3)

The concept of a rigid boundary between two opposites, masculine and feminine, can be challenged. The association of masculine solely with men, and feminine with women, is debatable, as it ascribes divisions which are untenable in an equal opportunities culture. Welding in metal is often thought of as a masculine activity, but this does not mean that only men can do welding. Likewise, it should also be the case that sewing, seen as a feminine activity (especially embroidery), should also be accepted as a pursuit of men. As Parker (1984) goes on to discuss, this has been less acceptable. Men can be famous chefs and fashion designers, but 'patriarchal ideology' still prevents public acceptance of men as stitchers in fabric. (See also *Women as Designers*, Callen's (1995) discussion of William Morris and the Arts and Crafts Movement.) Is this attitude tenable in an equal opportunities framework? By subscribing to such stereotypes, are we party to the 'oppressive division of labour'?

Perspectives and positions on the issue of gender in design and technology: an overview

Most design and technology writing has taken a neutral or child-centred approach.

Research with an overtly feminist stance is sparse; indeed, feminist writing has been critical of the sexist nature of the subject's history (Attar 1990). Traditionally, discussion of gender issues in design and technology has overlooked the political dimension taken by feminist writing. This section seeks to engage with some of the issues that have sometimes been smoothed over, perhaps in a quest for consensus between an almost exclusively female home economics lobby and a predominantly male CDT lobby.

The 'denial of difference' perspective

It is claimed that boys and girls behave, learn and perform exactly alike in design and technology classrooms, and those who hold this view might regard discussion or action as therefore irrelevant. Riddell's case study of teachers' attitudes to sex differentiation in two secondary schools may still seem familiar (Riddell 1992). Physics, mathematics and technology teachers all claimed they were providing the same experiences for boys and girls, the same projects, the same teaching approach, and used this in denying that there was any need for change. Other teachers acknowledged that differences did exist but played down their importance – there were other more pressing concerns, other priorities. Growney (1995: 56), in her study of design and technology, found that there was 'a lack of interest in genuinely addressing the problem... The implementation of strategies was somewhat half-hearted'. Those who do recognise differences might pay lip-service to a more politically correct position, but be too busy to take action. Both of these groups' attitudes towards gender are negative.

The 'differentiation' perspective: the liberal-feminist position

Teachers who acknowledge differences in performance and attitude between girls and boys and try to take action, often adopt a differentiation perspective. Teachers try to use education in design and technology to help make a difference for pupils' individual needs, whether they are boys or girls. They see real differences, try to identify them clearly, and then try to mediate to support both boys and girls in appropriate ways. Actually trying to do something about it in the classroom is a positive position. Any caring teacher would try to accommodate individual differences between pupils. It is the approach taken by DATA:

> Although it may not be practical for teachers to plan an individual curriculum for every single student, it remains a considerable challenge for any teacher to ensure that the differing needs of students are considered and addressed as far as possible through differentiation.
>
> (DATA 1997: 3.3)

This statement can be called 'child-centred' because the individual child's needs are seen to be the key to effective implementation of equal opportunities. The responsibility for achieving gender equality is placed on the individual teacher. Is this fair, in situations in which the timetable, the environment, and the social context within which the teaching is placed might militate against ever achieving the goal? Kelly (1987) has criticised the individualised curriculum because it ignores constraints placed on the individual by his or her social context. It may not be any more than a short-term solution.

Acker (1994, 1998) has also drawn attention to the limitations of the 'child-centred' stance which has been most popular in primary schools. She comments on Skelton's study of primary teachers and their failure to challenge gender inequality: they were encouraged to believe that attention to children's individual differences, needs and development was paramount. The logic of this stance effectively rules out positive action, that is gender-appropriate tasks, because, if pupils are truly treated each as individuals, then it is impossible to discriminate against or in favour of a whole group, such as girls or boys as a whole. Acker's (1994: 99) commentary draws attention to the contradiction here, which applies to all ideologies about child-centred learning. The dilemma remains to be resolved.

The 'social-feminist' position

The *Design and Technology Head of Department's Handbook* (DATA 1997) goes on to reference questions from 'Genderwatch!' (Wilkinson *et al.* 1992), in which attention is drawn to the complexity of the social, cultural and political environment and its effect, and so it goes beyond child-centred/differentiation approaches to gender issues.

A position that takes account of the situational complexity involved in achieving gender-equal experiences for children, is often identified as the social-feminist position (Acker 1994). A teacher's best intentions for the pupils may be subverted by institutional factors such as the option system, timetabling, room allocations, funding discrepancies etc. The political dimension to equal opportunities is often ignored in design and technology, but various writers have shown how much it needs to be considered (Riddell 1992; Paechter and Head 1996).

The 'positive action' stance

Positive action, to encourage more participation by girls in the non-traditional areas of the curriculum, has been the subject of a number of curriculum development strategies and funded initiatives. The interventions within the GIST (Kelly *et al.* 1994) and WISE projects have been well publicised. These initiatives made an assumption that there was a deficit, on the part of girls and women, to be addressed. The reverse side of this view might instead ask questions about the nature of the curriculum, and access to it for both boys and girls, with regard to issues of justice and equal access. Indeed, current concern over the underachievement of boys has highlighted that a culture of 'blame', in which underachievers are seen as victims of their own destiny, is not a productive approach. That positive action on the part of curriculum planners (including teachers) is required, was spelt out by Riddell (1992: 221) in her case study of two secondary schools.

The 'radical-feminist' position

The radical-feminist position precedes all discussion of overt differences between girls and boys by reference to the power dimensions and oppression (of women by men) over the centuries. Feminist writing, which has insights to offer to design and technology in a post-modern society, resides outside the design and technology arena, in journals specific to curriculum and/or gender (see Paechter 1993). The power of influential policy makers (mostly men) to make curriculum decisions that favour boys, has been the subject of much protest during the development of the National Curriculum. Those who take the radical-feminist position regard positive action as the way to change established attitudes. However, most design and technology writing has taken a moderate, child-centred approach.

Summary

It may be useful to compare the characterisations, outlined above, with Acker's (1994) analysis of key distinctions in feminist thinking:

- The liberal-feminist position holds that women's liberation can be achieved without major changes to educational and political structures.
- The socialist-feminist position holds that class, race and gender oppressions interact in a complex way.
- The radical-feminist position holds that gender oppression is the oldest and most profound form of exploitation.

Table 10.1 summarises the main beliefs, attitudes and stances regarding action in relation to gender issues in design and technology teaching.

Some gender issues of current concern in design and technology

For many people the subject of technology has represented the most gender-stereotyped subject on the school curriculum. The gendered nature of the subject's history (Harding 1997: 20) provides an interesting dimension. A wealth of opportunities opened up, following the development of the National Curriculum, in a new subject with a broader base and the potential to unite the design-based subjects in the curriculum under a common banner. Consider your own specialist expertise or subject area within design and technology: does it cross the masculine–feminine divide?[4]

Thomas has drawn attention to the traditional divisions between English or physics in higher education; many of her comments could be read in terms of the gendered areas of design and technology (Thomas 1990). She quotes Segal's analysis of army recruits' training (Segal 1987), in which the training regime often uses overt sexism and contempt for women ('just like a girl', 'girl's blouse' etc.) to be tough and strong (masculine characteristics). The sergeant-major inculcates a

Table 10.1   Summary of beliefs, attitudes, and stance regarding action, in relation to gender in design and technology

Beliefs about gender differences in design and technology	How is attitude revealed?	Action taken	Where can further evidence be found?
Believe gender differences do not exist	Denial: argue with any evidence to the contrary.	Defend the status quo. Hostile to action	Riddell (1992) Acker (1994)
Believe gender differences remain unproven	Denial: discount research results	Preserve the status quo. Take no action	Growney (1995) Kelly (1988) Riddell (1992)
Recognise few gender differences	Devalue the relative importance of gender differences	Provide equal opportunities. Action is low priority	Growney (1995) DATA (1997)
Recognise some gender differences	Attempt to even out identified gender disadvantages	Child-centred approach. Action is low priority.	DATA (1997) Withey (2000) Clark and Millard (1998)
Believe gender differences are important	Identify complex interaction between gender differences and other social factors	Positive discrimination. Positive action is taken within the context	Wilkinson *et al.* (1992) Acker (1994) Withey (2000)
Believe gender differences are crucially important	Precede discussion of overt differences with reference to power dimensions and oppression (of women by men) over the centuries	Positive action to change the context. Restructure curricula. Empowerment strategies	Attar (1990) Paechter and Head (1996) Wilkinson *et al.* (1992)

fear of being considered feminine (compare this with the derogatory implications tied up in the term 'effeminate'). However, the result is to get the recruits, as soldiers, to conform to a passive, obedient, and subservient state – which is more often seen as conventionally feminine behaviour. She also quotes from Willis' (1977) study of teenage working-class boys to illustrate the paradox embedded in their rebellious attitudes: they class academic work as silly and cissy, and take pride in their masculine macho rejection of school and all things conformist. However, their lack of qualifications leads to low-paid jobs and little chance to exercise choice in their lives, thus leading to enforced social conformity despite the culture of rebellion in their behaviour.

Arnot (1982), though, takes a feminist position in arguing that to choose a typically feminine role, for example domestic and home-centred, can represent rebellion against the pervasiveness of macho stereotypes. She sees this as a brave standpoint and credits the working-class women of her study with guts for adopting this as their role. In this respect, a female teacher who chooses to teach design and technology, with its traditional masculine origins and associations, could be said to have conformed to pressure to value more highly that which is overtly masculine. The reaction that follows is often exaggerated conformism to the stereotype. She has to follow, even more so than the male design and technology teacher, traditional hierarchies and values. Paechter and Head (1996), discussing the stereotyped female role in home economics, have found 'an ultra-feminine ethos' emerging and drawn parallels with dance teaching in PE. Arnot's view is that, sadly: 'Whichever choice a woman makes, the traditional divisions will be reinforced' (Arnot 1982: 64–89).

Single-sex education or mixed schools and/or classes?

Research in the 1960s and 1970s considered the relative merits of single-sex or mixed schooling (Arnot and Weiner 1985). Single-sex schools offered girls less opportunity to study physics and chemistry compared with boys' schools. The argument was therefore that mixed schools were better as they provided a broader curriculum. In examining the figures for actual uptake of the sciences as examination subject options, Scaife (1998: 64) found that girls had a better chance of taking physics or chemistry, and boys biology, in single-sex schools. The opportunity was there in mixed schools, so why was each edged out, into stereotypical choices? A prevailing culture of conformity may be preventing them but perhaps there is an element of 'teacher expectations' here too. Riddell's (1992) analysis presents a picture of teachers in mixed schools, keen to preserve the status quo, who see environmental and social barriers to equal opportunities and so feel it is useless to try. Pioneering work in separate gender design and technology classes has been the subject of small-scale local initiatives (Withey 2000). It demands an attitude of positive discrimination, which depends on either a whole-school approach, or some more funding for projects. The current government's concern about the underachievement of boys may lead to further progress in this area.

Gender issues and curriculum organisation in design and technology

The evidence of children conforming to highly specific stereotypical behaviour from an early age has fundamental implications for design and technology, because pupils have to make choices of subject area: for instance, whether to take GCSE in electronics or textiles, food or resistant materials. It is in choosing the options that many teachers and pupils unquestioningly adopt stereotypical choices. The choice of a non-stereotypical gender option may lead to embarrassment, teasing from others. Pupils sometimes become uncomfortable with the associated gender identity that this confers on them, and need support to be courageous or rebellious enough to stand up for their preferred choice. Do design and technology departments condone gendered expectations? Might this be classed as sexist behaviour? What strategies might teachers use to support pupils in non-stereotypical gender choices?

Within the National Curriculum, design and technology as a foundation subject is compulsory up to, and including, Key Stage 4 (except in Wales). One of the principal aims of the National Curriculum for design and technology was to ensure that both boys and girls were given equal opportunity to study all areas of the subject: woodwork, metalwork, food, textiles etc. The consultation document iterated the aims of the new National Curriculum as being to ensure that:

> ... all pupils, regardless of sex, ethnic origin, and geographic location, have access to broadly the same good and relevant curriculum.
>
> (DES 1987)

Prior to the introduction of the National Curriculum, technology subjects were segregated into home economics and CDT and taught as individual elements. This segregation resulted, as many writers have documented (Riddell 1992), in a gender-biased selection of subjects by pupils, and gender stereotyping in relation to the representation of teaching staff within each element. It could be argued that the design and technology curriculum has overcome earlier concerns, as it provides pupils with a holistic representation of the subject through its inclusion of traditionally male and female orientated subjects under the one subject banner. To a certain degree this may be true, with examination board statistics showing increasing numbers of girls opting to take resistant materials, for example, and slightly more boys opting for food technology. There is, however, continued segregation within design and technology, resulting in inequality of opportunity for pupils.

Workshop environments

As Withey (2000) has pointed out, the questions raised about the subject in Genderwatch! are still relevant:

> What messages does the design and technology learning environment give about whose work is valued and who has ownership?
>
> (Myers, K. 1987)

> How is the balance maintained between the valuing of women's and men's traditional experience of technologies in topics and course content?
>
> (Wilkinson *et al.* 1992: 139)

Study of the curriculum projects currently offered by schools at Key Stage 3 often reveals well-intentioned but highly gender-biased design and technology projects. The Genderwatch! report highlighted the perception of girls in secondary schools:

> For the subject to be meaningful, female pupils stress the humanistic aspects of 'design problems' whereas male pupils tend to value technology as a

'technical puzzle' and/or as a means to a career. The CDT curriculum, as it is presently conceived and practiced by most teachers and pupils, is more suited to the interests and expectations and learning styles of most male pupils.

(ibid.: 135)

Evidence from Nuffield and Royal College of Art projects (Nuffield Foundation 1995; Technology Colleges Trust 1995) shows a wealth of open-ended project ideas which have more appeal for the learning needs of female pupils. Parker, in her study of making in textiles, points to a key dimension which made and probably still makes, embroidery and hand-sewing so popular as a pursuit for women:

> ... the bond that embroidery forged between women; sewing allowed women to sit together without feeling they were neglecting their families, wasting time or betraying their husbands by maintaining independent social bonds.
>
> (Parker 1984: 14)

The contrast with the noisy workshop, the stereotypical masculine domain, where work and projects are often on a larger scale, is clear. The machines make it too noisy for conversation, and the demands for safety mean that work is not of a sociable kind. Instead, the demands of embroidery often involve concentration and individualism, rather than any notion of group activity.

Do you think this is true? Are the majority of design and technology workshops like this? Are there areas, activities and materials in design and technology that allow opportunity for quiet working that could involve some conversation? Is cooperative group work possible in the typical masculine domain?

Traditional option choices?

During Key Stage 3, all pupils are required to study all elements of the technology curriculum so that, at the end of the key stage, they are able to make informed choices concerning their options for Key Stage 4. In design and technology this relates to the area of the subject in which pupils will specialise. The syllabuses currently offered by the majority of examination boards under the design and technology criteria contain the following options: food, textiles, resistant materials, graphics products, electronic products, and systems and control. It is commonly accepted that these are gendered, thus pupils often fall into traditional option choices. The fond hope of the Genderwatch! authors for design and technology was as follows:

> In time the barriers between the different technology disciplines should disappear, resulting in the formation of mixed-sex teams of technology teachers. This alone will provide a powerful example and image for teachers.
>
> (Wilkinson *et al.* 1992)

When reflecting on the doubts expressed in 1992 by the 'Genderwatch!' team, one questions whether perpetuation of gender stereotyping at option uptake has been at all reduced in the development of new syllabuses:

> Although the National Curriculum holds out the promise that all students will have access to a common technology curriculum there is no longer an entitlement to a full GCSE course at KS4. Schools will wish to give careful consideration to the choice of courses at this stage to avoid the perpetuation of gender stereotyping in option take-up.
>
> (Wilkinson *et al.* 1992: 134)

Teachers as role models?

A case study, written by a student in teacher training indicates what might be one solution to the perceived problem: under-recruitment of girls into typically male option choices at GCSE level.[5] The student's solution:

> Throughout education, and especially in Design Technology [*sic*], it is my belief that boys need positive male role models in subjects such as food and textiles and need to be aware of the importance of these subjects in relation to the outside world. Let us train our future Design Technology teachers in these subjects, and at the very least offer men, like myself, the opportunity to do so within a general Design Technology course. Without such action, it is my belief that schools will continue to see a decline in the achievements and attitudes of boys within education as a whole, but especially within specific subjects such as Design Technology.
>
> (Gallagher 1998: 8)

As total recruitment into ITE (initial teacher education) has dropped, it seems that schools are getting fewer women applying for food and textiles posts, rather than more men. Note also the comment that:

> Many girls' schools have downgraded food and textiles in favour of Resistant Materials and IT, and have done so in the name of equal opportunities, not recognising or valuing the success which girls have traditionally enjoyed through making with these materials.
>
> (DATA 1997: 3.3)

The issue of lack of status and/or the lower status accorded to the traditionally 'feminine' areas of the curriculum is called into question by both of these examples. It seems evident that a more radical feminist and political approach to curriculum planning is required to solve the problem.

Learning styles and pupil assessment issues: the lesson for design and technology and gender issues

Assessment evidence has revealed that different forms of assessment task favour one gender over another (see Chapters 8 and 9). Generally, it has been found that boys perform less well in coursework tasks that involve planning and organisation and presentation of their work (Cresswell 1990; Kimbell *et al.* 1991; 1996). Whereas girls are meticulous in graphics work, they are slower to embark on making. They take more time planning design work, rather than generating diverse ideas. Boys' reaction to making tasks has been observed: they cannot wait to get started and find little relevance in prior planning. Evidence of boys' superior performance in multiple choice tests has been commented on by many writers (Head 1996; Harding 1997). The APU work (Kimbell *et al.* 1991) drew attention to the gender differences in:

1   Using reflective skills. Tasks requiring reflection suited girls best: where the task required the identification of a need or the evaluation of a product, girls participated with confidence and demonstrated good capability. Tasks that suited boys were 'active' tasks that involved doing and making: this was when they participated with confidence and showed capability.
2   The context in which the task was set. Girls outperformed boys in a people context and boys outperformed girls in an industry context.

Murphy comments:

> Typically girls tend to value the circumstances that activities are presented in and consider they give meaning to the task. They do not abstract issues from their context. Boys as a group conversely do consider issues in isolation and judge content and context to be irrelevant.
>
> (Murphy 1996: 150)

Teachers can control purpose, content and context and so have it within their power to plan inclusive curricula. Scaife (1998: 60–79) outlines a variety of approaches to designing curriculum experiences in science, which might apply to design and technology projects. The essential element is that teachers recognise the support that is required, and acknowledge the gender implications for design and technology teaching.

The issue of career choice and career aspirations

Equal Opportunities Commission research has continued to point out the need to challenge gender stereotyping in subject, career and occupational choice (Rolfe 1999). The findings from research on relatively new mainstream programmes, such as the modern apprenticeships, show that there is heavy occupational segregation by gender:

> For example, over 97% of young Engineering Manufacturing apprentices are male and 92% of Hairdressing apprentices are female. Occupational choices such as these are not in themselves a 'bad thing' if they are freely made, but even then they have an impact on individual economic prosperity and a strong influence on the continuing pay gap between men and women.
>
> (ibid.)

Their recommendations for change tackle careers practice and claim that it has not had a sufficiently high profile in recent years. The also point to the lack of a clear agenda from the DfEE (Department for Education and Employment):

> The DfEE should provide clear guidelines on the principles behind Equal Opportunities … The Department should also emphasise that it is as committed to Equal Opportunities and gender equality as it is to current policies on disaffection and underachievement.
>
> (Rolfe 1999)

Conclusion

Equal opportunity: why is this not enough?

Imagine a scrupulously fair situation in which, in every design and technology lesson, each pupil gets an equal share of time from the teacher, gets equal access to tools and equipment, and has an equal number of design projects that he or she enjoys and can benefit from. Will this satisfy the concern for equal opportunities? This would be a fair system, but only at a very simplistic level, in which each pupil is assumed to start with equal advantages. Many writers have drawn attention to the naiveté in the approach to equality through equal offerings:

> Given the very different out of school experiences of girls and boys, to give them at school, the same offerings, resources and advice was not likely to affect them equally.
>
> (Yates 1985: 212)

Experience of teaching makes us aware that some pupils need more time to understand a task, and so a greater share of teachers' time goes to clarifying the requirements for these pupils and showing them how. There are those who do not need so much access to tools because they work faster and get the wood joint right first time, whereas others make mistakes and need to recut the wood, or sand it for longer. Many writers admit now that 'equal opportunities' was too simplistic a concept in an unequal world. There needs to be real consideration of equality in input, equality in process and equality of output of the teaching situation, to achieve true equality. And it is taking positive action to ensuring equal access that is at stake in many cases.

Positive discrimination as a solution

Methods to achieve equality in design and technology, often with the best of intentions, have used positive discrimination techniques towards certain pupils. The arguments in favour of positive discrimination in design and technology rely on the assumption that life and experience have handicapped some more than others, so the ones without the advantages need a 'leg up' the ladder to redress the balance and allow them to reach the same end point. Thus, the teacher scrutinises the curriculum, sees that systems and control is an area where girls need special inputs to get them to the same level as boys, and books the WISE bus to come to the school. Many surveys of design and technology in the past have revealed that girls' attitudes are 'less positive than boys' (Head 1985). Indeed the Manpower Services Commission (MSC), in *Equal Opportunities in TVEI*, stated that:

> Unless special measures are taken, the negative attitudes towards technology which girls already reveal, will undermine the objectives of TVEI.
> (MSC 1987)

There are drawbacks: a culture of 'blame', in which underachievers are seen as victims of their own destiny, may not be a productive approach.

More research as a solution?

In her discussion and overview of gender as a topic in educational research, Delamont describes the four paradoxes that confront educationalists working in this area (Delamont 1996: 8–17):

1   The boom in research on women and girls that has had little or no effect on the mainstream of the subject. As Acker has pointed out, most of this research is read by those interested in 'women's studies'; it is marginalised (Acker 1984).
2   The credibility of the database is questionable, due to methodology that is suspect, small sample size etc., and therefore many of the assertions are questionable. Delamont feels that this is a poor advocate for feminist research.
3   Feminist methodology: if it is always qualitative it prevents any research by females or on females being taken seriously by mainstream education circles. Delamont also thinks that the research agenda should encourage men to do more research on gender in order to authenticate it, as it will be written off if it is always done by women!
4   There is a serious shortage of work on men and boys as males. There is, in contrast, a plethora of research that assumes that boys are representative of the population at large and so it does not show how boys' experience is different from girls. The irony of the absent male! Delamont points to the variety of projects designed to encourage girls in mathematics and science and technology, and says it is equally important to attract and retain boys in 'needlework, cooking and foreign languages'. 'We are a long way from understanding the role of masculinity in education' (Delamont 1996: 14). However, she also points out that there has been some progress in providing a focus on these issues.

Taking positive action

Acker's discussion of resistance to attempts to introduce gender equality strikes a familiar chord. Most of the challenges outlined above rely on introducing changes to ways of teaching, things that teachers have held dear, fundamental aspects of their practice and their beliefs about the subject, 'tantamount in some cases to admitting years of malpractice. We cannot expect such conversions to come easily' (Acker 1994: 96). The clues in this statement are twofold:

- 'Malpractice', that is teachers are accused of erroneous, wrong strategies. They are made scapegoats for situations on which they have no guidance.
- 'Conversions', which has the implication of a complete change of beliefs. To alter someone's set of fundamental beliefs is to expect miracles. Most studies from which Riddell quotes equate younger teachers with such revisionary attitudes:

> There are various reasons why this might be so, including greater exposure of younger teachers to the women's movement and feminist ideas, and older teachers more likely to be in management positions, with a greater stake in the status quo.
>
> (Riddell 1992)

The child-centred approach to design and technology, with its emphasis on differentiation in tasks, in process, in resources, and in outcomes, can limit teachers' horizons in relation to real equality of access to the design and technology curriculum. This is the stance of the liberal feminist, who believes that justice can be achieved without disturbing the status quo, without change to established systems and structures in the curriculum and schooling in design and technology.

A real challenge confronts teachers who want to make a difference to the imbalance of option choices. The subject emphasis of design and technology projects and their assessment ought to allow more boys to study food and textiles if they want to, and girls to study construction materials or electronics if they want to. Teachers have to confront the political agenda implicit in traditional subject choices, the damaging stereotyping of certain media areas in design and technology, GCSE syllabus structures and cultural and societal norms. This is an enormous task, which must require a radical approach. The National Curriculum may have made a difference to design and technology, by uniting female home economics subjects with male CDT subjects and the positive outcomes may be celebrated, but most teachers recognise that there is further yet to travel to reach a state of equality. The journey is not yet over. Gender is still an issue, and as a human issue it is bound to be controversial.

Questions to consider

1   Analyse the design and technology teaching environment(s) in your school. What messages are conveyed about gender?
2   The WISE bus takes positive action in favour of girls to allow them to develop

knowledge, understanding and skills in systems and control. How might this preferential treatment affect boys' attitudes to systems and control?

3   Are such initiatives patronising towards girls? Such initiatives derive from an assumption, as Harding (1997) has pointed out, that the problem is with girls rather than with subject content. Girls' negative attitudes to systems and control may be because they want to question the assumption that new technology is necessarily a good thing. In any well-meaning programme of 'remedial technology', questions should be encouraged rather than stifled.

4   Industrially sponsored initiatives and resources tend to steer girls away from the familiar territory of environments and human contexts (in which the APU found girls performed well), taking instead an industrial emphasis. This is a good thing in that it exposes girls to an area of uncertainty in which they naturally problematise the knowledge and skills involved, rather than take them for granted. Do such initiatives undermine the values inherent in the domestic side of technology? Do they undermine the credibility of 'home technology', for example food and textiles production in a domestic context, by making it seem 'folksy' in comparison with the white heat of engineering on a big scale?

Notes

1   Journal of Design and Technology Education, International Journal of Technology Education, IDATER (International Design and Technology Educational Research).
2   Staffordshire LEA Guidelines (1997) state that: 'Gender is the socially or culturally defined difference ascribed to females and males. There is no scientific evidence that girls and boys are born with innate differences other than anatomical details but they do learn gender differences.'
3   The Royal College of Art Schools' Technology Project and the Nuffield Design and Technology Project have set a good example in tackling a broad range of issues that question established values, including gendered assumptions.
4   As a textiles specialist, in charge of a home economics course, I moved into design and technology, at the onset of the National Curriculum. My motives in moving into design and technology were very pragmatic, in some senses, as I wanted to remain a textiles specialist and contribute to the debate from within the new subject; on reflection, however, this position could be said to legitimise the apparent 'takeover' of the female, domestic, home-economics emphasis, in favour of the masculine, CDT/construction-based/systems-and-control emphasis that now exists.
5   The extract below (Gallagher 1998: 8), taken from a case study of one student teacher's experience of schools, illustrates how boys lose out in the food and textiles area:

> While an increase in the number of female design and technology teachers, especially in resistant materials and graphics, has resulted in girls observing positive female role models within these subjects, the existence of male teachers, especially in food and textiles, has been virtually non existent. Recent reports concerning the underachievement of boys suggest they lack male role models… I would suggest one… proposal would be to urge governing bodies to address the occupancy of male role models within traditionally female orientated subjects. Food and textiles, for example, procure insufficient male teachers, and would, I believe, see increases

in the number of boys valuing these subjects and wishing to study them, if more males could be encouraged to teach within these areas. Because schools have expended much of their efforts in recruitment and retention of female teachers in technical subjects, I believe governing bodies have neglected the issue of male role models within traditionally female subjects.

References

Acker, S. (1994) *Gendered Education*, Buckingham: Open University Press.

Arnot, M. (1982) 'Male hegemony, social class and women's education', *Journal of Education*, **164** (1): 64–89.

Arnot, M. and Weiner, M. (eds) (1985) *Gender and the Politics of Schooling*, London: Hutchinson in association with the Open University.

Attar, D. (1990) *Wasting Girls' Time*, London: Virago.

Callen, A. (1995) 'Sexual division of labour in the Arts and Crafts Movement', in Attfield, J. and Kirkham, P. (eds), *A View from the Interior: Women and Design*, London: Women's Press, pp. 151–65.

Cresswell, M. (1990) *Gender Effects in GCSE: Some Initial Analyses*, paper pesented at the Nuffield Seminar, June, University of London: Institute of Education.

DATA (Design and Technology Association) (1997) *Design and Technology Head of Department's Handbook*, Wellesbourne, DATA.

Delamont, S. (1996) *A Woman's Place in Education*, London: Avebury.

DES (Department of Education and Science) (1975) *Equal Opportunities Act*, London: HMSO.

DES (1987) *National Curriculum 5–16: A Consultation Document*, London: HMSO.

DES (1992) *Choice and Diversity*, London: HMSO.

Gallagher, A. (1998) *Equal Opportunities in Design and Technology*, unpublished course assignment.

Growney, C. (1995) 'Gender equality in technology: Moving forward', in Smith, J. (ed.), *IDATER 95: International Conference on Design and Technology Educational Research and Curriculum Development*, Loughborough University of Technology, Loughborough, pp. 52–7.

Harding, J. (1997) 'Gender and design and technology education', *Journal of Design and Technology Education*, **2** (1): 20–5.

Head, J. (1996) 'Gender identity and cognitive style', in Murphy P. and Gipps, C. (eds), *Equity in the Classroom: Towards Effective Pedagogy for Girls and Boys*, London: Falmer Press.

Kelly, A. (1987) *Science for Girls*, Buckingham: Open University Press.

Kelly, A., Whyte, J. and Smail, B. (1984) *Girls into Science and Technology: Final Report*, Manchester: Manchester University Press.

Kimbell, R., Stables, K., Wheeler, A.D., Wozniak, A.V. and Kelly, A.V. (1991) *The Assessment of Performance in Design and Technology*, London: Schools Examinations and Assessment Council andHMSO.

Mahony, P. (1985) *Schools for the Boys? Co-education Re-assessed*, London: Hutchinson.

MSC (Manpower Services Commission) (1987) *Equal Opportiunities in TVEI*, London: Manpower Services Commission.

Myers, K. (1987) *Genderwatch Materials*, Manchester: Equal Opportunities Commission.

Nuffield Foundation (1995) *Nuffield Design and Technology*, Harlow: Longman.

Paechter, C. (1993) 'What happens when a school subject undergoes a sudden change of status?', *Currriculum Studies*, **1**: 349–64.

Paechter, C. and Head, J. (1996) 'Gender, identity, status and the body: life in a marginal subject', *Gender and Education*, **8** (1): 21–9.

Parker, R. (1984) *The Subversive Stitch*, London: Women's Press.

Penfold, J. (1988) *Craft, Design and Technology: Past, Present and Future*, Stoke on Trent: Trentham.

Riddell, S. (1992) *Gender and the Politics of the Curriculum*, London: Routledge.

Rogers, R. (1986) (ed.) *Education and Social Class*, Lewes: Falmer Press.

Rolfe, H. (1999) *Gender and Equality in the Careers Service*, Manchester: Equal Opportunities Commission.

Scaife, J. (1998) 'Science education for all?', in Clark, A. and Millard, E. (eds), *Gender in the Secondary Curriculum*, London: Routledge.

Segal, L. (1987) *Is the Future Female?* London: Virago.

Staffordshire LEA (1997) *Guidelines*, Stafford: Staffordshire LEA.

Technology Colleges Trust (1995) *Royal College of Art Schools Technology Project*, London: Hodder and Stoughton.

Thomas, K. (1990) *Gender and Subject in Higher Education*, Buckingham: Open University Press.

Walkerdine, V. (1986) 'The family and the school', in Wilkinson, S. (ed.), *Feminist Social Psychology*, Buckingham: Open University Press.

Weiner, G. (1985) *Just a Bunch of Girls: Feminist Approaches to Schooling*, Buckingham: Open University Press.

Whyte, J. (1986) *Girls into Science and Technology*, London: Routledge.

Withey, D. (2000) *Opportunities for Gender Equality in Design and Technology: An Evaluation of the Newley Secondary Schools Initiative*, unpublished PhD thesis, Manchester Metropolitan University, Manchester.

Wilkinson, S. (1986) (ed.) *Feminist Social Psychology*, Buckingham: Open University Press.

Willis, P. (1977) *Learning to Labour*, London: Methuen.

Yates, L. (1985) 'Is "girl-friendly schooling" really what girls need?', in Whyte J., Deem, R., Kant, L. and Cruickshank, M. (eds), *Girl-friendly Schooling*, London: Routledge.

Further reading

Atkinson, S. (1995) 'Approaches to designing at key stage 4', in Smith, J. (ed.), *IDATER 95: International Conference on Design and Technology Educational Research and Curriculum Development*, Loughborough: Loughborough University of Technology, pp. 36–47.

Attfield, J. and Kirkham, P. (1995) (eds) *A View from the Interior: Women and Design*, London: Women's Press.

Clark, A. and Millard, E. (1998) *Gender in the Secondary Curriculum: Balancing the Books*, London: Routledge.

Gilligan, C. (1982) *In a Different Voice*, Cambridge, MA: Harvard University Press.

Kimbell, R., Stables, K. and Green, R. (1996) *Understanding Practice in Design and Technology*, Buckingham: Open University Press.

Lawler, T. (1999) 'Exposing the gender effects of design and technology project work by comparing strategies for presenting and managing pupils' work', in Roberts, P.H. and Norman, E.W.L. (eds), *IDATER 99: International Conference on Design and Technology Educational Research and Curriculum Development*, Loughborough University of Technology, Loughborough, pp. 130–7.

Measor, L. and Sikes, P. (1992) *Gender and Schools*, London: Cassell.

Riggs, A. (1998) 'Gender and technology education', in Banks, F. (ed.), *Teaching Technology*, Buckingham: Open University Press.

Whyld, J. (1983) (ed.) *Sexism in the Secondary Curriculum*, London: Harper and Row.

Whyte, J., Deem, R., Kant, L. and Cruickshank, M. (1985) (eds) *Girl-friendly Schooling*, London: Routledge.

Wilkinson, S., Farrell, A. and Grant, M. (1992) *Design and Technology in Genderwatch!*, Cambridge: Cambridge University Press.

Internet source

The Equal Opportunities website has free downloads of many of its research reports at http://www.eoc.org.uk

Part 4

Issues beyond the school

11 What has ethics to do with design and technology education?

Steve Keirl

Introduction

I believe that a high-quality design and technology education is essential for all school pupils no matter where in the world they might be. Having said 'all', this chapter is written for teachers of pupils of all ages – from the early years in which play, imagination and development of 'self' are the building blocks for the years ahead; through the primary years, in which an integrated curriculum and growth in skills and environmental awareness are valued; into the secondary years, in which pathways to future education and employment begin to emerge.

This chapter focuses on the *general education* of pupils. Of course, there are two senses in which an education might be 'general'. First, it is concerned with the compulsory years of schooling, those years concerned with the education of all pupils in their preparation for life as citizens in society. This is not to say that the post-compulsory years and the activities conducted therein are not considered – indeed they are highly significant. The chapter is written with the many pathways that are available to post-compulsory school pupils very much in mind. Second, although we teach in a specialised field called design and technology, we continuously contribute within that field to the general education of all pupils – their literacy, thinking capacities, socialisation, communication skills and so on. Thus, we, as design and technology teachers, contribute to our pupils' education in design and technology *per se*; to their education for life in society, even beyond the school years; and, between these two, to their education as future users and creators of designed and technological products.

So just what has ethics to do with design and technology? There are perhaps two interpretations of this question. First, is 'design and technology' a *subject*, a lump of curriculum content that is devoid of, separate from, or alien to, ethics? Second, is the *practice* of teaching design and technology devoid of ethics – can we teach it in a values-free or 'neutral' way? To conclude my question-asking, teasing-out of the key issues, I offer another fundamental, and ambiguous, question – why teach design and technology? Thus, why does our curriculum include something called 'design and technology'? Alternatively, why do *you* personally teach design and technology? Is it, like Everest, 'because it's there'? Is it because you like it? Is it because you believe in it? As one answers such questions one is formulating a *rationale* for one's work as a professional design and technology educator. Is there a place for ethics in this rationale?

Ethics

Interests in ethics have fuelled philosophical discourse for millennia and, although ethics dropped somewhat from public discourse during the 1970s and 1980s, it has regained some of its currency of late. This is hardly surprising, given the technological, economic and environmental developments that have occurred over those decades. It is probably true to say that the mentioning of 'ethics' to many people suggests an outdated, even inappropriate, use of language, and though we might believe that ethics is important, it is nevertheless something which is neither easy to articulate nor seems readily applicable to the 'real world'. By this last understanding, I mean either that it is seen as 'out of touch' – with which philosophers are generally charged – or, that those very technological innovations (or, more subtly, their consequences) happen faster than it is possible for the necessary associated ethical discourse to develop. Just because ethics has traditionally been, and will continue to be, an area of philosophical contestation, does not mean that it cannot manifest itself as practical and personal action – of which, more below.

Any study of ethics inevitably embraces associated terms, such as morality, goodness, right and wrong, obligation, ideals and values, and each warrants analysis of its meaning and role in ethical discourse. Although this chapter cannot entertain more than the briefest of reviews of this philosophical area, it would be unreasonable to proceed without some acknowledgement of the field.

Slote (1995: 591–5) contends that perhaps the '… major problem… of moral philosophy… is coming up with a rationally defensible theory of right and wrong action', and he identifies four current dominant basic views or theories:

- Utilitarianism, which has always been controversial, wherein the right action is understood in terms of human good, pleasure and satisfaction of desire. Any means can be justified by a good enough end.
- Kantianism, which contrasts with utilitarianism in arguing that moral rightness is a matter of consistent and rational behaviour, less a matter of happiness than duty.
- Intuitionism, or common-sensism, which counters the above views in arguing that there can be no unifying account of moral obligation. The only general moral principles are prima facie ones such as 'it is prima facie wrong to harm others'.
- Virtue ethics, which traces its roots to the Ancient Greeks and notions of 'situational sensitivity', how we should 'be', and draws upon inner traits (virtues) rather than being referenced to some external rule system.

Of course, the field of ethics is much more extensive, subtle and fascinating than this. Humanist, existentialist, post-modern theory – all contribute, and alternative perspectives to the philosophical emerge through religious, race, gender and class agendas. Inasmuch as anyone may be interested in the quality of our existence and, indeed, of our coexistence, then we are faced with ethical questions and, thus, some degree of engagement with ethical discourse.

To the assertion that philosophical approaches may be out of touch with the real world comes a significant refutation from Singer (1993), whose text is squarely placed among the issues of today and the future. Singer is concerned about the quality of life issues, which abound today, and argues that by living in an ethically reflective way it is possible to defeat the individually and collectively self-defeating goals of self-interest. He contends that:

> Ethics is practical, or it is not really ethical. If it is no good in practice, it is no good in theory either. Getting rid of the idea that an ethical life must consist of absolute obedience to some short and simple set of moral rules makes it easier to avoid the trap of an unworkable ethic. An understanding of ethics that allows us to take into account the special circumstances in which we find ourselves is already a major step towards attaining an ethics that we really can use to guide our lives.
>
> (Singer 1993: 204)

This 'practical' view is well supported. Warnock (1978: 135) concluded her text noting that ethics since the 1960s had become 'a practical subject' and inferred that a new language of ethics was in the process of being developed. Her recent (1998) text articulates clearly her practical focus on moral philosophy.

So it is that ethics is seen as being far from 'out of touch' and that it has a place in life and work. As Singer puts it:

> I share Parfit's (1984; see references) view, that in the advancement of ethics lies the possibility of a new and more hopeful turn in world history; but it must be an advancement, not only in ethical theory, but also in ethical practice.
>
> (Singer 1993: 20)

Thus, philosophers themselves are positive about the capacity of ethics to play a central role in human enterprise and development in the coming years. This calls for a blend of *reflection* and *action*.

What might be a 'good' design and technology curriculum?

For reasons both political and philosophical, 'good' is not necessarily a *good* adjective to use for such an emergent and dynamic field of education. Design and technology is currently exposed to the agendas of a variety of stakeholders (of whom, more below) and thus the political tensions which can exist for the profession at both systems and school levels. To use the phrase 'good design and technology' is, at best, to beg some questions and, at worst, to provoke impassioned argument.

It is important to recognise the value judgements that can come with the use of the word 'good', and it is particularly useful to draw on the following discussion from the ethics literature. This example is drawn from Frankena's (1973: 82) account of the uses of 'good', in which he distinguishes between *moral values*, that is things which he contends are good on moral grounds, and *non-moral values*, which he illustrates with sub-categories. Frankena puts it thus:

> … one may commend a thing or say it is good on various grounds. If the thing is a person, motive, intention, deed, or trait of character, one may commend it on moral grounds; then, one is using 'good' in the moral sense… One may also commend something on nonmoral grounds, and then one may apply the term 'good' to all sorts of things, not just to persons and their acts or dispositions.
>
> (Frankena 1973: 81)

He distinguishes six sub-categories of the use of 'good' on non-moral grounds. I make use of five of these here and offer (in brackets) what I perceive to be examples of design and technology education for each:

1   Utility values: things which are good because of their usefulness for some purpose, for example a stick may be a good lever. (Some skills gained may be useful for maintaining a dwelling.)
2   Extrinsic values: things that are good because they are a means to what is good, for example going to the dentist twice a year is a good thing to do. (Design and technology education may lead to a career.)
3   Inherent values: things that are good because the experience of contemplating them is good or rewarding in itself, for example a good work of art which, because of its goodness, brings pleasure. (The appreciation which can be gained from a genuinely good product – here, I have deliberately avoided clarification of the nature of the appreciation and of the identity of the maker.)
4   Intrinsic values: things that are good in themselves, or good because of their own intrinsic properties, for example learning. (This matches Layton's (1994) last stakeholder category of liberal educators, below.)
5   Contributory values: things that are good because they contribute to the intrinsically good life, or are parts of it. Thus they may be the means to achieving a good life, for example earning money or gaining knowledge may, initially, be the means to attaining happiness. (Aspects of learning within design and technology may be engaged in by pupils as a means to realising their final design. The intrinsic value of design skills may not be apparent to pupils, however the contributory value of these to a successful outcome may be apparent.)

Having some awareness of how we use the word 'good' is critical, but the terms 'design' and 'technology' are quite disputable too and are certainly never neutral. As with the case for 'ethics', space does not allow exploration of these terms in depth, however it is appropriate to note some of their central characteristics and problems.

Design

'In English the word design can mean many things.' (Design Council 1991: 3). The Council, presenting its case for design in education, recognises the curricular difficulties for design as it had neither an established subject base nor the academic status of some other subjects. Today the word frequently occurs in curricula, for example product design, industrial design, design and technology, engineering design, design awareness, art and design. Whereas definitions are available in some educational texts or documents, they are noticeably absent from others.

Mayall (1979) gives a careful and educationally very useful breakdown of ten principles of design in his book. The impressive clarity of the principles and their distinct relationships, set apart from, say, art and science in education, demonstrate the powerful case for design in schools. Implicit in Mayall's analysis lie the ethical issues concerned with 'designing' in professional contexts such as engineering and architecture.

In some countries, as far as design and technology education is concerned, design may be viewed as a distinct curriculum activity, as a partner with technology, or as an educational tool within technology. Whatever its position or purpose, it is prone to interpretation and remains 'under tension from aesthetic and technological formulations' (Donnelly and Jenkins 1992: 47). Nonetheless, 'design' is now significantly and centrally established as a part of technology education in curriculum policies across the world (Design Council 1992; AEC 1994a; 1994b; Layton 1994; Ministry of Education 1995).

Technology

In common with 'design', 'technology' has societal, industrial and educational derivatives and the resulting understandings are many and varied. Definitions abound and few are mutually compatible. For example, the extent of the field for technology in Australian schools is summarised by the Australian Education Council (AEC) thus:

> Technology in the school curriculum combines theory and practice. It includes much that is scientific, ethical, mathematical, graphical, cultural, aesthetic and historical. It explores the synthesis of ideas and practices, and the effects of technology on societies and environments.
>
> ... The process of designing, making and appraising is central to technology. It is a dynamic process whose elements overlap and have no set sequence. As the elements interact and combine they generate ideas which can be converted into action.
>
> (AEC 1994b: 2)

Ethics, technology and design are all dynamic and contested terms, and before moving to argue the interwoven nature of ethics–design–technology issues in education, it is necessary to offer something of the global and societal context from which much ethical concern arises today. The extent of the available literature is huge and it derives from many fields. Its clarity and richness cannot be ignored when considering the education of future generations.

Global and societal concerns

Several famous names come to mind when one seeks to portray global concerns. These people have in common a capacity to have provided critiques of our own mass understandings (those we collectively hold from within our 'Western' perspective) of the cultural, economic, technological and political world beyond. Toffler (1971), Schumacher (1973), Papanek (1974), Singer (1993) and Suzuki (1997) have all articulated global concerns for increasing numbers of people who are realising their cultural, economic, technological and political inter-connectedness and interdependence.

The degree to which authors' values are explicit varies. As Roy has argued:

> In a field such as politics and technology it is worth making a distinction between those books written by people who display a clear commitment to a particular political viewpoint or set of values and those written by people whose commitment is less apparent…
>
> (Roy 1977: 330)

It is time to turn to a range of observations about technology. Schumacher (1973), whilst discussing technology, posits:

> It tumbles from crisis to crisis; on all sides there are prophecies of disaster and, indeed, visible signs of breakdown.

> If that which has been shaped by technology, and continues to be so shaped, looks sick, it might be wise to have a look at technology itself. If technology is felt to be becoming more and more inhuman, we might do well to consider whether it is possible to have something better – a technology with a human face.
>
> (Schumacher 1973: 122)

Schumacher's text concerns itself with 'economics as if people mattered' and his global perspective links many facets of human endeavour, technology being just one. Noble's (1977) thesis, equally, links technological production with capitalism, arguing that the 'drive' which propels technological determinism (to which I return below) comes, in large part, from the market-driven economies of the world. These authors challenge the economic systems, to which they see technology as integral, on ethical grounds.

Similarly, in discussing globalization, Redclift and Benton (1994), who develop their challenge to technological determinism and call for careful examination of *consequences* of economic systems which remain solely quantitative, look for qualitative aspects in the global environment. Indeed, they articulate technology as one of four dimensions of cultural relations. Meanwhile, the technological impact on social relations is documented by Siraj-Blatchford and Patel (1995) when they describe:

> The so-called 'Green Revolution', which has meant high yield varieties of grain have made farmers dependent upon provision of seeds, pesticides and fertiliser, provides a good example of technological imperialism and shows how the consumer sometimes has no free choice, and how technologies can change social relations. It has impoverished small peasant farmers and turned them into landless labourers who are often unable to afford to buy the product themselves.
>
> (Siraj-Blatchford and Patel 1995: 26)

Of course in the few years since this observation we have become increasingly aware of two major, ethically contentious, developments. First, there are governments today issuing patent rights (sometimes granted to themselves) over the plant and human genes of other peoples, as in the case of the US government and the DNA of a Papua New Guinean. 'The US government has granted itself exclusive rights over a foreign citizen's cell line' (Penenberg 1996: 44–50). Second, with regard to plant material, sterilisation is now established practice to maximise profits and control markets. Genetically modified organisms (GMOs) are rapidly gaining attention – notably because of the 'terminator technology' to which Monsanto will own the rights in scores of countries. In this technique, a transgene is introduced which allows plants to grow normally and produce a harvest but, because the grain is biologically sterile, farmers must buy new, patented seed annually. It would seem that Monsanto is to become the Microsoft of biotechnology 'providing the proprietary "operating systems" ... that will manage the new generation of plants' (Berlan and Lewontin 1999). Not only farmers, but nations, are in danger of becoming dependent on transnationally controlled technologies which govern the market and suppress genetic diversity.

The notion of technological imperialism is embraced too by earlier writers. In their discussion of the possibilities and limitations of 'alternative technology', Entemann *et al.* (1977) identify the need for determining 'new values and priorities' but argue that this is not 'merely a matter of moral argument'. They contend that it is political and economic too. So, for a country which may be a candidate for alternative technology, the differential value systems of respective cultures may be an issue, as exemplified by Toffler (1971):

> ... a tacit technological policy... [can be]... a brutally unsophisticated policy, and as a result all kinds of new machines and processes are spewed into the society without regard for their secondary or long-range effects.
>
> (Toffler 1971: 391)

In 1991, Jonas argued that:

> ... form and matter of technology alike enter into the dimension of ethics. The questions raised for ethics by the objects of technology are defined by the major areas of their impact and thus fall into such fields of knowledge as ecology... demography, economics, biomedical and behavioural sciences (even the psychology of mind pollution by television)
>
> (Jonas 1991: 115)

When Redclift and Benton (1994: 3) said: 'the preoccupation of economics with wealth-creation, efficiency in production, and the satisfaction of human *wants* [my emphasis] suggests the inescapability of a confrontation with the material conditions and setting of economic activity', they were careful not to say *needs*. The ethics embedded in 'quality of life' issues stemming from technology and its products are commonly discussed. As Montgomery (1974) put it:

> Tocqueville thought that the American concern with technology meant the equation of 'good' with 'goods' and social critics have continued to object to the elevation of the machine to eminence as the symbol of progress and the source of national virtue.
>
> (Montgomery 1974: 17)

Turnbull (1988), a merchant banker, argues ethically when he draws together technology, Australian society and quality of life with his view for the next century:

> Quite obviously there is a limit to the amount of goods and services individuals can or want to consume...
>
> ... the technology of the future in Australia will need to be increasingly concerned with improving the quality of life rather than living standards. Individual freedoms and choice are aspects of the quality of life. These aspects can be profoundly influenced by the ownership, control, management and type of technology.
>
> (Turnbull 1988: 280)

The incarnation of products for 'consumption' is only one part of the picture, as the 'after use' aspect of designed products is a matter of concern for many people. The ethical aspects of designing are articulated by Mayall (1979) and Whiteley (1993), both of whom identify the need for designers' values to match clients' values in the design-manifestation process. However, the bigger picture raises questions of (designed) obsolescence, disposability and environmental degradation. Almost three decades ago, Toffler (1971) made succinct observations about the 'throw-away society' and argued the ethical case for future societies by identifying key questions which would need carefully thought-through answers. At about the same time Papanek (1974) noted that:

We know that the twin concepts of 'designed aesthetics' and 'designed obsolescence' are heavily interrelated, and that this connection becomes very apparent both in basic research and in the manufacturing process… Today we are taught that ageing (be it of products or individuals) is subtly wrong.

(Papanek 1974: 235–7)

As one reflects on technology and the comments made by writers on its manifestations and effects, it would seem that hardly a technological act or product can occur without there being an associated ethical connection. This view is not shared by some, for example those who consider technology to be 'neutral' and who argue that it is to the *users* of technology that the ethics should apply. Holders of this view separate the product from the act of using it.

From the discourse of commonality and difference between science and technology, one key factor which has emerged has been the essential characteristic of 'purpose' in technological activity, that is, the design or intention which is behind the technological act (Black and Harrison 1994; Cardwell 1994; Mitcham 1994; Gardner 1995). It is technology as 'action' which adds further ethical dimensions for the field. It is clearly no longer acceptable to operate within the solely *manufacturing* phase of activity and apply the classic technological criterion of success: 'does it work?' Questions of consequence are increasingly important too. Thus one might ask: 'What are the *intentions* of the designer and, in turn, our roles as consumers or purchasers of these products and systems (Whiteley 1993; Keirl 1997a; 1997b). So the ethical issues might be explored on a technology continuum of intention–design–manifestation–application– (and possibly) – consequence (though there are consequences at each stage).

However, it is not simply a matter of 'the design' or 'the technology' alone. The ways in which knowledge of this field is constructed and applied must be understood. The prevalence of positivist and technicist approaches to technology is a major concern for feminist authors who have written about the alienation of women by, and through, technology (Cockburn 1991; Wajcman 1993; 1994; Weiner 1994). Grant writes of the disenfranchisement of 'women from the politics of technology' (Grant 1983: 217) and Apple (1992: 110) talks of the 'feminization of poverty'; Whiteley (1993) embraces the ethics of green design, critiques of patriarchy and the feminist criticisms of the positioning of women in society by market-led design and designers.

One can also explore the uses of technologies for purposes that they might not have been originally designed. Although it is common now to use the domestic telephone for mutual surveillance, the developments at (inter)national levels continue apace. The issue of 'dataveillance' is discussed by Nixon (1996) and he notes how systemic is the surveillance of citizens through their data-based transactions – purchasing, banking, internet use, telephone, social and political membership – and through video monitoring. Riviere (1999) demonstrates that the extent and sophistication of *non*-military surveillance is now extreme. There is a requirement in many countries that 'every telecommunications operator… install a permanent listening "interface" ' in phones – not only to 'listen' but also to provide number, caller *and location* (if mobile) data. Meanwhile, of the twenty-one-plus US surveillance satellites currently in use, three of the latest have a resolution of just 12 cm.

Have we the will…?

The concept of determinism, though having its roots in philosophy (and not being highly regarded in ethical discourse, at least not by Raphael (1981) or Warnock (1998)), has been adapted and applied to technology. The notion is given currency by those who maintain that the flow of new technologies and their accompanying change are 'all inevitable'. Thus, one cannot change or challenge technology's course and one should 'go with the flow'. There is a strong undercurrent which supports this view, whether it stems from a feeling of powerlessness on the part of individuals or is actively driven by those with particular agendas, for example businesses promoting their products or governments fearing a loss of 'competitive edge'. The feeling of being 'left behind' or 'not up with the times' manifests itself at every level from the individual to the national. Such thoughts and feelings help sanction the concept of 'technological determinism'.

The question here is whether we actually do have the power, or the will, individually or collectively, to determine what technology influences and does. Similarly, the whole question of 'choice' and whether we actually have such a *freedom* in the democratic sense, or even in the practices of design or of education, is interwoven with this concept. Political solutions remain problematic too because, as Cardwell (1994) points out, any government which intervened to slow or stop the spread of a technology which people wanted (on, for example, the grounds that it was actually a *want* and not a *need*) would be deemed by those people to be authoritarian. As Beynon and Mackay (1992) say:

> Technological determinism diverts attention from such questions as the relationship of technology to human need. Implicit in technological determinism is that there is no choice about the technology we have.
>
> (Beynon and Mackay 1992: 12)

On a matter which many would argue to be a 'quality of life' issue, it is appropriate to make mention of an ontological facet of technological practice which, whilst not directly an ethical matter, has apparent ethical connections. Over 100 years ago William Morris gave a critique of the dehumanising nature of some work and work situations. He was particularly concerned with those involved in the creation of products with hand and machine. He valued people and the work they did, indeed, he valued work of which people themselves could be proud (Morton 1979). A century later, Graves (1986), Apple (1992) and Roszak (1996) provide salient cautions about the deskilling and depersonalising nature of computers in the context of current economic policies. Meanwhile, Fry (1992) offers an excellent perspective of our very separation *from* technology, in a craft sense, which contributes to a dehumanising of our 'selves'. Inasmuch as creating, bringing into being, and producing are personally fulfilling, then they must play a part in our very being and existence. This deeper personal, even spiritual, dimension to technological practice is so often absent from the agendas of those who would dictate the field. This absence must, too, constitute an ethical concern.

It might be possible to summarise this section on a note of doom and pessimism. However, this is not an option I wish to entertain as it would be neither professionally defensible nor very helpful. The majority of the authors cited offer cautionary tales and write with positive views of the future which are, of course, premised on positive actions for the future. These matters of quality of life for *all* people cannot be tackled without wisdom and commitment and there can be no doubt that educators have a key role to play. Singer urges that 'narrow self-interest' not be considered in its limited sense of personal pleasure or individual satisfaction, seeing these as self-defeating for both individuals and society generally. Rather, he argues the case for 'enlightened self-interest'. He considers the seeming meaninglessness of life – whether perceived by existentialists or by disillusioned adolescents – and suggests:

> Here ethics offer a solution. An ethical life is one in which we identify ourselves with other, larger, goals, thereby giving meaning to our lives. The view that there is harmony between ethics and enlightened self-interest is an ancient one, now often scorned. Cynicism is more fashionable than idealism. But such hopes are not groundless, and there are substantial elements of truth in the ancient view that an ethically reflective life is also a good life for the person leading it. Never has it been so urgent that the reasons for accepting this view should be widely understood.
>
> (Singer 1997: 30)

Having sought to demonstrate the potential interwoven nature of ethics and design and technology it is time to turn to schools and our own professional practice.

Who decides what is design and technology curriculum?

I preface this section by saying that the organisation of education within a democracy is neither a straightforward matter nor are its problems and challenges new. There are many ethical and political issues which are contestable and these contestations are mirrored within sections of curriculum such as design and technology . In her exploration of 'Education, Democracy and the Public Interest', White (1973) points out that:

> There is at least *one* policy which *must* be in the public interest in a democracy. This [policy] is an appropriate education for a democracy.
>
> (White 1973: 237)

It is possible to value not just White's conclusion that a 'must' for the public interest in a democracy is 'an appropriate education for a democracy', but also her argument that the determination of what might constitute that 'appropriate education' must not be left to 'experts' '... to be worked out much as the value of the gross national product is calculated' (White 1973: 223). As public interest policies are about things that the public *ought* to have, White argues that they are, therefore, by and large, value judgements. Thus, moral judgements must be seen to be fundamental to the determination of the core policy (education) of a democracy. It turn, moral judgements call for moral arguments, and so ethics forms the basis for determination of education for, and within, a democracy.

The centrality of ethics to good design and technology education

Given that the field of technology is so pervasive, it is hardly surprising that there are multiple interests in its delivery in schools. A whole range of tensions and competing agendas becomes clear when one examines the literature, and I have argued (Keirl 1999b) that professional design and technology educators have a significant role to play in determining a high-quality curriculum for our field. What, then, are the values on which the following 'actors' in our 'curriculum drama' are based? Taking Layton's (1994) theatrical metaphor, used in reporting the landmark international research study by the United Nations Educational, Scientific and Cultural Organization (UNESCO) of the emergent worldwide phenomenon of technology education, he identified the following key stakeholders:

- *Economic instrumentalists,* whose concerns lie with national economic competitiveness and wealth creation, and for whom design and technology education and vocational education become almost synonymous.
- *Professional technologists and engineers,* who often see design and technology education as contributing to national economic growth and also seek to shape it to enhance the professional standing of their field.
- *Sustainable developers,* who seek to ensure the compatibility of economic growth and environmental protection.
- *Girls and women,* whose representation across the field of design and technology education remains minimal, yet towards whom so much technological development, in the product and systems sense, is directed.
- *Defenders of participatory democracy,* who identify the empowering dimension of design and technology education as being a necessary safeguard against the dominance of a technocratic elite. The burden being placed on technology education in relation to democratic decision making in the future is formidable.
- *Liberal educators,* who laud the intrinsic merit of design and technology education; they argue that technological activity involves a distinctive form of cognition, which is unique and irreducible. As such, all children should have access to it as a matter of right and in order to develop their full human potential.

By taking each group in turn, not only might we see the defensible case for each (though, undoubtedly, there will be potential differences between our own personal and professional values and one or more of these 'actors') but we can also witness the tensions which exist for us in trying to deliver 'good' design and technology. As each may have a legitimate claim to the curriculum, who will arbitrate the competing claims and how?

The point is that, while each group of 'actors' will ultimately argue that theirs is the worthy claim, any claim to *worthiness* must ultimately draw upon judgements of value and upon moral argument. As some of these claimants have the potential to be exclusive of others, there is the question of whether all six can be addressed within the general education years. When one reflects on Frankena's analysis of the uses of 'good' and which senses of the word may be legitimately applied to each claim then it is possible to begin detecting the relative moral, and/or non-moral, strengths of each one.

Conclusion

Curriculum challenges are ethical challenges

In introducing this chapter a few questions were posed. The question in the title had, it was suggested, two interpretations. First, is design and technology alien to, or devoid of, ethics? Well, possibly it could be, if one were just to teach skills in some teacher-centred way without giving pupils any empowerment through designing or decision making. Even then, some sort of values system has decided that it be a skills-based curriculum – which raises the further question of who decides which skills. Whether this is ethically defensible may warrant discussion. Second, and regardless of whether the content of the subject be deemed 'ethics free', is the practice of teaching design and technology devoid of ethics – could we teach it in a values-free or neutral way? This might be quite a challenge.

There are, however, other ways to develop ethical discourse. Perhaps we ought to acknowledge that technology is values-rich, that all technologies have undesirable attributes and that technological practice is so central to our very existence that ethical questions must come as part and parcel of the whole business. To illustrate new ways of exploring our curriculum and teaching I shall take one example. There has been a steady flow of writing on the topic of 'technological literacy' over the last twenty years (for a brief overview, see Keirl 1999a) and authors who critique (technological) literacy discourses now link ethics, politics and technology. As Layton puts it:

> School technology... is subject to a range of competing influences and the politics of technological literacy – who creates and controls the meanings of the phrase, how the imposition of meaning is attempted – is a central concern of technology education today.
>
> (Layton 1994: 13)

Luke (1992) elaborates on 'cultural' and 'functional' literacy (for an elite and for the masses respectively, and constructed to meet political agendas), whereas

Apple (1992) is unequivocal in making the political picture clear, pointing to the marginalisation of democratic curricula and teacher autonomy by economic and ideological pressures. Beynon (1992), citing Albury and Schwartz, gives a critique of technological literacy and uses their work to explore some of the roots of the current position. They state:

> Because Science and Technology were mythologised by the Victorians as intrinsically progressive we have been accultured into not interrogating them as to their moral justification and actual social usefulness.
>
> (Albury & Schwartz in Beynon 1992: 15)

Thus we might construct technological literacy not as a mere functional 'skilling for the workplace' but, rather, in a rich and critical format that supports the very interrogation of design, technology, and the curriculum itself by staff and pupils alike.

Some would argue that a values–morals–ethics approach is not the *core* business of present-day design and technology educators and that this should be conducted at the periphery of the subject. Meanwhile, others might contend that it is not the business of design and technology educators at all but rests with social studies. Olson (1997) rebuts this notion and cites Barnett, who said:

> … an arrangement by which responsibility for practical capability rested with Technology, and for critical awareness with subjects such as Social Studies, History or Religious Education i.e. where values had been driven into exile from out of Technology, would be undesirable. This would tend to confirm Technology as a ghetto for ingenious, specialist tinkerers, and the Humanities as the natural home for anti-technologists.
>
> (Barnett, cited in Olson 1997: 388)

Indeed, as Olson concludes:

> We have to understand what human welfare is. This is the moral horizon for technology which cannot be set aside, neither in the world, nor in education.
>
> (Olson 1997: 89)

The Design Council offers an explicit agenda for exploring underlying values from a different perspective, when, in arguing the centrality of design-related activity to general education, it says:

> Design decision-making cannot and does not operate in a vacuum. Every decision effects in some way a social preference or value, and an economic priority. Design can explore and reflect the underlying values which go towards the way societies organise their environments, communications, and patterns of production and consumption…

However the questioning of existing ideas which form part of many design projects, can sometimes lead to challenging and uncomfortable questions being asked...

(Design Council 1992: 9)

Questions to consider

So one might conclude with another of the questions posed in the introduction:

1 Why teach design and technology? Is it there as part of a democratic curriculum for a democratic society founded on ethical principles? Or, is it there simply for a couple of non-moral values, to meet the perceived needs (wants?) of pupil or teacher, or one of the 'curriculum actors'?

Perhaps the biggest question on which both the student and practising teacher might reflect:

2 Why *do* you teach design and technology? What is your ethical rationale for your professional work and curriculum delivery as a design and technology educator?

References

AEC (Australian Education Council) (1994a) *A Statement on Technology for Australian Schools*, Carlton: Curriculum Corporation.

AEC (1994b) *Technology – a Curriculum Profile for Australian Schools*, Carlton: Curriculum Corporation.

Apple, M. (1992) 'Is the new technology part of the solution or part of the problem in education?', in Beynon, J. and Mackay, H. (eds), *Technological Literacy and the Curriculum*, London: Falmer Press, pp. 105–24.

Berlan, J.-P. and Lewotin, S.C. (1999) 'Menace of the genetic-industrial complex', *Le Monde Diplomatique* Jan: 8–9.

Beynon, J. (1992) 'Introduction: learning to read technology', in Beynon, J. and Mackay, H. (eds), *Technological Literacy and the Curriculum*, London: Falmer Press, pp. 1–37.

Beynon, J. and Mackay, H. (1992) (eds) *Technological Literacy and the Curriculum*, London: Falmer Press.

Black, P. and Harrison, G. (1994) 'Technological capability', in Banks, F. (ed.), *Teaching Technology*, London: Routledge, pp. 13–19.

Cardwell, D. (1994) *The Fontana History of Technology*, London: Fontana.

Cockburn, C. (1991) 'The gendering of technology', in Mackay, H., Young, M. and Beynon, J. (eds), *Understanding Technology in Education*, London: Falmer Press, pp. 41–65.

Design Council (1991) *Design Education at Secondary Level*, London: The Design Council.

Design Council (1992) *Design Focus in Schools*, London: The Design Council.

Donnelly, J.F. and Jenkins, E.W. (1992) *GCSE Technology: Some Precursors and Issues*, Occasional Paper No. 4, University of Leeds School of Education, Leeds, pp. 1–68.

Entemann, E., Gordon, F., Greeley, K., Valdes, R. and Ward, P. (eds) (1977) 'Alternative technology: possibilities and limitations', in Boyle, G., Elliott, D. and Roy, R. (eds), *The Politics of Technology*, London: Longman, pp. 319–28.

Frankena, W. (1973) *Ethics*, Englewood Cliffs, NJ: Prentice-Hall.

Fry, T. (1992) 'Green hands against dead knowledge', in Noris, I. (ed.), *Craft in Society, An Anthology of Perspectives*, South Fremantle, WA: Fremantle Arts Centre Press, pp. 254–68.

Gardner, P. (1995) 'The relationship between technology and science: some historical and philosophical reflections', in *International Journal of Technology and Design*, **5**: 1–33.

Grant, M. (1983) 'Craft, design and technology', in Whyld, J. (ed.), *Sexism in the Secondary Curriculum*, London: Harper and Row, pp. 216–27.

Graves, J. (1986) *Liberating Technology: Steps towards a Benevolent Society*, London: Peter Owen.

Jonas, H. (1991) 'Towards a philosophy of technology', in Thompson, W. (ed.), *Controlling Technology*, Buffalo, NY: Prometheus Books, pp. 98–119.

Keirl, S. (1997a) 'We are what we use', in *Proceedings of the Second Biennial Conference of the Home Economics Institute of Australia (HEIA)*, Macquarie, ACT: HEIA, April 1997, pp. 125–30.

Keirl, S. (1997b) 'Critical practice in design and technology education: yarning or weaving?', *Design and Education*, **7** (1): 3–13.

Keirl, S. (1999a) 'Determining Technology Education: knowing the orthodoxies, the interests, and the potential', in Johnson, B. and Reid, A. (eds), *Contesting the Curriculum*, Sydney: Social Science Press, pp. 74–89.

Keirl, S. (1999b) 'The fruits of technological literacy: wild varieties or crops of mass production', in Benson, C. and Till, W. (eds), *Proceedings of Second International Primary Design and Technology Conference*, Birmingham University of Central England, Birmingham, pp. 72–7.

Layton, D. (1994) (ed.) *Innovations in Science and Technology Education*, Vol. V, Paris: UNESCO.

Luke, A. (1992) 'Literacy and work in "new times" ', *Open Letter*, **3** (1): 3–15.

Mayall, W.H. (1979) *Principles in Design*, London: Design Council.

Ministry of Education (1995) *Technology in the New Zealand Curriculum*, Wellington: Ministry of Education.

Mitcham, C. (1994) *Thinking Through Technology: The Path between Engineering and Philosophy*, Chicago: University of Chicago Press.

Montgomery, J.D. (1974) *Technology and Civic Life: Making and Implementing Development Decisions*, Cambridge, MA: The MIT Press.

Morton, A.L. (1979) *Political Writings of William Morris*, London: Lawrence & Wishart.

Nixon, M. (1996) 'Dataveilance', *22.C Scanning the Future* **2**: 30–6.

Noble, D.F. (1977) *America by Design: Science, Technology and the rise of Corporate Capitalism*, Oxford: Oxford University Press.

Olson, J. (1997) 'OP-ED: Technology in the school curriculum: the moral dimension of making things', *Journal of Curriculum Studies*, **29** (4): 383–90.

Papanek, V. (1974) *Design for the Real World: Human Ecology and Social Change*, St. Albans: Paladin.

Parfit, D. (1984) *Reasons and Persons*, Oxford: Clarendon Press.

Penenberg, A. (1996) 'Gene piracy', *21.C Scanning the Future* **2**: 44–50.

Raphael, D.D., (1981) *Moral Philosophy*, Oxford: Oxford University Press.

Redclift, M. and Benton, T. (1994) *Social Theory and the Global Environment*, London: Routledge.

Riviere, P. (1999) 'How the United States spies on us all', *Le Monde Diplomatique*, Jan: 2–3.

Roszak, T., (1996) 'Dumbing us down', *New Internationalist*, **285** (Dec.): pp. 12–15.

Roy. R. (1977) 'A guide to the literature', in Boyle, G., Elliott, D. and Roy, R. (eds), *The Politics of Technology*, London: Longman, pp. 330–4.

Schumacher, E.F. (1973) *Small is Beautiful*, London: Abacus.

Singer, P. (1993) *How are we to Live? Ethics in an Age of Self-interest*, Port Melbourne: Mandarin.

Singer, P. (1997) 'The drowning child and the expanding circle', *New Internationalist,* **289** (Apr.): pp. 28–30.

Siraj-Blatchford, J. and Patel, L. (1995) 'Understanding environmental education for the primary classroom', in Siraj-Blatchford, J. and Siraj-Blatchford, I. (eds), *Educating the Whole Child: Cross-curricular Skills, Themes and Dimensions*, Buckingham: Open University Press, pp. 115–33.

Slote, M. (1995) 'Problems of moral philosophy', in Honderich, T. (ed.), *The Oxford Companion to Philosophy*, Oxford: Oxford University Press, pp. 591–5.

Suzuki, D. (1997) *The Sacred Balance: Rediscovering our place in nature*, St Leonards, NSW: Allen & Unwin.

Toffler, A. (1971) *Future Shock*, London: Pan Books.

Turnbull, S. (1988) 'The meaning and implications of technology', in Miller, P., Holmes, H. and Stamford, P. (eds), *Preparing Australians for a Future with Technology*, Sydney: University of Sydney, Warren Centre, pp. 279–80.

Wajcman, J. (1993) 'Feminist critiques of science and technology', in McCormick, R., Newey, C. and Sparkes, J. (eds), *Technology for Technology Education*, Wokingham: Addison-Wesley, pp. 60–72.

Wajcman, J. (1994) 'Technological A/genders: technology, culture and class', in Green, L. and Guinery, R. (eds), *Framing Technology: Society, Choice and Change*, St Leonards, NSW: Allen & Unwin, pp. 3–14.

Warnock, M., (1978) *Ethics since 1900*, Oxford: Oxford University Press

Warnock, M. (1998) *An Intelligent Person's Guide to Ethics*, London: Duckworth.

Weiner, G. (1994) 'The gendered curriculum: developing a post-structuralist feminist analysis', *The Australian Educational Researcher,* **21** (1): 63–86.

White, P.A. (1973) 'Education, democracy, and the public interest', in Peters, R.S. (ed.), *The Philosophy of Education*, Oxford: Oxford University Press, pp. 217–38.

Whiteley, N. (1993) *Design for Society*, London: Reaktion Books.

12 Values and attitudes in design and technology

Mike Martin

Introduction

Technology exists as a result of human activity and is developed and used in social and environmental contexts. As such, it is shaped by our beliefs, values and attitudes and, in turn, has a significant effect on shaping our culture and environment.

Education about design and technological activity attempts to mirror the processes that are undertaken in developing technology in the world outside schools. Given that technology is bound up in our beliefs and values, technology education must involve the exploration of beliefs and values towards technology and the exercise of value judgements. There is no escaping these facts. The question is about the extent to which values are made explicit. The degree of exposure of values depends on our view of what technology is and what kind of practical questioning and discussion activities pupils should be involved in. It is important to remember at this point that technology education is shaped by the values of those in authority and the existing political climate.

During the last ten years a wide range of views about the nature of design and technology education have been aired, reviewed, revised and often dismissed. All, however, have kept two key elements explicit: first, that technological knowledge and skills are involved; and, second, that transferable process skills are also involved. The balance between these two has been the focus of considerable debate, a debate that still continues today. A third, sometimes hidden or incoherent, element is that of developing attitudes towards, and ways of thinking about, technology. Providing opportunities for pupils to consider the work of other people (a process of 'valuing'), including those in different cultures and periods of history, is important in two ways: first, in developing a broad understanding of technology; and, second, in enabling pupils to improve their own designing and making capability by learning from the work of others.

It could be argued that a design and technology education that fails to recognise the importance of values and attitudes is reduced to technical training – of little value on its own for a generation growing up in a rapidly changing technological society.

This provocative statement sets the scene for this chapter, which explores the significance of values and attitudes within design and technology. The author makes the case that aesthetic, economic, social, moral, political and even spiritual values are an essential part of design and technology education.

Views of technology

As has been said above, the significance of values and attitudes in relation to technology education is closely linked to our personal view of what technology is. Ask a group of pupils to write down five examples of technology. Assemble the results and look at the list. It is quite likely that one of the examples will be a computer. This is no surprise, given the domination and hype of this medium of communication in the UK. Perhaps pupils have included the table they are working at? Possibly the bag that holds their books or shopping? Less likely would be a vase of flowers or a snack product eaten at break time. This exercise highlights the point that technology is often seen as discrete objects.

Technology as objects

To see technology purely as a collection of objects or products is a common viewpoint. This is understandable, as it is the tangible products that we see around us that are the visible outcome of technological activity. It is, however, a rather narrow view and hides the fact that technology involves complex systems of physical resources and human interactions. The motor car, for instance, would be useless without the network of petrol stations and garages across the country.

Technology as products and processes

Highly technological consumer products in the UK are, in the main, designed by teams, produced in mass quantity, distributed over a wide area and marketed through a variety of media. To view technology as not only the product, but also the process that bring it about, is therefore logical. This, however, is still not really enough to explain the variation in technological products between different countries, cultures and social groups.

Technology as culture

All the technological products that we see around us reflect the values of our society, the values of the designers and manufacturers involved and the perceived values of the end users (their views and lifestyles):

> Technology does not spring, ab initio, from some disinterested fount of innovation. Rather it is born of the social, the economic, and the technical relations that are already in place.
>
> (Bijker and Law 1992: 11)

It is clear, therefore, that consideration of economic, social, moral, environmental and other values issues is an important part of technological activity. Those responsible for developing products and bringing them to the marketplace will make decisions related to such issues: take an everyday example (say, training shoes) and consider the issues involved in their production.

The author Arnold Pacey, in *The Culture of Technology* (1983), highlighted three important aspects of technology practice: technical, organisational and cultural. He claimed that to view technology practice only in terms of technical skills and knowledge was to have a restricted view.

If technology education is to align closely with the reality of technological practice in our societies, then a model of technology education practice, similar to that used for technology practice, should be useful. Based on Pacey's (1983: 6) ideas, technology education practice should also include the three main aspects of technology practice:

1   Technical aspect: acquisition of the technical knowledge, skills and techniques, including the use of tools and machines.

This aspect alone gives a very restricted view of technology education.

2   Organisational aspect: developing capability in the use of design strategies and processes.
3   Cultural aspect: considers attitudes and values, and includes acquiring the skills of valuing.

Together, these three aspects give a much broader, more general view of technology education and help to clarify the place and importance of values, attitudes and valuing processes in the domain of technology education practice. Which of the technical, social and organisational statements reflects the true nature of design and technology education?

In reality, all three elements, technical, organisational and cultural, are integrated. The curriculum of the day reflects the relative emphasis given to each of these elements and the extent to which they are exposed. For those responsible for teaching the subject of design and technology, a broad understanding of the term 'technology' is essential.

Technology education without values?

Surely we can teach about technology without needing to address values? This is not possible, as values may be buried but will always be present. To suppress values issues would promote a blinkered view and deprive pupils of the opportunity to develop a comprehensive view of technology's place in society. Design and technology education with little or no discussion of values is effectively technical training and promotes a deterministic view of technological development in which we are passive consumers of products.

Care needs to be taken to achieve an appropriate balance. If discussion dominates too much, the subject will become theoretical and lose its practical base. It is continuous action and reflection that makes design and technology the unique subject that it is.

Values through designing and making

The most important, and perhaps the most difficult, areas of design and technology in which to undertake work with values are those in which pupils are engaged in their own design and make activities.[1] One of the best ways of assessing the impact of values work with pupils is to look at the way in which their designing and making has been informed by the exercise of value judgements and a sensitivity towards end users. Have they, for example, considered the impact of their design ideas on people and the environment before they start making?

There are three obvious ways in which pupils can be encouraged to explore value judgements, namely:

- during the exploration of the context for designing and making;
- at the point of making decisions during planning and making;
- while evaluating the outcomes of their own work.

The exploration of contexts

Design and technology always takes place in a human, social and environmental context. We may choose to ignore the wider aspects of the context in which technology is situated, but the social, cultural and environmental issues are, nevertheless, always there.

In the first National Curriculum order (1990), it was expected that pupils would take part in activities in one of a number of contexts:

> Pupils should be able to identify and state clearly needs and opportunities for design and technological activities through investigation of the contexts of home, school, recreation, community, business and industry.
>
> (DES 1990: 3)

The lack of meaningful guidance from government at the time and the general lack of understanding about process-driven design and technology led to much meaningless activity through broad contexts. Mistakenly, the notion of contexts was seen as a problem rather than a matter for interpretation. As a result, there has been little reference to contexts in subsequent curriculum documents.

One of the consequences of this has been that designing and making activities have become somewhat decontextualised. Pupils might, for example, make a model vehicle or a timing circuit without any reference to possible applications. Unit 16 of the DATA *Guidance Notes for Key Stage 3* (DATA 1995), for instance, is on time and timing. The following information is given:

The Context: The activity focuses on the use of electronic timing and control systems.

The Activity: This focuses on the 555 timer…

Although there is no doubt that a great deal of learning will take place through such activities, they do not help pupils to understand the relationship between technology and people, and there will be little opportunity for them to exercise judgements and make decisions of their own, given that the outcome (555 timing circuit) is already prescribed to a large degree.

In the revised curriculum we see the return of contexts as an important facet of design and technology education for at least some pupils:

> During the key stage, pupils should be taught the knowledge, skills and understanding through… design and make assignments in different contexts.
> (QCA 1999: 138)

It is essential to set some design and make activities in real contexts. This is quite easy to set up, because the school and local community present a wealth of opportunity for pupils of all ages. Even once placed in context, the way in which design and technological activity is introduced can make a significant difference to the opportunities available for pupils to engage in valuing and the discussion of issues.

Working within contexts

The choice of starting point for design and technological activity can play a significant role in opening up opportunities for pupils to engage in valuing and discuss a range of issues. Starting with an issue, rather than a fixed brief, provides opportunities for valuing to take place. For example, consider a design and make activity on the theme of 'carrying' in which the teacher intends pupils to develop a carrier from textile materials. How is the activity presented to pupils? Here are two possibilities:

1   Design and make a bag to hold a range of foodstuffs.
2   Address the issue of an elderly shopper who needs the means of carrying his/ her shopping back home from the supermarket.

Both design activities may result in pupils making very similar products, but the second activity presents a much richer situation in which pupils can explore and discuss a range of issues. The product to be made is not defined and will be determined by pupils' decision making. There are ways of addressing such an issue without making something, and it is important that pupils realise that a product may not always be the best way of satisfying a particular need.

The disadvantages of what might be called 'context-rich' approaches are that activities will be more difficult to manage with greater discussion and the likely use of a wider range of resources. This highlights the point that, although all work related to values may be rewarding, it is not always easy!

Success criteria

To ensure the genuine evaluation of a pupil's own work, the development of 'success criteria' is essential. In essence, how can the success of a design and make activity be judged? Such criteria should go beyond the traditional one-line brief and include user requirements and teachers' assessment criteria, as well as pupils' own learning agenda. Extensive and comprehensive criteria can only be generated if potential users are involved from an early stage and the context is considered in depth.

Decision making

The processes of designing and making involve a great deal of decision making. Choices need to be made on the way to proceed to the next stage, for instance choosing what to make:

> In technology, pupils are constantly making decisions: 'What do I want to make?' 'Which material shall I use?' 'How should I design this artefact?' In deciding how to proceed, pupils, like all designers and technologists, are making judgements. 'If I make the product out of cheap material, it may look good, but has it limited life?'
>
> (Conway and Riggs 1994: 228)

At its simplest the choice may be between the use of new and recycled card. More complex decisions could involve weighing up a range of interconnected criteria such as use of recycled material, weight, cost, durability, user expectations and ease of disassembly for reclamation purposes.

One very successful strategy that teachers have used with pupils involves the consideration of winners and losers when a technological product or system is introduced. This is most widely known through materials produced by the Nuffield Design and Technology Project (1995) and involves filling in a target diagram (Figure 12.1). Here, for example, is how one pupil evaluated her design for a disposable waterproof hat for hikers, using a target chart. First, she listed all the people who would be directly affected if her design were to be mass-produced. They included hikers, the people who own or work in the factories which would make the hats, the people who produce the plastic material and the shopkeepers who would sell the hats. These were written in the first (inner) ring of the target (Figure 12.1). Next she thought of others who might be affected indirectly, such as the people who manufacture rival products, people who might find the hats thrown away on their land, the people affected by the plastics industry and so on. She wrote these on the next (outer) ring. She then looked at each group of people to decide if they were winners or losers and highlighted the winners yellow and

Evaluating outcomes – winners and losers

Winners and losers target chart

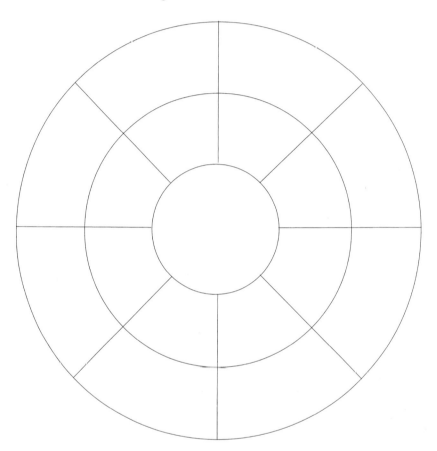

- Write the product name in the middle.
- Write those people directly affected by the design in the spaces in the inner ring.
- Write those indirectly affected by the design in the spaces in the outer ring.
- Highlight the winners in one colour and the losers in another colour.
- Use the colour balance to decide if the idea is a good or bad one.

Figure 12.1 Target diagram to consider the 'winners and losers' when a technological produce or system is introduced. Nuffield Design and Technology 11–14 Teacher's File (© 2000 The Nuffield Foundation) Winners and Losers Resource Task (SRT38).

the losers blue. At the end she was able to use her chart to help her evaluate her idea.

Of course, none of this thinking will take place without the 'appropriate' attitudes from both pupils and teachers. This is discussed later in the chapter.

Evaluation of making – looking at consequences

It may be felt that asking pupils to evaluate their own work is easier than looking at the work of others. This is only true on a superficial level. To ask difficult questions of pupils' own work, related to human and environmental issues, is quite challenging and needs to be handled carefully. Indeed, for pupils to evaluate their own work alongside commercially produced products can be not only difficult but disheartening!

In drawing comparisons between commercially produced products and those made by pupils it is essential that similarities are highlighted first, before differences. Care also needs to be taken so that deeply held beliefs and constructs are not exposed and pupils ridiculed by others as a result. Consideration of what happens to their product at the end of its useful life is important. Can the materials be reused or recycled? Perhaps the product is biodegradable? Could it be used for another purpose afterwards?

Evaluating the products of design and technology

As well as designing and making products themselves, pupils need to be given opportunities to look at the work of others. This has two purposes: first, to inform their own designing and, second, to provide them with a broad understanding of the role of technology in society. For example, by looking at snack-food products pupils can learn about ingredients which provide energy and, at the same time, gain an appreciation of the power of marketing and repackaging existing products.

The processes of evaluating products provide rich opportunities to explore values issues in the widest sense. Technology has been described as 'values made visible'. If this area is broadened to the evaluation of the products of design and technology, then it will include the systems and environments also created by design and technological activity and the effects of technology beyond those intended. By looking at the work of others, pupils can:

- appreciate the ways in which different products meet the same need;
- see how their own work relates to the world around them;
- develop observation and communication skills;
- widen their 'success criteria'.

Analysis or evaluation?

The revised curriculum (QCA 1999) sees the removal of the phrase 'investigation, disassembly and evaluation activities'. In its place we have 'product analysis', a term that is open to interpretation. This could be seen as essentially attribute analysis, taking place outside of the context in which the product is used, and could be quite scientific in nature. There is likely to be more educational value in *product evaluation* that considers not just 'how does it work?' and 'is it aesthetically pleasing?', but also whether the product meets an identified need from the point of view of users.

Making comparisons

Making comparisons between products is useful. Take, for example, a number of different torches. All have essentially the same key function but differ according to the context for which they were designed. Each torch will reflect the values of the designer(s) and the perceived values of potential users. By looking at the similarities and differences between a collection of torches and/or lights, pupils can engage in a dialogue about the value they would place on each torch or light and the reasons for their judgements.

Using questions

Questions need to be structured and of a type that is appropriate to pupils' age and capability. They should be encouraged to come up with their own questions whatever their age. Teachers might suggest the following questions:

- What is my initial reaction? Do I want to touch/taste/use/discard it?
- Who might the owner be?
- Why might someone buy it?
- Would I want to own and/or use it?
- Is it really needed?
- Can it be part of a sustainable world?

(DfEE 1995: 3)

Supplementary questions can be useful in clarifying pupils' responses to products and exposing deeper beliefs and values. Great care needs to be undertaken with such activities as revealing pupils' personal constructs can make them vulnerable to ridicule and prejudice:

> Of course, strongly held, conflicting values will sometimes be identified and an open, dialogic approach is required of the teacher. An educational climate of tolerance and mutual respect must be developed.
>
> (Siraj-Blatchford 1995: 200)

A particularly interesting strategy is to ask pupils to describe who they think the owner of a particular product might be. Something as simple as evaluating different shopping bags can reveal deeply held beliefs about our society from primary age pupils:

Working with small groups of five children and using carrier bags from three different retail outlets – Mark's and Spencer's, Morrisons and Netto, together we evaluated the bags… The question that prompted children into revealing the social values they attached to these products was 'what kind of person do you think might use this bag?' The responses were immediate. The M&S shopper was 'rich, posh and selfish'; the Morrisons shopper was the sort of person that goes 'to a usual type of shopping place' but the Netto shopper was 'thick'. When questioned further about what they meant by thick, they said 'stupid'. People who used Netto bags were also deemed to be 'tramps' and people who had to walk to the shops. By classifying others these children were simultaneously classifying themselves.

(Allison 1997: 5)

Product evaluation activities are likely to be more effective when pupils are encouraged to be open towards different ideas. Developing such attitudes takes time, and considering pupils' prior experience is critically important. This highlights the need for careful planning through the years.

Evaluating products in terms of their environmental impact and sustainability is important and provides useful information that can be used when pupils reflect critically on their own designing. This is now recognised in the curriculum as being a significant area for design and technology in terms of its contribution towards education for sustainable development:

… through developing knowledge and understanding of the principles of sustainable design and production systems, developing skills in creative problem solving and evaluation, and exploring values and ethics in relation to the application of design and technology.

(QCA 1999: 9)

Looking at technology in different cultures

Pupils can learn a great deal from looking at design and technology in different cultures. Particularly useful examples of this come from Intermediate Technology, a charity working with local people in Africa, Asia and South America on sustainable development projects. The pack *Creating Art, Creating Culture* (Martin and Rea 1994), for example, illustrates the work of a women's textile cooperative in Bangladesh. Pupils are able to learn a great deal about the processes of textile production and, at the same time, are presented with positive images of design and technology in different cultures, in this instance, relating to textiles. When pupils are looking at different cultures, the approach taken is of critical importance. Looking at comparisons before differences can avoid some of the potential for tokenism and the reinforcing of stereotypes.

Is it appropriate?

A particularly useful strategy for looking at work in different cultures, including our own, is to use the concept of appropriate technology, which links technology with contexts. Whether or not a technology is judged to be appropriate depends on the extent to which it meets criteria such as those given in Figure 12.2. Pupils, as a group, could perhaps draw up their own criteria, then generate questions to help evaluate their own work. Details of such criteria can be found on the Values in Design and Technology Education (VALIDATE) website: www.data.org.uk/values.

Making it happen – planning for values

Attitudes

Exploring values through design and technology needs to be seen as a positive thing in which pupils are involved. Overcoming potentially negative attitudes of staff, parents and governors is critical in embedding good practice in policy documents and the ethos of the school as a whole.

Building confidence

Whatever opinion is formed about the importance of controversial issues, it is likely that all teachers will, at some point, have to face difficult questions from pupils, given the highly technological society within which we live and the profound effect that technology has on our lives. How can teachers deal with these issues?

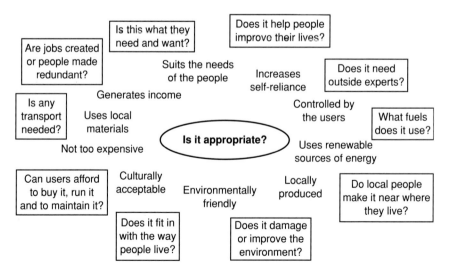

Figure 12.2 Is it appropriate? Criteria to use when judging whether a technology is an appropriate one to use.

- Seek advice from subject leaders, teachers of drama, etc.
- Try giving pupils different 'hats' to wear – with which to view products from different perspectives.
- Recognising that there are limits to how much knowledge it is possible to retain (that is, teachers cannot know everything – particularly in design and technology).

It is important to present a broad picture of technology to pupils. Exploring technology unfamiliar to both pupils and teachers, however, can make teachers feel vulnerable as they may only know as much information as their pupils. Although finding out about products before they are evaluated by pupils is a good idea, it should be recognised that it is impossible to know everything.

Pre-judging

When looking at the work of other people it is important to recognise that evaluation is undertaken from a specific cultural viewpoint. This means that it is likely that we may pre-judge some aspects. Pre-judging is not necessarily a 'problem' if it is recognised. One approach to dealing with this is to ask pupils (and possibly teachers) to look at a product from the viewpoint of different people, including users, designers, manufacturers, those indirectly affected, green activists, etc. In this way, pupils could start to appreciate that their own views on a product depend on how they are affected by it. With this kind of work there are clear opportunities to work with, or seek the support of, teachers of drama.

How controversial?

Design and technology is an inherently controversial subject as it deals with the development, manufacture, use and effects of technology in human, social and environmental contexts. There are many examples of technological products, such as the mobile phone, that are controversial. Some people feel that mobile phones are both intrusive and bad for our health. Others say that they feel more secure as a result of having instant communication at hand. For most technological products that we use, from the paperclip, to the disposable nappy, to a high-speed train, there will be a range of opinions about a wide variety of issues. Is it the role of teachers of design and technology in schools to deal with these issues? The arguments against dealing with complex issues include:

- the consequences of technology are best discussed and dealt with by adults;
- the role of teachers is to teach skills and knowledge, not to indoctrinate pupils;
- dealing with controversy is best dealt with in other curriculum areas, for example PSHE (personal, social and health education);
- there is precious little time to teach skills, let alone for prolonged discussion.

Arguments in favour of dealing with controversial issues include:

- the need to reflect 'real-world' technological activity in the classroom (technology itself being controversial);
- developing critical thinking in pupils so they become discerning users and not just passive consumers;
- the importance of understanding other people's viewpoints;
- crucial distinctions between technical training and technology education.

How can teachers help pupils discuss controversial issues?

Auditing existing schemes

Policy documents

There should be statements in policy documents, at both departmental and whole-school level, about the development of attitudes and values. This is currently good practice, but will be essential in the future for Ofsted purposes – particularly in relation to citizenship and other cross-curricular issues.

Progression

> As pupils move through the key stages there should be a growing ability to justify the choices they are making with reference to values and beliefs and a growing acceptance of responsibility for the consequences of technological activity.
>
> (Conway and Riggs 1994: 236)

What makes product evaluation activity easy or difficult? Table 12.1 suggests some possible lines of progression. These are put forward as ideas and it is recognised that there is a need for research to be undertaken in this area. In the meantime, however, such activities appear in the statutory curriculum and teachers will be expected to tackle issues of progression themselves to the satisfaction of Ofsted.

Assessment

In the current political climate, issues of assessment are of importance. If valuing activities cannot be assessed then their survival in the classroom may be questionable. On the other hand, are we in danger of promoting only those things which can be assessed? How can we assess pupils' understanding of values in design and technology?

Assessing product evaluation capability

How can pupils' ability to evaluate products be assessed? The lack of guidance from QCA, and its predecessors, on issues of progression and assessment of pupils' ability to evaluate products gives cause for some concern. This is especially so

Table 12.1 Lines of progression in product evaluation

→ Progression →	
From	To
Familiar products	Unfamiliar products
Simple products (one piece)	Complex products (many parts)
Comparison with similar products	Comparison with different products
Using given evaluation criteria	Developing and using own criteria
Evaluate for use by self	Evaluate for use by others

because the outcome of assessment may not be quantifiable as it may be, for example, a record of attitudinal change or a particularly sensitive response to a given design context. If an outcome cannot be assessed, then how can the effectiveness of teaching strategies be measured? To address this issue, the following criteria for assessing pupils' progress in evaluation are suggested:

- dialogue and reasoning (from subjective reaction to objective argument);
- number and type of evaluation criteria used (inclusion of pupils' own criteria);
- consideration of wider issues (from purely functional to environmental, moral etc.);
- supporting information (evaluation backed up by other sources);
- helping other work (incorporation of ideas/information/strategies into designing).

Conclusion

Looking at the technology that surrounds us we can see that the values of individuals, organisations and society have formed and shaped all designing and making activities. The extent to which we recognise this is affected by our understanding of technology: as products; the systems that bring them about; or as a part of our culture. Acceptance of the view that values are inextricably linked with technology can only support the view that values issues should be a part of design and technology education in the school curriculum. Whatever our personal views, it is important to recognise that technology education without discussion of values, or recognition of the importance of contexts, can become deterministic and essentially technical training.

Several ways of exposing values and initiating discussion have been outlined above. The exploration of contexts and evaluation of products are particularly significant and immediately applicable to existing schemes of work. In applying such issues it is important to work towards a coherent whole-department approach that takes account of assessment and progression issues. Careful thought needs to be given to the way in which activities are undertaken. Teachers need to be particularly sensitive in looking at products and technological activity in different cultures and in dealing with pupils' viewpoints and personal constructs.

Overall, it can be said that it is important for teachers to adopt an approach to technology education that encourages critical thinking and questioning so that young people are aware that technology has a relationship with people, society and the environment. How pupils *value* technology will shape their future and they should be entitled to discuss such issues in the classroom.

Questions to consider

How can pupils' ability to evaluate products be assessed?

1   Look at a range of teaching packs and identify the assessment schedule that they provide. Do they address the asessment issues identified in this chapter?
2   What makes product evaluation easy or difficult?
3   How can teachers help pupils to discuss controversial issues?
4   Take a topic, such as waste disposal, and get groups of pupils to complete a winners and losers chart. Ask half to take the role of winners and the other half losers. Write down or discuss the views and feelings of each group.

Note

1   The author uses the term *activities* in preference to *assignments* to emphasise the open-ended nature of pupils' designing and making rather than the potentially narrow character of teacher-directed assignments.

References

Allison, Y. (1997) 'What values do primary children attribute to everyday objects within their experience?', in Smith, J. (ed.), *IDATER 97: International Conference on Design and Technology Educational Research and Curriculum Development*, Loughborough University of Technology, Loughborough, pp. 4–9.

Bijker, W. and Law, J. (1992) *Shaping Technology/Building Society: Studies in Socio-Technical Change (Inside Technology)*, Cambridge, MA: MIT Press.

Conway, R. and Riggs, A. (1994) 'Values in technology', in Banks, F. (ed.), *Teaching Technology*, London: Routledge.

DATA (1995) *Guidance Notes for Key Stage 3*,Wellesbourne: DATA Publications.

DES (1990) *Technology in the National Curriculum*, London: HMSO.

DfEE (1995) *Looking at Values through Products and Applications*, London: DfEE Publications.

Martin, M. and Rea, V. (1994) *Creating Art, Creating Culture*, London: Intermediate Technology Publications.

Nuffield Design and Technology Project (1995) *Student's Book*, London: Longman.

Pacey, A. (1983) *The Culture of Technology*, Oxford: Basil Blackwell.

Siraj-Blatchford, J. (1995) 'Kelly's repertory grid: a technique for developing evaluation in design and technology', in Smith, J. (ed.) *IDATER 95: International Conference on Design and Technology Educational Research and Curriculum Development*, Loughborough University of Technology, Loughborough, pp. 195–200.

QCA (1999) *The National Curriculum: Handbook for Secondary Teachers in England, Key Stages 3 and 4*. London: QCA.

Further reading

Budgett-Meakin, C. (1992) *Make the Future Work*, London: Longman.

This was the first book written to support teachers in their teaching of the wider dimensions of technology education such as the concept of appropriate technology. Detailed examples of technology from other cultures are presented alongside examples of classroom activities. The chapter on values is of particular interest.

Lury, C. (1996) *Consumer Culture*, London: Polity Press.

The book explores the way an individual's position in social groups, structured by class, gender, race and age, affects the nature of his or her participation in consumer culture. It goes on to develop the view that this has contributed to changes in the way in which individuals belong to these social groups. Consumer culture is thus seen to provide new ways of creating social and political identities.

MacKenzie, D. and Wajcman, J. (1999) *The Social Shaping of Technology*, Milton Keynes: Open University Press.

This book demonstrates how social relations in the workplace have shaped technology. It explores the effect of the social context on the development of technology and the relationship between technology and gender.

Papanek, V. (1997) *The Green Imperative*, London: Thames and Hudson.

This book discusses the significance of design in our lives and the ways in which design can be used to benefit people and the planet. The chapters 'Is convenience the enemy?', 'Generations to come' and 'The best designers in the world' are particularly interesting.

13 Links with industry

To what extent is it possible to establish effective links to benefit all partners?

Sue Shore

Introduction

The idea of educational links with industry raises the question: 'How can it be done when the curriculum already expects so much?' Since the introduction of the National Curriculum in England and Wales, existing woodwork, metalwork, technical drawing and home economics teachers have had the task of adapting, first, to the introduction of the curriculum and then to ongoing changes focusing on not only the importance of design but the need for technology. A number of schools, making way for what they thought was the 'new subject' with less emphasis on manual skills, sold their machinery. However, developments in design and technology, leading to the Dearing Committee's review in 1995, placed emphasis on the value of practical skills as a part of the overall subject.

As far back as 1884 John Moss understood the need for linking education to industry:

> The school workshop... should be an integral part of the education system adapted to the requirements of industrial communities. It should be a means of illustrating scientific principles and of applying in practice theories which of themselves, too often appear to the pupils as useless dry bones.
>
> (Moss 1884)

For schoolchildren, knowledge of what was happening in industry, in both design and production, was seen as relevant to gaining a full understanding in a realistic context. The words 'business' or 'industry' are often used today as general expressions for 'the world of work'. They may include manufacturing industry and also commerce and service industries; they may also mean the design industry, including the media and the arts. Is it always advantageous for industrial companies to be involved in education or schools to be involved with industrial companies? The report *All Our Futures: Creativity, Culture and Education* (DfEE 1999) makes it plain that there is great value in links with industries as they are part of the community in which we live.

However, often in our technological world there has been a lack of understanding on both sides due to changes constantly taking place. Ian Lynch of the City Technology College's Trust had concerns for both parties:

There are different perspectives which can inevitably lead to heated differences of opinion which are not helped in instances where each side is ignorant of the other's modus operandi.

(Lynch 1998)

When pupils are old enough to take part in work experience, it is advantageous for pupils to be aware of roles in various workplaces, and for employees within such companies to be aware of the changes which have taken place within education. The following issues seem important:

- What are the origins of industrial links, and what changes have occurred during the development of design and technology education since the introduction of the National Curriculum?
- How useful and suitable are the links for all partners: industrial companies and teachers and pupils from primary to secondary education?
- In what ways can teachers of design and technology deal with industrial links?

These questions will be examined in this chapter and reinforced by considering some examples in which education and industry have worked together, both in the UK and in other countries.

Origins of links between education and industry

The Great Exhibition in 1851 played an important role in the many changes in industry and education and was seen as an important way of assisting future improvements. The government recommended the establishment of schools for the training of teachers in design. By 1860 there were eighty such teacher training schools with around 80,000 students. The design syllabus caused controversy in that there were a number of different views of what was meant by 'design' and how it should be linked to society. Some believed that design students should have direct contact with industry concerning production, whereas others believed in concentrating on style. It could be said that the same debate is still taking place today.

Chapter 2 describes how 'design' and production were seen to separate during the Industrial Revolution. Previously, products were often designed and made by the same craftsmen, and sometimes the craftsmen had workshop assistants to help them in making the products. The role of the industrial designer was that of an inventor and, in the early 1900s, it became separated from production. Pulos (1994) noted that, once industrial design had separated from production, specialist training was required in a chosen field. Apprenticeships were offered for many of the practical roles within companies but never for the positions of specialist designers. Technological development in industry subsequently decreased the need for workers specialising in any one role and encouraged those who were adaptable, able to cope with change and able to work in various roles.

Although major changes were taking place in industry, many were also taking place in education. In 1976 James Callaghan, initiating the 'Great Debate' in education, which then led on to the 1988 reforms and the introduction of the National Curriculum, voiced concerns about the purpose and direction of education since the 1944 Education Act:

> The goals of our education, from nursery school through to adult education, are clear enough. They are to equip children to the best of their ability for a lively, constructive place in society and also to fit them to do a job of work. Not one or the other, but both.
>
> (Callaghan 1976: 332–3)

In 1977 the 'Green Paper' mentioned the need for educational links with industry and the importance of such issues when training teachers:

> More attention should be given in initial teacher training to the national importance of industry and commerce, to helping them (the prospective teachers) in their responsibility for conveying this to their pupils.
>
> (DES 1977)

By 1983 the TVEI (Technical Vocational Educational Initiative) had been introduced for fourteen- to sixteen-year-olds:

> For much of our previous history those young adults would in the main have been engaged in the working life of the community at that age. It is not, therefore, surprising to find that the interests of many of them are in things which are relevant, which bring a sense of achievement, which can be seen to relate to the world outside school.
>
> (Woolhouse 1984)

Many schools developed vocational education within TVEI and continued with successful industrial contacts. But doubts were still being raised about the effect of industrial knowledge:

> There is some confusion between industrial and educational perspectives on the activity. In education the concern is to expose pupils to design and technological experiences in order that they may develop understanding and capability. In industry that design and technological capability is directed towards the manufacture of a product or system. Whilst the product is of less importance than the process to education we must recognise the interdependence of these two perspectives on the activity.
>
> (DES/APU 1988)

More recently, Layton (1990) has drawn attention to the different purposes within which the claims for greater links between industry and education are situated:

- Economic: the claim that economic prosperity is founded in vocational preparation is used as an argument for enhancing industry-based work in schools.
- Educational: the educational value of links with industry and a focus on real-life and practical skills is used as an argument.
- Socio-cultural: the socio-cultural argument centres on the need to build a culture of respect for industry, which can only be achieved by young people developing positive attitudes to working in industry.
- Social: the social argument is often framed with reference to new technologies, in that links with industry will help young people understand the impact of technologies on social change. Their decisions will therefore be more informed.
- Political: political arguments focus on the value to society of more young people being readily employable.

Can industrial links be useful for both education and industry?

During the Industry Year of 1986 numerous schools became involved in establishing links between education and industry. Once the links were established many of the schools saw real benefits and continued to develop them further. During the development of the National Curriculum it seemed important not only to link subjects to each other but also to the 'outside world' of economy, industry and community. Cross-curricular themes were devised as part of the 'Whole Curriculum' (NCC 1990a). One of the cross-curricular themes, Education for Economic and Industrial Understanding (NCC 1990b), was often linked to design and technology:

> Education for economic and industrial understanding is an essential part of every pupil's curriculum. It helps pupils understand the world in which they live and prepares them for life and work in a rapidly changing, economically competitive world. It is needed at all key stages…
>
> (NCC 1990b)

Such developments revealed an opportunity for design and technology to make a major contribution to pupils' understanding of industry and the economy. Too often children have been taught in an enclosed environment where they have very rarely seen, or understood, what was happening in the 'outside world'. Teachers have faced the question from children: 'why are we learning this?' When faced with the question how has it been answered?

> A good education should prepare young people for adult life in our increasingly complex industrial and technological society – it is the teacher's job to help pupils to understand this complexity. This is recognised in the National Curriculum for England and Wales, which requires young people to have an understanding of the workings of industry and commerce, in order to equip them as future citizens.
>
> (Webucators: http://www.webucators.co.uk/ind._mats.html)

However, industrial links might benefit not only education but also companies that are actively taking part. When companies are seen to be making a contribution to society the developing culture of business may be recognised and accepted by all parties. Another way of looking at acceptance could be to consider educational and industrial links as a partnership. David Blunkett, as Secretary of State for Education, talked about raising standards and how links with business and industry could aid the future of the country:

> The government is determined to raise standards in education. But we cannot achieve this alone. Business Partnerships have a vital role in preparing young people for the world of work. Industry needs a skilled and adaptable workforce and, equally, young people will gain enormously from real experience in the workplace.
>
> (Blunkett 1997)

Blunkett felt that the industry links which had taken place with education in the 1980s had lost their momentum:

> … perhaps some of the impetus of education–business partnerships have been lost over the last decade. Many local educational authorities developed partnerships in the 1980s and these need to be revitalised… Our aim is threefold. First, we intend to develop in all our young people the knowledge, skills and understanding required for adult and working life. Second, we intend to use education–business link activities as a vehicle for motivating disaffected young people. Third, we intend to improve the quality and coherence of link activities.
>
> (ibid.)

Finally, Blunkett talked about the benefit to teachers of placements in business and industry and also the benefits to people within companies and the companies themselves:

> It is essential that government, business and education work together to ensure that young people are better motivated and therefore more employable. It is essential, too, that we work together to change the negative and, in some cases, ignorant attitudes which many young people have towards industry. They must see the relevance to adult and working life of what they learn at school and the qualifications they acquire.
>
> (ibid.)

Developments in this area have led to many partnerships between education and industry, for example Science and Technology Regional Organisations (SATRO), Understanding British Industry (UBI), Economic Awareness and Teacher Education (EATE), Schools Council Industry Project (SCIP), Careers Research and Advisory Council (CRAC) and others.

How might industrial links with education take place?

By 1997 there were a number of official companies dealing with education–industry links, for example the Education Business Partnership, the Confederation of British Industry and Business in the Community. This brought more coherence to the activities and improved the overall monitoring. Also, by this time, a pilot scheme, Pathways Towards Adult and Working Life (devised by the London Enterprise Agency with backing from such government departments and professional bodies as DfEE, SCAA and Ofsted),[1] had been involved in linking business or industrial companies with schools. Some examples are listed below from the two pilot years, which took place in Cheshire:

1   Gorsey Bank County Primary School linked with Manchester Airport in an introduction to the world of aviation. Through a 'behind the scenes' tour, schoolchildren saw places that they would not normally see. They designed a number of 'safe' products relating to their experiences at the airport.
2   Hallwood Park County Primary School children worked at Halton Hospital kitchens as part of an inter-schools topic on food. They considered suitable food for sick people and looked at hygiene in the kitchen.
3   St. Helen's County Primary School, Newchurch County Primary School and Culcheth High School linked with a representative from Cheshire's In Your Own Words project to design a welcome booklet for Culcheth High School. They spent some time considering graphical processes and production for presentation to others.
4   Woodford Lodge High School and Greenfields Primary School worked with a number of local businesses to produce mirrors with decorative frames for marketing at a trade fair. Representatives from business and industry assessed the marketing potential of the products at the trade fair (Figure 13.1).
5   St Wilfrid's Primary School worked with Gallifords on buildings and structures. Pupils had to look at the real problem situation then come up with some ideas to resolve such problems.
6   Weaver County Primary School, Brine Leas High School and South Cheshire College worked together to produce a Shakespearean play, including designing, directing and building set models and the operation of computerised lighting systems and sound systems.
7   St Helens CE (Aided) Primary School and Culcheth High School worked with Scotia Haven to develop a new fruit and nut snack. This had to be produced as a balanced, healthy food product, which was also packaged in an appealing way. During another project, linked with Whitbread's brewery, students were set the challenge of developing a new non-alcoholic cocktail suitable for children.

Technical Vocational Educational Initiative (TVEI)

As has been mentioned previously, the TVEI was successfully up and running in a

Figure 13.1 Pathways projects production of novelty mirrors. Reproduced with permission from the *Winsford Chronicle*.

number of schools by the late 1980s.[2] One example was Chesterton High School, which worked with various companies for some years. Being on the outskirts of the Potteries (Stoke on Trent), an appropriate link was for the school to work with Royal Doulton. The industrial experience module included a visit to one of the factories, followed by a few staff from Royal Doulton working with pupils in the school for a number of regular lessons. It was felt that this would help pupils to understand how pottery was made and decorated, at the same time as learning about the machines, tools and equipment used in production.

The introduction to the school's *Work Based Learning* booklet relates what was being done to interest pupils of all abilities, but especially those who found it difficult to concentrate just on academic subjects. The school saw the introduction of the National Curriculum as the opportunity to overcome various problems which had often affected individuals who did not always 'fit in' with academic achievement:

> The National Curriculum provides a framework within which learning opportunities are made available to individuals to develop their abilities and practical skills to their full potential and prepare them to participate effectively in a society, which is in constant change. The purpose of Work Based Learning is the utilisation of the workplace to facilitate learning and to enhance the relevance of the curriculum to the benefit of young people. Consideration is now given to how this work base can be used to provide and develop learning opportunities.

> In the beginning, it is necessary that students should be given an understanding of how the manufacturing process is organised in relation to a particular product. This will be achieved by a factory visit which will give particular emphasis to Quality Control. Careful preparation will be required prior to the visit in order to achieve the required degree of focus and interest. The follow up to the visit will involve members of the company working with students in the school environment.
>
> (Chesterton High School 1993)

The same school was involved with another local firm, Lucas Rists Wiring Systems. In this project pupils were able to see the layout of wiring systems that were to be placed in motor cars during a visit to the company, having seen a video showing the full production and assembly process prior to their visit. They met various people who worked for the company and learned about their roles. They saw how each department had a quality control section and were later to copy such a role during the follow-up sessions which took place during lesson times at school.

Young Engineers Clubs

Many young children show enthusiasm and interest in 'engineering', though they may not identify it in these terms, when they enjoy using such things as Lego and Meccano. In design and technology lessons this interest can be included in National Curriculum work, and so can be passed on to those who have not had the opportunity to discover such educational toys. Industrial links can develop pupils' interest, knowledge and understanding of engineering. When asked to draw a picture of an engineer, often pupils will see them as men in dirty overalls wearing hard hats. It is important for pupils to understand that there are both male and female engineers, that it is not necessarily a 'dirty' job, and that often computers are an essential part of engineering.

City Technology Colleges (CTC)

The introduction of the city technology colleges (CTCs) in the late 1980s was designed to involve education with business and industry as far as possible. Landau Forte College in Derby is supported by local businesses and industries and is constantly working with local companies. For example, companies such as Rolls Royce, Thorntons, British Telecom and many more local businesses have been involved in design and technology projects with pupils. Each year the college coordinates a trade fair (see Figure 13.2), involving a number of subjects and many industrial companies. The design and technology department instigates a 'design and make' project which is shown to company representatives at the trade fair. During lessons in other areas of the curriculum links are made between businesses, which is also a good way to show teachers and pupils how other subjects can be, and are, involved in technology.

Notes on industrial links with education in other countries[3]

New Zealand

Design and technology in New Zealand is a relatively new subject. Although New Zealand has a history of technical education for various groups, from primary up to senior, technical education for all is quite recent. In fact, in the late 1990s there were still a number of boys' schools which did not have the facilities to work in food technology and girls' schools that were not equipped with resistant materials workshops. However, other subjects have been involved with some areas of overall 'technology'. Science has been, and still is, involved with technology. The most common area of technology with which science deals is structures and mechanisms. Intermediate schools (children aged ten to twelve) are covering technology with form teachers in various areas of the curriculum, for example healthy food and structures and mechanisms:

> Technology has a major influence on individuals, on communities and on the wider society. It influences the needs and wants of people in their immediate and larger communities, and people influence technology.
>
> (Jones 1997)

Figure 13.2 Landau Forte CTC Trade Fair.

Is it possible that that the subject is losing its real context because there are areas of technology which specialist teachers are not addressing? Could it be said that if design is not also included with all technological areas, the subject loses its momentum? Perhaps others might argue that technological knowledge is meant to be more factual than the creativity of design and technology?

> Technology provides a context for the integration of knowledge and skills from many school subjects and from out-of-school experiences. It is a rich source of understanding and questions which would contribute to better teaching and learning. Students who work from their existing knowledge, skills and understanding as they carry out technological activities will be motivated towards aquiring further knowledge and skills in order to resolve problems in an individual and innovative way.
>
> (ibid.)

Considering materials technology, Welby Ings shows that the current concern for purchasing current technological products in schools is influenced by 'technology' education:

> Technology education in New Zealand schools opens up a large market in terms of plant and with that comes a concern that we do not confuse the purchase of current technological products with technological education. The curriculum deals with the development of processes of thinking and doing, not purchasing and using. While there is an understandable push by industry to encourage schools to buy new plant, as educationalists it is important that we are able to assess these presentations in the light of the aims of our programmes. Current technology in plant does not, by implication mean quality education in curriculum.
>
> (Inges 1997)

Here Ings expresses his concerns for education if industry is trying to encourage schools to buy new technological products, which may not be suitable for educational purposes. New Zealand has been aiming to link education to industry in many schools. The Secretary for Education outlines why these links are required:

> The nature of work, and the workplace that students can expect to enter, are rapidly changing in response to technological developments and changes in trade relations and the economy. To respond to these changes, schools need to develop in students the knowledge and skills that enable them to be self reliant and adaptable participants in working life, whether paid or unpaid.
>
> (Fancy 1999)

A New Zealand design technology document for the Year 11 School Certificate, under a section headed 'The Nature of Technology and its Effects on Society', states:

> Candidates must relate their activities to allied industrial processes, and must make some investigation of the effect of industrial technology on people's lives. Workbooks must show evidence of such a study.

In 1994, the Institution of Professional Engineers (IPENZ) launched an initiative called the Neighborhood Engineers Scheme with the idea of linking with education. By 1998, Technology Education New Zealand (TENZ) saw the potential for future technology projects to ensure national coverage through links with IPENZ. Gary O'Sullivan from Massey University College of Education in Palmerston North is conducting a study of New Zealand education and industry links:

> In New Zealand along with western English speaking countries there has been a shift in education policy; this shift is away from a liberal-humanist education towards a more vocationally focused curriculum. The change has come about partly as a response to economic targets and objectives set by national policy makers. An example of this shift can be seen in the growing emphasis on making education more responsive to the needs of industry and business. This policy has led to the development of a variety of school industry partnerships or links. Although not a new idea links have found prominence in the recent addition of the New Zealand national curriculum framework essential learning area of technology education.
>
> (O'Sullivan 1999)

Although the notion of industrial links continues to be an aspiration of education, the falling employment rates in manufacturing industry in Western Europe, and a social shift towards service industries and flexible working, may be having an impact on links with schools.[4] A continuity of contact, which would make forming links with people relatively straightforward, is sometimes lacking, thereby making communication difficult.

Summary of the benefits of industrial links with education

Benefits for teachers

- Many teachers have not worked in any area other than education, so it is an advantage to broaden their understanding of commercial and industrial practice.
- Teachers gain knowledge of the environments in which commerce and industry take place, and of the machinery and equipment used.
- Teachers learn about current business and industrial practices.
- Opportunities for teachers to develop new skills using real-world technology.

Benefits for pupils

- Increased motivation to learn.
- Design and technology contexts are real ones.
- Better preparation for pupils' adult and working life.
- Greater confidence in their ability to contribute to society.
- Clearer understanding of the world of work.
- Opportunities to develop communication skills with adults other than parents and teachers.

Benefits for people in business and industry

- People in business and industry become aware of the changes that have occurred in education since they were pupils.
- There is potential for the development of new ideas, and new approaches.
- There are opportunities for business people to gain insights into the reaction of potential consumers to their product range.
- An advertising element is present – the company may gain from publicising its brand name to future consumers.
- Often a company is keen to encourage young people to consider it as a career opportunity, and this can be a direct benefit if recruitment is low, for example in unpopular areas of manufacturing.

(from Banks 1994)

How can teachers establish effective industrial links?

Schools may already have contacts with various organisations which link education to industry. It is always worth an individual teacher investigating these avenues first of all, to build on established networks that already exist. Sometimes organisations have passed on resources to senior members of schools or heads of departments. Such people may be waiting for interested staff to use their initiative, rather than forcing extra work on anyone who may feel pressurised into participating. In general terms, if there are no established education and industry contacts, it is worth establishing what local companies do and which areas of the design and technology curriculum might be linked with industry. Before approaching companies, it might be worth having project ideas in mind. The investment in time and effort will pay off because once links are established they tend to continue year after year. Ask yourself, first of all:

- Which local companies have previously worked with education?
- Which local companies would be willing to work with the school?
- Are pupils' parents employed within local companies or do they know of suitable companies with which to link to the school?

Conclusion

There are thousands of schools in the UK which are already involved in educational links with business and industry. All secondary schools deal with careers and work experience at Key Stage 4, but often Key Stage 3 and primary schools do not have any contacts. Younger pupils may be missing the chance of developing their knowledge and understanding of the world outside of school and home. Industrial links can develop not only pupils' knowledge of particular local companies but also ways of communicating with adults, personal presentation and presentation of work. Group work is a major part of the world of work and group work is often necessary for pupils involved in industrial links. Pupils learn about roles, at all levels, within industrial companies. When taking part in industrial links at school, they may be given a role, or they may have to choose a suitable role for themselves. In developing pupils' knowledge schools may need to work with different companies and compare roles and responsibilities to facilitate their understanding.

Most ideas and views on linking education to industry are positive. Criticism sometimes arises over the time required for planning and completing industrial links. Also, visits to places connected to the industrial links may overlap with other subject lessons. Using pictures, videos, CD-ROMs, websites and visits from people within the company can help to alleviate this problem. People in local business and industries are often willing to be involved in education. After all, local schools are busy educating and developing many of their future workers. If teachers, pupils and local companies start forming links early in the education process and continue such links, then there will be a greater awareness on all sides of future developments as they happen.

Questions to consider

There is an increasing number of industries which provide resources for use in primary and secondary schools, for example the UK Steel Association, British Telecom and industry-sponsored websites, such as Technology Insight (www.technology-insight.com) where pupils can experience a virtual visit to industry:

1   Investigate what resources are available to link with your projects and evaluate the materials by using some of them with a class of pupils.
2   Is the material useful and educational? Or is it just promoting the company? What do your pupils think?
3   What messages does it convey about the industry? Does it raise any issues that are controversial and, if so, how does it deal with them? Which of Layton's categories does the material most relate to?

Notes

1   'Pathways' had a trial period of two years in Lewisham, Doncaster and Cheshire. Since the trial the project has continued to develop in the aforementioned areas through the knowledge and experience gained and will expand to all other primary and secondary schools. The project receives support from companies such as British Telecom, Marks & Spencer, Consignia (formerly The Post Office) and Unilever. It was felt that Pathways catered for the non-statutory areas of the curriculum: 'The Pathways' framework provides for all schools, whether primary or secondary, a means of drawing together into a coherent learning strategy all those vital areas of learning in a school which are not statutory, yet which form an important part of a young person's development…' (Finance & Education Services 2000). *Pathways 2000* was aiming to be accepted and used in as many schools as possible by the year 2000. Within the North and Mid-Cheshire Training and Enterprise Council's area, there are many school links with business and industry as well as the Pathways pilot scheme.

2   The UK Steel Association has been involved in education and compiled some resources following a pilot scheme in 1995. They then produced packs called 'Steel in Your Life' and 'Discovering Steel'. During the first year it was estimated that around 100,000 children in primary and junior schools had used the packs. The third resource, 'Design in Your Life', is aimed at secondary schools and was completed in 1999: 'As well as providing a valuable resource for teachers to use, the Steel Industry's Education Programme (SIEP) is changing steel's image in the classroom. In a recent survey, 93% of teachers said that they had a positive image of the steel industry having used some of SIEP's educational packs. Only 28% said that they felt that way before they received the information.' Joe Eason, SIEP's chairman, said: 'Teachers and educationalists have guided every stage in the development of our education packs. That's how we have ensured that they are really useful teachers' aids, covering many of the materials that we use in our daily lives, not only steel' (UK Steel Association: http://www.uksteel.org.uk/nw11.html).

   British Telecom (BT) have been involved in education for some time. They have updated their *Education News* magazine, incorporating many photographs of BT employees and school pupils celebrating achievements. In 1998 the editor, after outlining BT's financial contribution to various areas of education, ended with the following words: 'Funding is important but the involvement of people marks the difference between a hand-out and an added-value contribution. It is this that ensures that "partnership" is not just a current "feel-good" term but the essence of the relationship between business and education: it is the key to making a difference.' (Weir 1997).

3   Schools in Australia have been involved in industrial links for a number of years. The emerging school–industry links programme in Australia is part of a worldwide movement to establish closer links between education and industry. It is important

for us to realise that though the reason for the recent upsurge in the degree of school–industry cooperation may vary from one country to another, in general terms there is one underlying catalyst responsible for this activity: the restructuring of the international economy (Price 1991).

4 At the 1997 Educational Conference 'Living and Working in Europe', which took place in Kostelec, in the Czech Republic, there were representatives from Germany, the Netherlands, Switzerland, France and Britain. The agreement made at the conference was to 'undertake a number of joint educational projects for the mutual benefit of partner institutions' students and business, industrial and wider communities.' (Ellingham and Oberreiterova 1997).

References

Banks, F. (1994) *Teaching Technology*, London: Routledge.

Blunkett, D. (1997) 'We need business to help us raise standards', *Times Education Supplement*, 12 June.

Callaghan, J. (1976) 'Towards a national debate', *Education* 22 October.

Chesterton High School (1993) *Work Based Learning*, Stoke on Trent: Chesterton High School.

DES (1977) *Education in Schools: A Consultative Document*, London: HMSO.

DES/APU (Department of Education and Science Assessment of Performance Unit) (1988) *Design and Technological Activity*, London: HMSO.

DfEE (1999) *All Our Futures: Creativity, Culture and Education*, Sudbury: DfEE.

Ellingham, R. and Oberreiterova, A. (1997) 'Living and Working in Europe', Educational Conference, Kostelec and Orlici.

Fancy, H. (1999) Secretary for Education, New Zealand Ministry of Education, in http://webster.state.nh.us/govenor/summit/p6.html

Finance & Education Services (2000) *Pathways 2000*, Chester: Cheshire County Council Education Services.

Inges, W. (1997) 'Materials technology: are you sitting comfortably?', in *Technology Education in the New Zealand Curriculum: Perspectives on Practice*, pp. 128–40.

Jones, A. (1997) 'Technology education in the New Zealand curriculum,' in *Technology Education in the New Zealand Curriculum: Perspectives on Practice*, pp. 48–59.

Layton, D. (1990) 'Science education and the New Vocationalism', in Jenkins, E. (ed.), *Policy Issues and School Science Education*, University of Leeds, Centre for Studies in Science and Mathematics Education, Leeds, pp. 53–62.

Lynch, I. (1998) Technology Science Education and the World of Work, London: City Technology Colleges Trust.

Moss, J. (1884) [1981] 'On the value of special and general workshop instruction in elementary, higher and evening schools. The equipment of school workshops.' Second report of the Royal Commission on Technical Instructions, in Hamilton, J. (ed.), *Perspectives and Priorities*.

NCC (National Curriculum Council) (1990a) *Curriculum Guidance 1: The Whole Curriculum*, York: NCC.

NCC (1990b) *Curriculum Guidance 4: Education for Economic and Industrial Understanding*, York: NCC.

O'Sullivan, G. (1999) 'Technology education and community links: developing the inclusive curriculum', paper presented at the second biennial conference of Technology Education New Zealand, 'Pathways to Technological Literacy', pp. 240–2.

Weir, L. (1998) 'BT Community Partnership Programme', *Education News*, 48.

Useful websites

Technology Insight: www.technology-insight.com
UK Steel Association: http://www.uksteel.org.uk/nw11.html
Webster: New Hampshire State Government Online: www.state.nh.us
Webucators:http://www.webucators.co.uk/ind._mats.html

14 The professional nature of teaching

Issues for design and technology teachers

Diana Burton and Steve Bartlett

Introduction

As a new or trainee design and technology teacher you will have a rich and varied knowledge base that, with careful analysis, can be used to enhance the work of your department and school. As new technologies are introduced to deliver design and technology, you will be keen to exploit them to the full. You might be considering your long-term career and the possibilities for you in middle management. Identifying your own training needs so that you feel confident with new processes, materials, health and safety requirements and so on is part of your professional responsibility as a teacher. Helping other teachers to audit their own personal professional strengths and needs might be part of your role as a primary coordinator (Cross 1998: 96) This chapter covers some definitions of the professional nature of teaching, including the political and theoretical/pedagogical context of teacher professionalism.

The chapter then goes on to outline some of the issues to consider during your induction year and beyond. Career development concerns, including fast-track initiatives and performance management, are discussed. The increasing emphasis on evidence-based practice is considered and current inspection orthodoxy is briefly introduced. Aspects of your general professional development are specified within the DfEE Standards for the Award of QTS (qualified teacher status; currently Area 'D', but due to change in 2001–2). These standards are reviewed briefly. For further reading on this topic, support is available from the professional association DATA (the Design and Technology Association), and a selection of their publications is included in the bibliography. These are useful, in particular, for those who aspire to become heads of department or primary coordinators. It is recommended that you contact current websites for up-to-date information, and a brief list of useful sites is to be found at the end of the chapter.

The term 'profession' is frequently applied to the work of teachers. It is first worth considering to what extent teachers may be regarded as professionals. Becker (1962) saw professionalism as merely a symbol for an ideology used to justify actions and behaviours. He noted that many occupations trying to become professions used the symbol in an attempt to increase their autonomy and raise their prestige. They would try to take on as many parts of the symbol as possible. Becker may well have considered teaching to be such an occupation.

There have been many attempts to identify the features of a profession. Bottery (1996) suggested that at least seventeen different criteria have been claimed at one time or another to describe professional behaviour. Salient characteristics included subscription to a specialised body of knowledge exclusive to the occupation, which required learning in higher education. There was a code of professional conduct and ethics with a strong emphasis on service. There was a high degree of self-regulation by the professional body itself over entry, qualifications, training and members' conduct. It is perhaps worth examining how teachers have matched up to these professional criteria.

In 1957, Tropp (1957) felt that teachers had, since the Second World War, through steady development, reached the status of professionals. Teaching was seen as a worthwhile occupation. There were teaching associations whose aim was to raise professional standards. Teachers had fought for educational progress and been engaged in continuous research and evaluation. He felt that at work teachers had gained almost complete independence. They had earned their licensed autonomy and inspectors from HMI (Her Majesty's Inspectorate) were regarded as helpful senior colleagues. Tropp saw this professional development and independence within education as a safeguard to democracy and protection against the growth of dictatorship. This position prevailed in the 1960s and 1970s but was to alter radically through the 1980s and 1990s.

A number of occupations have developed higher levels of training and standards of practice to enhance their claims to professional status. However, Wilensky (1964) said that many of these groups rested on a knowledge base which was either too general and vague, or too narrow. They lacked autonomy and were supervised by those without professional status themselves. Etzioni (1969) preferred to classify these occupations as 'semi-professionals'. These workers, in his view, were characterised as working in bureaucratic organisations, a large number of them were likely to be female, training was usually less than five years, and the knowledge base was weak and not directly used by the worker. Significantly, they had restricted autonomy because they were controlled by those in higher ranks. Their working day was tightly regulated and they were subject to checks in areas where their work was least visible. Teachers may be seen as being prime examples of semi-professionals. Such things as the need for teachers to report to parents on their child's progress, school inspections by Ofsted and the publishing of pupils' performance in league tables help to regulate the autonomy of teachers.

Perhaps in realisation of the fact that teachers did not really match the model of the established or more traditional professions, there have been attempts to redefine the term 'professional' or to present different kinds of professionalism. Much of this discussion has focused on the actual practice of teaching. The modern professional, according to Schön (1983), constantly questioned and reflected upon practice. This involved the professional regarding his or her work from the point of view of the client or as an outsider. The purpose of this was to understand all aspects of the process resulting in greater professional insight. This whole procedure, involving evaluation, criticism and ultimately self-development, required openness and trust between those involved. Hoyle (1980) differentiated between two sorts of teachers. Restricted professionals are conscientious practitioners but are limited in outlook. Extended professionals seek to improve their practice by learning from other teachers and professional development activities. They are keen to be involved in practitioner research and to link theory to practice.

The political context of teacher professionalism

Throughout the Conservative administrations of the 1980s and 1990s many changes have been noted in the work process of teachers (see Ozga and Lawn 1988). Their ability to control the pace, content, volume and assessment of work declined. Routine administrative tasks grew in number. Schools' managements became more supervisory and concerned with performance levels, in keeping with their industrial counterparts. Teaching jobs became less secure, with redundancy, redeployment and retraining issues attacking the professional. Within education Hoyle (1995) saw the meaning and use of the term 'professionalism' as having altered. The focus was now on, and not beyond, the classroom. It had come to mean a form of management-assured quality delivery. Teachers had now, in Dale's (1989) terms, moved from licensed autonomy, trusted by the state and allowed relative independence, to a more regulated autonomy, subject to greater external monitoring. Ozga (1995a) characterised teachers as bureaucratised, state professionals. It was the relationship with the state that she saw as most significant. The state had effectively retained strategic control of teaching, the curriculum and assessment while using school heads to develop the market strategy. This process involved cooption of management and the growth of managerialism. As market success required smooth production and eradication of problems, Ozga (1995b) suggested that deviations from policy were less likely to be tolerated. Thus, under the guise of empowerment and collegiality, teachers were subject to increasing monitoring and surveillance. She suggested that the growth of management teams and supervisory functions may have 'extended' the professionalism of some but deskilled others. Bottery (1996) explained that these changes have involved retrenchment due to reduced budgets, increased scrutiny in terms of costs and efficiency, changes in contract which have redefined power relationships in favour of management, and greater content control over work.

It could be argued that the Labour government has reduced emphasis on the market but continued to develop control from the centre (Avis 1999). However, given the shortage of teachers, Labour has recognised the need to raise the status of teaching through, for example, the establishment of the General Teaching Council (GTC). The GTC is the new professional body for teachers and started work in September 2000. A majority of the Council's sixty-four members are teachers, most of them elected. It is an independent body funded by teachers' registration fees. Teachers in maintained schools will be required to register with the GTC. The GTC will advise the government on professional development, induction, career progression and performance management in the drive to raise standards of achievement. It will have powers to remove teachers from the register for serious misconduct or incompetence. There is still debate about how independent of government control the GTC will actually be and how its functions will relate to those of the DfEE and the TTA (Teacher Training Agency). Once again, a government is talking of the teacher as a professional. However, Bottery and Wright (1999) see this as a restricted view of professional activity. Emphasis is on the classroom and the techniques of teaching.

Thus, there have been differing views presented on the nature of teacher professionalism. Hoyle (1995) suggested that policies, which could be seen by some as 'deprofessionalisation', could be regarded by the policy makers as making those occupations more professional in relation to the needs of their clients, that is, as part of a process of reprofessionalisation. Whitty suggests that it is best to see these differing views existing as competing versions of teacher professionalism rather than 'seeing any one as fitting an essentialist definition… and others as detracting from it' (Whitty 1999: 2). He suggests that which version different individuals support will be influenced by their political beliefs, values and position in relation to government reforms. Helsby (1996) states that local contexts, and in particular departmental cultures, are influential in shaping teachers' sense of professionalism. She contends that mutual support is important because it engenders self-confidence.

Operating as groups or individuals within schools, teachers are affected by and react to wider issues. However, they are not totally determined by them. They form judgements, take decisions and act according to their own circumstances and perceptions. Undoubtedly the work of teachers became far more regulated during the Conservative administrations. Under Labour the talk is again of teacher professionalism though it would appear to be of a restricted form. This restricted professionalism may remain a straitjacket or may develop into the more licensed position which existed before.

The last twenty-five years have thus seen many changes in the nature of teacher professionalism. It can be argued that teachers are no longer encouraged to take a wider perspective and that years of criticism have encouraged a culture of the restricted professional. Ultimately, however, all teachers carry their own philosophy about their work, schools and the education system in general. Hopefully, this is shaped and reviewed in the light of accumulated professional experience. Good teachers seek out and use professional challenges and development opportunities.

Professional development through a theoretical understanding of pedagogy

Over the past decade there has been increasing emphasis on 'technical-rational' explanations of, and justifications for, current educational thinking and legislation. Technical rationality emphasises utilitarianism and favours mechanistic explanations of teaching, learning and assessment. McNiff (1993) has explained that the assumption, inherent in the technical-rational approach, that what works well in one situation will work well in another, is not applicable in teacher education since:

> ... learning involves the evolution of understanding and professional development involves considered reasons for action within teachers' context-specific situations.
>
> (McNiff 1993: 13)

Zeichner (1993) has described the externality of the technical-rational approach as limiting the dialogic relationship of theory and practice. This approach separates learning from teaching, reducing teaching to a mechanistic set of competences centring almost exclusively on the teacher's actions without enquiring into the effect on learners.

This anti-intellectual or anti-theoretical tendency can be detected both in the implementation of the National Curriculum (Ball 1994) and in the 1992 changes to initial teacher training (Lawton 1994). Garrigan and Pearce (1996) found that school-based mentors of trainee teachers:

> ... retain a very strong concept of themselves as practitioners – proud to make that distinction between themselves and theorists, reinforced in the culture in which they have worked. This leaves them with a sense of somehow betraying other practitioners, not realising that by being suspicious of theory or even rejecting it out of hand they are not only limiting their own professional development... but they are also failing to inform the corpus of knowledge
>
> (Garrigan and Pearce 1996: 30–1)

The demise of a theoretical perspective can be traced back through changes to teacher education curricula from the 1960s to the present day. The inclusion of discrete psychology of education courses alongside sociology, philosophy and history of education in the 1960s and early 1970s gave way in the next decade to professionally applied versions of these disciplines such as curriculum design, behaviour management and contextual studies. Since the late 1980s this applied form of education studies has given way to the even more attenuated conception of professional development, with its exclusive emphasis on the school-based acquisition of hands-on classroom craft skills (Carr 1997). Darling-Hammond (1994) has called for a 'professionalizing of teachers' through:

> ... a stronger understanding of how children learn and develop, how assessment can be used to evaluate what they know and how they learn, how a variety of curricular and instructional strategies can address their needs and how changes in school and classroom organisation can support their growth and achievement.
>
> (Darling-Hammond 1994: 17)

Professional development occurs within a shifting educational scene, in terms of policy and pedagogic practices, especially since the introduction of the National Curriculum and its attendant assessment. Pollard (2000) claims that the modern education system may have unintended but damaging consequences because it fails to take account of individual children as learners, placing instead more emphasis on the curriculum. As a new teacher it can be especially daunting to have to get through all the prescribed curriculum content. The tyranny of the scheme of work can obscure the focus on learning. It can be argued then that professional development activities should encourage teachers to consider how much time pupils spend talking about their learning and what evidence there is that pupils are internalising lesson content (written, verbal, physical). Teachers should consider, during their training and beyond, research findings about how pupils learn, in addition to their study of subject knowledge, skills and pedagogy. Joyce and Showers (1988) set criteria for effective in-service training, which emphasised the need for trainee teachers to develop an understanding of the theory underlying the method, to practise new methods in the safety of a university or college environment, and to be coached in the method they are applying in the real situation of their own schools. University provision of such specific in-service training has to some extent waned because financing arrangements have encouraged the growth of 'in-house' training by schools.

Current policies of professional development: a managerial approach?

The government launched a major review of professional development in February 2000 that seeks to 'transform educational standards and raise achievement in every school' (DfEE 2000: 3). It is predicated on ten principles; these include a need for teachers to take ownership of their development, to 'learn on the job' from expert practitioners, to harness the potential of ICT (information and communications technology), and to plan and evaluate their development programmes. The government pledges a commitment to fund and support teachers' professional development through a culture of entitlement. Fundamentally the goal is to raise the standards of pupils' achievement. The parameters for this are the individual teacher's needs and aspirations, the needs and priorities of individual schools and national strategic priorities. DATA is in broad agreement with the government's suggestions but feels there is insufficient emphasis on the updating of subject knowledge that is so vital within design technology (DATA 2000: 28–9).

Area D of the QTS Standards (DfEE 1998) lays down a requirement that teachers undertake responsibility for their own professional development. As noted earlier, the current government characterisation of professional development differs from the approach of previous years in which in-service short courses for enhancing subject knowledge and pedagogy were available through the LEA. Now the frame of reference is the career framework with the emphasis on individual teachers charting their way through its stages and phases. The model thus embraces responsibility for NQT (newly qualified teacher) induction, individual career development within an increasingly diverse set of progression routes and management of teacher performance.

The induction year

The DfEE (1999a) has established clearly the expectations of newly qualified teachers during their induction year. Although teachers attain qualified teacher status at the end of their training, successful completion of the induction year is required for newly qualified teachers to be eligible for employment in maintained schools. The head teacher is responsible for monitoring and supporting progress and for recommending to the LEA (Appropriate Body) whether the requirements of the induction year have been met. The LEA is then ultimately responsible for deciding whether the induction standards have been met.

Each newly qualified teacher has an induction tutor who should normally be the head of department or a senior experienced colleague with whom there is considerable contact. He or she has the operational responsibility for supporting and monitoring progress. The newly qualified teacher should be observed teaching at least once every half-term and have three summative assessment meetings during the year. The career entry profile (CEP) completed at the end of training is an important document during the newly qualified teacher year. The school has a responsibility to respond to development needs laid out in the CEP as well as to those that emerge during the year. The targets identified for improvement must be worked on and observed in action. Objectives designed to meet the induction (NQT) standards are set and should be reviewed every half-term. Schools and colleges organise regular meetings for newly qualified teachers which can be helpful as self-support groups. The newly qualified teacher is entitled to a reduced timetable in the first year – 90% of a normal timetable. There should be an agreed programme for how the remaining 10% of time is spent in support of professional development.

There are several layers of support for a newly qualified teacher. The LEA will offer meetings and in-service training (INSET) courses that bring together all its newly qualified teachers. These are an excellent source of peer support as well as being instructive in pedagogical terms. Head teachers are not obliged to allow newly qualified teachers to attend LEA meetings and courses but most are happy to take advantage of them. The DfEE (1999a) guidance document on newly qualified teacher induction, the supporting handbooks published by TTA (2000) and Dennis Hayes' *Handbook for Newly Qualified Teachers* (Hayes 2000) offer detailed guidance on the induction year. Hayes' book provides plentiful practical ideas and advice. It is worth noting that some evaluations of the levels of support given during the induction year have not always matched the entitlement newly qualified teachers should receive. Such findings call into question the sufficiency of a model of professional development in which the systematising of support through a statutory framework fails to take account of the complexity and realities of school life.

The professional ladder

Teacher education is increasingly conceptualised within an extended framework from initial training, through induction, to the newly qualified teacher year, and beyond into qualified teacher status. Routes through to subject leadership and beyond are now formalised, with standards existing for subject leaders, special education needs coordinators (SENCOs) and head teachers. The effect of the government's plans on performance management (see below) will be to create a plethora of routes to promotion and a diversification of remuneration for teachers. Advanced skills teachers (ASTs) will be eligible to earn up to £40,000. The grade has been created to provide a career path for the best classroom teachers who do not want to move into a management post. Advanced skills teachers are not intended to have management responsibilities over and above those of classroom teachers.

There is also a plan to create a 'fast track' through the profession to early subject leadership, pastoral roles and on to headship. This route requires a commitment to extra training, but carries with it greater opportunities (see DfEE 1999b). Top-quality graduates and 'the most talented serving teachers' will be selected for their commitment to teaching, excellent subject knowledge and talent to communicate, to inspire and to lead. Fast-track teachers will move through a number of designated challenging teaching posts to gain a range of varied experience. They will undertake extra CPD (continuing professional development) activities out of school hours and during school holidays such as short placements outside teaching, study for additional higher-level qualifications and courses offered by the new leadership college. They can reach the performance threshold within five years and progress to advanced skills teacher status or a leadership post shortly after.

Thus, for those who want to craft a career through to subject or key stage leadership and beyond there will be a structure to guide them, clear professional development opportunities and courses, and an expectation that learning will be recorded through portfolio building and validated possibly through further qualifications. The creation of the advanced skills teacher and fast-track posts is a controversial initiative because it can be argued that the creation of a few highly paid posts militates against a collegiate approach to school improvement. A situation in which a few high-fliers are dubbed experts may lead to the disillusionment of many committed but less ambitious teachers who may leave the development work to those who are better paid. It is significant that very few schools have appointed advanced skills teachers to date.

Performance management

The government is currently pursuing plans for teacher performance to be linked to pay. This means that if pupils meet the necessary performance indicators a teacher may be eligible for year-end incremental rises. All teachers will be subject to annual performance review, but not all will necessarily opt for, or qualify for, salary enhancement through performance. A teacher has to be at the final incremental point of the main professional salary grade to apply to be assessed at the performance threshold. Schools will have to implement a performance management system from September 2000 that will set targets and evaluate their outcomes for each individual teacher. School heads and senior teachers will be expected to set objectives for individual teachers relating to various year groups and subject areas, for example a teacher might be set the objective of developing a different approach to a teaching topic. Alternatively, a small group of pupils not meeting expectations might be targeted for extra attention or a specific classroom management technique. Assessment and benchmarking data derived from Ofsted inspections, SATs (Standard Assessment Tests) scores and GCSE results will be used to set targets in the school's development plan, and objectives for individual teachers will fit with these overarching goals. The scope of objectives will relate to a teacher's responsibilities so head teachers will have objectives for pupils' progress at school level, whereas heads of subject may look at progress by year group and teachers within departments focus on work with cohorts, groups or individuals (DfEE 1999c). Objectives are expected to cover pupils' progress and teachers' professional development. The latter might involve observing other teachers' good practice or signing up for some particular training.

This model of professional development is controversial because it assumes a simplistic causal relationship between teacher input and pupil attainment. In Hoyle's (1995) terms, it encourages restricted rather than extended professionalism. We know that there is a host of factors influencing pupils' performance that are beyond the control of the teacher, from the amount of television they watch to their attendance pattern and the extent of the support they receive from parents. We also know that teachers contribute more to a pupil's development than that which can be measured through examinations. Teachers have a concern for the whole person that includes his or her self-esteem, physical and emotional well-being, and cultural and spiritual development.

The performance management model also promotes a focus on the individual teacher as opposed to the subject or year team, yet we know that much of the creative pedagogic and curriculum development work emanates from a team approach. It is also the case that teachers often support each other through team teaching situations within the design and technology workspaces. This focus on individual development contrasts with a 'total quality management' model of development which emphasises collaboration and teamwork (Scholtes 1995). The system is here to stay but more sophisticated ways of assessing the contribution of a single teacher to a pupil's learning will need to be found if the profession is not to be fractured by what could become a very divisive methodology.

The ideology of performance management sits well within a technical-rational approach and the desire to itemise discrete teaching skills and teacher behaviours through, for example, QTS and NQT Standards. Many have argued that this atomisation provides an impoverished and partial model of the teacher and that the whole is greater than the sum of the parts. This dominant ideology has spawned a report commissioned by the DfEE to determine what makes an effective teacher. It has recently reported findings that come as no surprise to many serving teachers but which may be useful for trainees, newly qualified teachers and for school managers who are assessing teachers' performance. The government used early findings to set the standards for the new performance threshold and to inform its performance management appraisal system. HayMcBer conducted detailed interviews with 172 teachers and observed around 120 of them. Five thousand questionnaires, completed by teachers, pupils and others, were also analysed. A summary of the report can be found at the www.dfee.gov.uk/teachingreforms/mcber website. The findings are grouped into three factors that affect pupils' progress: a teacher's 'professional characteristics', 'teaching skills', and 'classroom climate'. The teaching skills thought to be particularly significant amongst effective teachers at both primary and secondary levels are high expectations and effective use of homework. Additionally, at primary level, strong time and resource management and good pupil assessment were most important while good planning was cited as being a key teaching component at secondary level (Barnard 2000).

Evidence-based practice

Within the teaching profession greater emphasis is being put on 'evidence-based practice', which, at its simplest, means analysing what teachers are doing with pupils to ensure that there are good reasons for a particular approach or task. Alternatively, they may be trialling a new way of teaching, a design project read about in a professional journal or observed as being successful for another teacher. Being mindful of evidence within a teacher's practice includes taking careful note of the attainments of each pupil. Each school now receives from Ofsted a PANDA report (*performance and assessment*) which shows the school's performance data in comparison with national averages and with schools in similar contexts. Heads are expected to use the data as a management tool in the cycle of evaluation and improvement. Consideration is given to the 'value added' to each individual pupil or group of pupils. 'Performance indicators' are identified on which teachers can focus with the subsequent year's classes in order to make year-on-year comparisons. Data from the school's PANDA are expected to help teachers to measure the effectiveness of a department or year group.

The DfEE is currently making available, to teachers, funds to assist their small-scale research into good practice in their classrooms (Best Practice Research Scholarship Scheme). Many teachers who are undertaking further study for qualifications may find this initiative helpful. It is also intended to help disseminate good practice within the school and beyond. There is some scepticism within established research communities, however, about how secure the methodologies and theoretical frames of reference will be for such investigations. Bottery and Wright (1999) note that the drive to transform teaching into a research- and evidence-based profession, while being desirable in aiming to improve the craft of teaching, remains narrowly focused. There is little scope for reflection beyond the classroom and for wider pedagogical debate. This remains a 'technical-rational' approach to teaching.

Inspection

Most teachers experience an institutional inspection at some point in their career. It can be argued that inspection is a necessary and objective element of the cycle of evaluation and therefore an important part of a teacher's professional development. Increasingly, however, the methodology and conduct of Ofsted inspections has come under fire from many quarters. The press has run stories about the harrowing effects of inspection on individual teachers and the previous Chief Inspector, Chris Woodhead, repeatedly fell foul of teachers with his robust and often antagonistic statements about the parlous state of teaching and learning. Many teachers have become disillusioned with the inspection process because opportunities which used to exist for inspectors and teachers to share in discussion of appropriate pedagogy have been subordinated to its function as a monitoring and assessment tool.

Inspections provide the evidence for the national evaluation of schools. The findings of all inspections are synthesised within the annual report of Her Majesty's Chief Inspector of Schools in England (HMCI) and thematic reports are published periodically which can provide useful comparative data on, for instance, assessment, behaviour, subject issues and so on. School inspections are governed by the School Inspections Act 1996, since amended by more recent legislation. All maintained schools are covered by the legislation on inspection and must be inspected at least once every six years. Section 10 of the Act says that a school's educational standards, the quality of the education provided, its management of the financial resources and the spiritual, moral, social and cultural development of its pupils should be reported upon. The Ofsted publications in the reference list provide detailed information about the conduct and objectives of inspection.

Ofsted claims that 'an inspection provides an independent, external view of the school and the standards it achieves' (Ofsted 1999: 4). Inspectors report a school's strengths, weaknesses and the evidence for their conclusions. Lessons are evaluated on a seven-point scale, from excellent to very poor and the inspector records data on how well the lesson is being taught, the impact on pupils' learning, pupils' attitudes and behaviour and the standards they reach. Most schools are judged to be 'effective', some are judged to be 'under-achieving', a few are judged to have 'serious weaknesses', and fewer still to be failing and therefore to require 'special measures'. It is worth noting that a school designated as requiring special measures cannot provide induction for an newly qualified teacher unless HMI specifies in writing that the school is suitable to do so. The inspection methodology can be said to reinforce the technical-rational approach to teaching because it separates components of teaching from each other and from their wider context.

Ofsted has recently been given a mandate to inspect, in conjunction with the Adult Learning Inspectorate, the work of colleges of further education. Ofsted also inspects LEAs; some have failed inspection and this has created opportunities for new entrepreneurial education businesses to offer management services to the government in these areas. This marketplace mentality inevitably presents ideological tensions for many teachers who hold a liberal view of the purposes of education.

Area D of the QTS Standards: other professional requirements

Trainee teachers' professional development is governed by area D of the QTS Standards (DfEE 1998). Even within the dominance of a technical-rational approach to teaching there is still a realisation of the broader professional responsibilities of teachers. Some elements of the standards take on greater significance at different points in the teacher's career. Thus, developing effective working relationships is of paramount importance from the beginning of the training period. Understanding the legal liabilities and responsibilities of teachers and taking responsibility for updating his or her own subject pedagogy take on greater significance once the trainee is fully fledged. Being alert to issues of ethnicity, gender and disability and knowing what constitutes discrimination has always been important, but the MacPherson Report into the Stephen Lawrence murder brings into even sharper focus the need to tackle institutional racism. Cole's (1999) edited collection discusses the professional issues of Area D from a range of perspectives and provides useful, accessible information relevant to trainees, teachers and their mentors. Space permits only a brief mention of some aspects of Area D here.

Increasingly, education is recognised as a multiprofessional sector with a variety of personnel liaising with teachers within schools. Teachers regularly liaise with the Child Protection Unit, special educational needs coordinator (internal), educational psychologist, school nurse, educational welfare officer, and social services contacts. Issues surrounding child protection are complex and it is especially important that teachers are familiar with school policy in this area. Trainees and new teachers are normally advised not to try to deal with issues of child abuse on their own and to avoid making promises of confidentiality if a pupil discloses information. The teacher's responsibility to the pupil is not to solve the problem but to refer the matter to the appropriate personnel (see Sweeney 1999).

Liaison with parents or carers requires that the professional conduct that is observed during interactions with pupils should extend to their parents. Parents should be treated with respect and as equal partners in the education of their children. They do not normally share the professional vocabulary of teachers so it is important not to exclude them from the discourse by the use of jargon terms.

Schools often employ teaching or classroom assistants on quite a large scale and this practice will increase because the government wants to develop this role within classrooms. It is important for trainees and new teachers to establish their working relationships with assistants and technicians early in the placement or teaching post. The school policy in this area can be interpreted within the design and technology working environment. Inevitably, pupils benefit most from classes in which the teacher and assistant plan carefully the tasks the assistant should undertake in advance of the lessons. Assistants will almost always be better established within the school than the trainee or new teacher but the teacher has to adopt the mantle of the expert. Assistants are expected to support teachers and pupils in a way that fits the teacher's approach.

There are also non-teaching personnel in school with whom the teacher must work effectively. Teachers need to relate well to key members of staff such as the school secretary, the caretaker, the cleaner who looks after their area and so on. These people are often very knowledgeable about the host of institutional systems that trainees and new teachers have to learn about. They can also act as gatekeepers to those in management posts or to useful materials or information. There has been some interesting work published on the power bases which exist within schools and newly qualified teachers' negotiation of them (Hodkinson and Hodkinson 1997). The micropolitics of school life is a fascinating study showing how power operates on different levels (Ball 1987; Bartlett 1998).

Area D requires trainees to understand the conditions of service they will encounter in the profession. The existence of education action zones (EAZs), city technology colleges (CTCs), specialist schools (technology, arts, languages, sports) and the development of improvement-focused and urban regeneration initiatives, such as Excellence in Cities, creates an increasingly diverse range of educational provision. The consequent demands on teachers vary according to the local situation and school in a way that was hitherto rare. Although local agreements on pay sometimes pertain, in maintained schools the *School Teachers' Pay and Conditions Document 2000* governs pay and conditions from September 2000. Guidance on this document can be found at the DfEE website. Consult Nixon (1999) for a full outline of conditions of service.

The standard length of the teaching year is 195 days, including five professional development days when the pupils are not in school. This can vary between LEAs and for public schools and CTCs. The Local Government Association has just published a report advocating radical changes to the school year in response to calls for examination periods to avoid the hay-fever season and for university admissions to be based on actual, as opposed to predicted, A level, BTEC and GNVQ results.

The notion of 'directed time' was introduced during the 1980s; this is set at 1,265 hours for the year. This was the first time that teachers' working time in relation to teaching, meetings, parents' evenings and break duties had been quantified. Directed time does not include lesson preparation, marking, report-writing and other activities related to the work of the teacher. Over the normal thirty-nine-week year (thirty-eight teaching weeks, five professional development days) 1,265 hours equates to approximately 6.5 hours per day. Prior to 'directed time', teachers spent whatever time was considered professionally necessary to carry out their role; for example, eating lunch with pupils or running after-school clubs was an accepted part of teacher professionalism. The introduction of directed time was a response to industrial action over pay taken by teachers in the mid-1980s. It signalled a significant shift in working conditions towards the greater regulation of teachers' professional activity. Thus, in Dale's (1989) terms a move from 'licensed' to 'regulated' autonomy.

Conclusion

Although, during the past decade, teachers have had more controls imposed upon them centrally, the act of teaching itself is still a largely autonomous activity in which the teacher is the final arbiter of his or her teaching and class management approach and one through which teachers are able to make a significant long-term impact on the knowledge and skills of other individuals. Notwithstanding the managerial model of professional development which prevails currently, adopting the view that teaching is itself a learning act is more likely to foster lifelong learning amongst pupils and to encourage teachers to take ownership of their own professional development.

Questions to consider

1   Preparing for appraisal sessions can be a positive and fruitful experience. Review your strengths and consider in what ways your performance could be optimised by further training.
2   'The tyranny of the scheme of work can obscure the focus on learning'. Consider what more you could do to improve pupils' learning in design and technology.

- What must you do to make it happen?
- Have you set clear and realistic targets?
- How can you monitor what is happening?
- What evidence will be available to show others?

3   Analyse PANDA data. Ask to see your school's PANDA report. Discuss with your induction tutor the implications of this comparative data for the school in general and for your area in particular. Work together on one particular performance indicator – how would you tackle it so that value is added to your pupils' learning?

References

Avis, J. (1999) 'Shifting identity: new conditions and the transformation of practice – teaching within post-compulsory education', *Journal of Vocational Education and Training,* **51** (2): 245–64.

Ball, S. (1987) *The Micropolitics of the School.* London: Routledge.

Ball, S. (1994) *Education Reform: A Critical and Post-Structural Approach.* Buckingham: Open University Press.

Barnard, N. (2000) 'Blueprint for the perfect teacher', *Times Educational Supplement,* 23 June, p. 22.

Bartlett, S. (1998) 'Teacher perceptions of the purposes of staff appraisal: a response to Kyriacou', *Teacher Development,* **2** (3): 479–90.

Becker, H. (1962) 'The nature of a profession', *Yearbook – National Society For The Study of Education,* **61** (2): 27–46.

Bottery, M. (1996) 'The challenge to professionals from the new public management: implications for the teaching profession', *Oxford Review of Education,* **22** (2): 179–97.

Bottery, M. and Wright, N. (1999) 'The directed profession: teachers and the state in the third millennium', paper submitted at the *Annual SCETT (Standard Committee for Education and Training of Teachers) Conference,* Dunchurch, November 1999.

Carr, D. (1997) 'The uses of literacy in teacher education', *British Journal of Educational Studies*, **45**: 53–68.

Cole, M. (1999) 'Where do we go from here?', in Cole, M. (ed.), *Professional Issues for Teachers and Student Teachers*, London: David Fulton, pp. 110–12.

Cross, A. (1998) *Coordinating Design and Technology across the Primary School*, London: Falmer.

Dale, R. (1989) *The State and Education Policy*, Milton Keynes: Open University Press.

Darling-Hammond, L. (1994) 'Performance-based assessment and educational equity', *Harvard Educational Review*, **64**: 5–30.

DATA (2000) 'Professional development consultation', *Datanews*, 14, 28–9.

DfEE (1999a) *The Induction Period for Newly Qualified Teachers*, Circular 5/99, London: DfEE Publications Centre.

DfEE (1999b) *A Fast Track for Teachers*, London: DfEE Publications Centre.

DfEE (1999c) *Performance Management Framework for Teachers*, London: DfEE Publications Centre.

DfEE (2000) *Professional Development: Support for Teaching and Learning*, London: DfEE Publications Centre.

Etzioni, A. (1969) *Readings on Modern Organisations*, Englewood Cliffs, NJ: Prentice Hall.

Garrigan, P. and Pearce, J. (1996) 'Use theory? Use theory!', *Mentoring and Tutoring*, **4**: 23–31.

Hayes, D. (2000) *The Handbook for Newly Qualified Teachers – Meeting the Standards in Primary and Middle Schools*, London: David Fulton.

Helsby, G. (1996) 'Defining and developing professionalism in English secondary schools', *Journal of Education for Teaching*, **22** (2): 135–48.

Hodkinson, P. and Hodkinson, H. (1997) 'Micro-politics in initial teacher education: Luke's story', in *Journal of Education for Teaching*, **23** (2): 119–30.

Hoyle, E. (1980) 'Professionalisation and deprofessionalisation in education', in Hoyle, E. and McGarry, J. (eds), *World Yearbook of Education 1980. Professional Development of Teachers*, London: Kogan Page, pp. 42–54.

Hoyle, E. (1995) 'Changing conceptions of a profession', in Busher, H. and Saran, R. (eds), *Managing Teachers as Professionals in Schools*, London: Kogan Page, pp. 59–70.

Joyce, B. and Showers, B. (1988) *Student Achievement Through Staff Development*, New York: Longmans.

Lawton, D. (1994) *The Tory Mind on Education 1979– 94*, London: Falmer Press.

McNiff, J. (1993) *Teaching as Learning: An Action Research Approach*, London: Routledge.

Nixon, J. (1999) Conditions of service of schoolteachers', in Cole, M. (ed.), *Professional Issues for Teachers and Student Teachers*, London: David Fulton, pp. 1–21.

Ofsted (1999) *Inspecting Schools: The Framework*, London: The Stationery Office.

Ozga, J. (1995a) 'New Age traveller', *Curriculum Studies*, **3** (1): 190–5.

Ozga, J. (1995b) 'Deskilling a profession', in Busher, H. and Saran, R. (eds), *Managing Teachers as Professionals in Schools*, London: Kogan Page, pp. 21–37.

Ozga, J. and Lawn, M. (1988) 'Schoolwork: interpreting the labour process of teaching', *British Journal of Sociology of Education*, **9** (3): 323–36.

Pollard, A. (2000) *Schooling for the 21st Century: Inaugural Lecture*, Graduate School of Education, University of Bristol, January 2000.

Scholtes, P. (1998) *The Leaders' Handbook: Making Things Happen, Getting Things Done*, New York: McGraw-Hill.

Schön, D. (1982) *The Reflective Practitioner*, New York: Basic Books.

Sweeney, D. (1999) 'Liaising with parents, carers and agencies', in Cole, M. (ed.), *Professional Issues for Teachers and Student Teachers*, London: David Fulton.

Tropp, A. (1957) *The School Teachers: The Growth of the Teaching Profession in England and Wales*, London: Heinemann.

TTA (2000) *Support and Monitoring of the Newly Qualified Teacher and Assessment of the Newly Qualified Teacher*, London:TTA.

Whitty, G. (1999) 'Teacher professionalism in new times', paper submitted to the *Annual SCETT (Standing Committee for the Education and Training of Teachers) Conference*, Dunchurch, November 1999.

Wilensky, H. (1964) 'The professionalization of everyone', *The American Journal of Sociology*, **LXX** (2): 137–58.

Zeichner, K.M. (1993) 'Connecting genuine teacher development to the struggle for social justice', *Journal of Education for Teaching*, **19**: 5–20.

Further reading

Cross, A. (1998) *Coordinating Design and Technology across the Primary School*, London: Falmer.

DATA (1997) *Secondary Design and Technology: Head of Department's Handbook*, Wellesbourne: DATA.

DATA (1996) *Primary Design and Technology: Coordinator's File*, Wellesbourne: DATA.

To order DfEE publications telephone 0845 602 2260 or e-mail dfee@prologistics.co.uk or visit the website at www.dfee.gov.co.uk

To order the Ofsted publications telephone 0870 600 5522 or visit the website at www.ofsted.gov.uk

To order TTA publications telephone 0845 606 0323 or visit the website at www.teach-tta.gov.uk

Useful websites

www.foodforum.co.uk
www.data.org.uk
www.naaidt.org.uk
www.nuffield.org.uk/primary
www.sln.gov.uk
www.dfee.gov.uk/teachingreforms/mcber

Index